ROSE WEST

JANE CARTER WOODROW

HODDER

First published in Great Britain in 2011 by Hodder & Stoughton
An Hachette UK company

First published in paperback in 2012

1

A CIP catalogue record for this title is available from the British Library.

ISBN 978 0 340 99248 7

Typeset in Bembo by Hewer Text UK Ltd, Edinburgh

Printed and bound by CPI Group (UK) Ltd, Croydon, CR0 4YY

Hodder & Stoughton policy is to use papers that are natural, renewable
and recyclable products and made from wood grown in sustainable
forests. The logging and manufacturing processes are expected to
conform to the environmental regulations of the country of origin.

Hodder & Stoughton Ltd
338 Euston Road
London NW1 3BH

www.hodder.co.uk

For Chad, Emily and Poppy

*Dedicated to the memory of Elizabeth (Betty) Malvina French, an
exceptional person and dear friend*

Contents

Part III House of Bodies: The Later Teen Years

Part IV A Portrait of the Young Girl
as a Grown-Up: A Misspent Youth

Introduction

No one old enough to understand at the time will ever forget the address 25 Cromwell Street, Gloucester, now synonymous with the 'House of Horrors' and surpassing in notoriety even 10 Rillington Place, home of serial murderer John Reginald Christie. Nor will they forget the macabre discoveries made at the family home, where body parts belonging to the victims of Rose and her husband Fred West were excavated from the cellar and garden.

That said, I must have been one of the few people in the country who did not follow the story when the full horrors were first relayed into our living rooms some seventeen years ago. Yet, ironically, I had been working in prisons around this time where, with my colleagues, I was trying to understand what led women and young girls into various types of offending, and what might have helped prevent it.

Some of the cases I had been dealing with, though rare amongst female offenders, were highly traumatic, i.e., child murder and paedophilia. After one particular case, I had begun to sleep with the light on. Alongside this, many of the women and girls I interviewed (serving a range of sentences from murder through to arson and burglary) had revealed stories to me on a daily basis of the abuse they'd experienced as children. As I began to understand the depths of depravity and cruelty that human beings were capable of inflicting on one another, I could not then bring myself to read about, or indeed listen to, what had happened to the victims at Cromwell Street. I walked out of a room whenever news of it came on TV, and turned over the pages of newspapers giving details of these most heinous of crimes. It may seem strange, a criminologist avoiding anything to do with what could undoubtedly be billed as the crime of the 20th century in Britain, but I really could not face it: enough was enough.

As it was, Fred hanged himself before the case came to court and Rose was found guilty of ten of the murders. It wasn't until many years later that, when stopping off in Gloucester, I took a shortcut from the shops to the car park and found myself on a paved walkway where the West house had once stood. This led to my pondering the case again and to wondering how a woman, and a mother at that, had come to commit such horrific crimes. This case exceeded that of Ian Brady and Myra Hindley and Beverly Allitt in terms of the number of victims involved, and Rose had even killed her own daughter and stepchild.

In the light of the recent high-profile child-abuse cases involving Vanessa George, a nursery worker from Plymouth, and that of Baby Peter and his mother, Tracey Connelly (though, unlike Rose West, neither of these women are serial killers), I decided to revisit the case. What was it that made Rose a killer? How did an ordinary little girl grow up to become someone who enjoyed tormenting and torturing other young women before finally killing them? It was a deeply chilling prospect, but I had to know.

Armed then with only the basics of the West case, I began my research. This included tracking down relatives, former neighbours, friends, victims and others who knew Rose during her formative years, and later as a teen mum. Some people felt able to speak about what had happened now that the dust had settled; others, understandably, wanted to forget. New information has come to light as a result, which is presented here and adds a further dimension to the story and to the phenomenon that is Rose West.

Finally, I wish to take this opportunity to thank the many people who have helped me with this book. I am especially grateful to Dr Rajan Darjee, Consultant Forensic Psychiatrist at The Royal Edinburgh Hospital, who has been a great source of help and support in the writing of it, and Andrew and Jackie Letts for all their kindness and generosity, and with whom I feel I have been on a journey of discovery. I would also like to say a very big thank you to Gill Job, Rita New, Joy McConnell, Priscilla Cloke, Diane Tucker, Caroline Roberts, Leo Goatley, the Blake family, Linda Margerison, Susan Greenhalgh, Rosemary Pritchard and the Newquay Old Cornwall Society, retired Inspector Bob Palmer and Inspector Julian Frost, as well as to all those who contacted me by various means, including those who wish to remain anonymous. A number of excellent books are cited in the text, which I recommend to the reader.

Jane Carter Woodrow, 2011

Prologue

ONCE UPON A TIME, in a pretty village between Bideford and Westward Ho! in north Devon, a baby was born whose olive complexion, large dark eyes and shiny dark hair made her look like a beautiful exotic flower: an orchid rather than a rose. An innocent little child who was welcomed into the world by her parents, Bill and Daisy Letts, to take her place in the family as the youngest of five children, with three sisters and a brother to look out for her and to play with. The year was 1953 and the baby was named Rosemary, though later abbreviated to Rose, or 'Rosie', as the family called her.

Except Northam wasn't quite the picturesque place that features on chocolate boxes, nor did the family live in the best part of it. Yet, with its rugged coastline, wild common land and the closeness of the community, it was still a good place to grow up in. And if some babies are born under a lucky star, Rosie's was blighted, and unlike a fairy tale, there was to be no happy ending but tragedy for so very many. Rose was obviously not alone in having a difficult childhood; countless others do, but they do not go on to kill, let alone become serial killers. It is also extremely rare for women to do so, and it would be easy to believe she had been complicit through coercion by Fred, or that she was nothing more than a cowering bystander, but this wasn't the case. How then did young Rosie, an innocent child, grow up to become this hideous monster?

To understand this I have retraced Rose's footsteps from childhood into adulthood, with information obtained from various sources as well as expert opinion in some of its interpretation. As Rose's young life began to unfold, it became an uncomfortable journey, but if we do not seek to understand, then we cannot prevent such appalling devastation from happening again.

A former Home Secretary told Rose she will never be released from prison, but will end her days there. From the pigtailed child to the plump middle-aged woman sitting in a cell with her knitting needles busily clacking away, this is a portrait of Rose West: Britain's most prolific female serial killer of our times.

PART I

Secrets and Lies: The Early Years

I

The Crimes

ON 26 FEBRUARY 1994, the police, searching for a missing 16-year-old girl, Heather West, excavated the garden of a house in Gloucester where, a few days later, they unearthed a thigh bone from a hole beneath the patio.

The pathologist, Professor Bernard Knight, reaching deep into another sludge-filled hole beneath pink and cream paving slabs, produced two more femurs. This led Knight to comment that either this was the world's first three-legged woman, or the police now had two victims on their hands.

Over the next few days, as the remains of yet more young women were discovered in small, vertical holes in the garden and beneath the concrete cellar floor, the public struggled to understand the events that had taken place at 25 Cromwell Street. At the same time, rumours began to surface that were as hideous as they were unbelievable: of abduction, sexual abuse and torture of the victims, before their young lives were cruelly cut short – all behind the façade of this very ordinary-looking family semi.

Most of the victims had been in their makeshift graves for over twenty years, dating back to the seventies; for as long, in fact, as the pair who owned the house had been married. And as each appalling rumour was confirmed as fact, so this case became – and remains – the stuff of worst nightmares. Yet it is a nightmare from which we can never awake; the depths of depravity and suffering that humankind is capable of inflicting on one another remain forever etched in our collective psyche from that time; an emotional as well as forensic archaeology at 25 Cromwell Street.

The pathologist had the grisly task of piecing together the heap of bones he'd collected to determine the number of victims involved, as well as their ages and sex. The cause of death was impossible to establish as the flesh had long since putrefied; thankfully, Professor Knight had no sense of smell. But as the excavation continued and further body parts were discovered, these revealed macabre indicators of what had happened to the victims before death.

The remains still had fetters and gags in place; duct tape mummifying one victim's head had a straw poked through the mask into a nostril, to allow just enough air to keep her alive during the torture; another had a wide leather belt strapped around her head and fastened beneath her chin. Most victims had been decapitated and one young woman had been scalped. In some cases, victims had been suspended from a hook in the ceiling to increase their pain before death, and at least one young woman had been kept alive for several days during the torture. All the bodies had been dissected and trophies kept of fingers, toes, kneecaps and other body parts which, to this day, have never been found. The victims had been dehumanised.

Some years earlier, on Radio 4's *In the Psychiatrist's Chair*, Professor Knight had said, 'I think the human race is pretty rotten. The more I see of it, the more rotten it becomes . . . We are a malignancy on the face of the earth.'

This case could only have served to confirm his view and, unsurprisingly perhaps, he then went on to say how he preferred animals to human beings.

By the time Professor Knight had assembled all the bones found at Cromwell Street and two other burial sites, the tally of victims had reached twelve. Identification of the bodies took some time as half the victims had not been reported missing, but they were all found to be the remains of girls and young women estimated to be between the ages of 15 and 25. They ranged from students passing through to young girls who had been in care, and others.

Yet, incredibly, these most heinous and sickening of crimes were said to have happened at the hands of the friendly, middle-aged couple who owned the house: Rose and Fred West, the smiling assassins, whose names were to become forever linked with evil. At the time, as pictures of the couple appeared on every news media, showing Fred, a slight man with curly hair and a gap in his teeth, with his arm around his wife Rose, a dumpy housewife, it seemed absurd to even begin to contemplate the notion.

But, more incredible still, when Fred West took his own life while on remand for the murders, it was widely held that the lesser charges brought against his wife would be dropped as there would not be enough evidence against her. Based on the fact that men are almost always the dominant partner in serial-killer relationships, many people believed that Rose would surely have been, at worst, complicit under coercion, possibly covering for her husband, who carried out the murders. But this wasn't the case. The prosecution brought charges against Rose West for ten of the twelve murders for which Fred was to have faced trial, including one she was alleged to have carried out on her own while Fred was in prison. A woman standing trial for 'stranger' murder is extremely rare, for serial murder is exceptionally so; and, as Rose pleaded 'not guilty', the public waited with bated breath for the outcome.

What Constitutes a Serial Killer?

Put simply, in the UK it is someone who kills a minimum of three victims on separate occasions with a 'cooling-off' period of at least thirty days between each death. (In the US it is defined as five murders over a set period of time.) A serial killer differs from a spree killer who kills a large number of people in a short space of time, usually in just a few hours and within the same geographical area. Spree killings also tend to be highly visible and usually result in the perpetrator killing themselves. These are cases such as the Dunblane tragedy, and, more recently, Derrick Bird in the Lake District, who slaughtered twelve victims within a few hours before turning the gun on himself. A serial killer is defined as someone like Peter Sutcliffe, the 'Yorkshire Ripper', who murdered thirteen women over a five-year span, with a cooling-off period of a few weeks or months between each murder.

Serial killers are also referred to as 'addictive killers'. This is because, once they have passed the psychological and moral boundary of the first murder, they then develop a taste for it and, to satisfy their hunger, kill again. While a spree killer usually has a build-up of psychological problems that come to a head before they set off on the rampage with a gun, serial killers often operate by stealth, so that we do not even know they are there. Examples include Dennis Nilsen, Dr Harold Shipman and, of course, Fred and Rose West.

The Rarity That Is Rose

Aside from Rose West, there have been only three other cases of women standing trial for serial murder in the UK in modern times. They are Myra Hindley (who, like Rose West, acted with a male partner); Beverly Allitt, a nurse convicted in 1991 of killing children in her care: an 'Angel of Death'; and Mary Wilson, an elderly woman in the north of England who killed a succession of husbands in the 1950s, falling into the category of a 'Black Widow'. None of these were mothers like Rose and, in each of these cases, the tally fell far short of the ten murders for which

Rose stood accused. And in the US and elsewhere across the globe there are fewer than a handful of such examples.

Standing in the dock at Winchester Crown Court in November 1995, the plump, 42-year-old Gloucester housewife and mother of eight, in her frumpy skirt, sensible shoes and oversized spectacles, looked as if she'd be more at home addressing a Girl Guide meeting, or up to her elbows in flour, rolling out pastry for a steak and kidney pie, rather than on trial for serial murder. But because the murders took place over twenty years earlier, she hadn't looked like this then – but had been a beautiful, slim, dark-haired teenager and young woman.

Rose had always denied any knowledge of the murders and because there was no hard evidence against her – no one had seen her kidnap the girls or take them down into the cellar, and there wasn't even a fingerprint to link them to her – the judge permitted the prosecution to try her on 'similar fact' evidence. This meant the jury would hear from other West victims whose attacks formed part of a pattern of behaviour repeated in the killings. A number of young women, all of whom had been lucky to escape with their lives from the Wests, then took to the witness stand, where they testified to Rose's grooming or abduction of them, and her sadistic sexual attacks on them. Two of these young girls had been a test run for the couple's appalling crimes, and all the victims spoke of Rose as having exceeded even the brutal excesses of her husband Fred. It was the grimmest of Grimm fairy tales.

As the jury returned to give their verdict on each murder over a period of two days, Rosemary Pauline West stood rigidly before them, staring straight ahead. Each time the foreman was asked, 'How do you find the defendant?', his reply was the same: 'guilty by a unanimous verdict' of the murders of Lynda Gough (19), Carol Ann Cooper (15), Lucy Partington (21), Thérèse Siegenthaler (21), Shirley Hubbard (15), Juanita Mott (18), Alison Chambers (16), Shirley Robinson (18), Charmaine West (8) and Heather West (16).

Rose was found not simply to have been an unsuspecting wife and victim of Fred, as she had maintained, but a primary player along with Fred in the murders of all the young women found at Cromwell Street, including her own daughter, Heather. In the case of her little stepdaughter, Charmaine, Rose was found to have killed her while Fred was in prison. This was at a previous address in Midland Road, Gloucester, where the remains of this once happy little girl were found buried beneath the concrete floor. The other victims had either worked for the couple or been plucked or lured off the streets by them, with Rose playing a leading role.

However, as Rose continues to maintain her innocence, startling new evidence has recently come to light which appears to lay to rest her guilt or innocence in at least one of these murders. It is a shocking eyewitness account and included in this book.

As the judge sentenced Rose to ten terms of life imprisonment for the murders, he told her, 'If attention is paid to what I think, you will *never* be released.' The gallery then erupted into cries of 'Hear, hear!'

Staring blankly back at him from behind her large plastic-framed glasses, the defendant was then taken down and driven away from the baying mob, to spend the rest of her days behind bars. Yet Rosemary Pauline West had once been a young girl full of hopes and dreams for the future, just like her victims. She'd even had a plan . . . Where did it all go wrong? And could it have turned out any differently?

2

New Beginnings

Bishop's Cleeve, Gloucestershire, January 1970

THE VILLAGE OF BISHOP'S Cleeve is just a few miles from Cheltenham and lies at the foot of the highest hill in the Cotswolds. To the south of the village is a new estate, built in the 1950s to house young families coming into the area to work in the growing industries there. This estate, The Smith's, as it is known, is surrounded by fields, fresh air and glorious views of the Gloucestershire countryside.

It was here as the swinging sixties petered out, bringing in the new dawn of the seventies, that a beautiful, slim dark girl jumped out of bed and yanked open the curtains to let in the day. Such was her excitement that she barely noticed the smoke rising from the neighbour's bonfire as it began forming a giant curl up to the sky. It was a crisp, sunny winter's day; the girl had been waiting for what seemed like an age for this moment, and had slept only in fits and starts the night before. Taking the rag dolls she'd made for her two little friends from the window ledge, she stuffed them into her bag, along with the few items of clothing she had and a pair of shoes. Then, taking a last look around the room and the bed she shared with her two younger brothers, she closed the door on her childhood forever.

Running down the stairs, the girl hugged her auntie Eileen and bade her mother, Daisy, a fond, if awkward, farewell. Her father stayed in the kitchen; he'd already let her know how he felt on the subject of her leaving. There was nothing more to be said. Her mother watched her go, worried: although her daughter was growing up, she was still very young in her ways. Even down to the white, knee-high schoolgirl socks she wore with her heels.

Kissing her little brothers Graham and Gordon goodbye, the girl set off towards the Gloucestershire hamlet of Stoke Orchard, humming 'I Say a Little Prayer for You' to herself, her long, dark hair billowing behind her in the breeze.

'Come back and see us, Rosie!' the boys called to her from the front gate.

Rosie turned and smiled at them. 'Promise!' she called back, not sure if her father would let her, then carried on her way, swinging her bag as she went, not a care in the world.

She had not long since had her birthday and today was the start of the new life she'd promised herself. Sweet 16 and she was off to meet her boyfriend. Well, a *man* in fact, some twelve years older than her, but who would protect her and take care of her, she was sure of that – just as her own father had . . .

'Forever, forever, you'll stay in my heart and I will love you; Forever, forever, never to part, Oh how I love you . . .' The words of the Aretha Franklin song swirled round in her head. Elated at the prospect of moving in with Fred and his two little girls, she was full of hopes and dreams for their future together. She had big plans, starting with finding a new, permanent home for them all.

Yet, little more than eighteen months later, at 17, Rosie, as the family affectionately called her, would kill her first victim alone and unaided. And a year later, she and her husband would entice and murder another two young girls, making Rose a fully-fledged serial killer while still in her teens: a disturbing, if unprecedented, accolade by any standards.

In her early twenties, Rose would kill again and again. Her last known murder was in 1987 when she was 33 years of age: the victim was her own daughter, Heather. But how did an ordinary teenage girl and young woman become a cold and calculating serial killer? Or was she never ordinary? What was it eating young Rosie West? To discover this we must go back further still.

Northam, north Devon, 1950s

In earlier times, the village of Northam had been an insular and remote community which, with its craggy coastline and surrounding countryside, was as wild and rugged as any described in *Wuthering Heights* and *Jamaica Inn*. Dark and desolate during the long harsh winters, with tales of smuggling, shipwrecks, drownings and jilted lovers, it was the place of the lost and the damned. Certainly Hubba and the Danes, who invaded there in the ninth century, must have thought so. The village still bears a plaque at 'Bloody Corner' to mark the mass slaughter of Hubba's army of almost a thousand men, now buried at Bone Hill near the back of the church. In later times, during the expansion of the British Empire, Northam boasted a railway line that came from neighbouring Bideford but went nowhere, the line closing almost as soon as it had opened. All in all, the stuff of Gothic fairy tales.

Yet, though the winters were difficult in Northam, the summers were a different matter, particularly in more recent times of the post-war years of the 1940s and 1950s, when the village and surrounding areas became a holiday destination. And, just as the tourists enjoyed it, so too did local families – particularly the children, who spent long hot days on the beaches or exploring the wild countryside of the Northam Burrows coastal plain, stealing rides on the horses that roamed freely there. There was also the excitement of finding unexploded Second World War bombs on the beach, when the children would rush off to tell their parents. The whole village had to stay inside until the army bomb-disposal unit detonated them, the children letting out a loud cheer as the window frames rattled as if to signal the all-clear.

This was to be the birthplace of Rosie Letts, who would join the ranks of the village's few famous inhabitants, including Sir Walter Raleigh, who once had a house there, and Charles Kingsley, author of the *Water Babies* and *Westward Ho!*, after which the nearby holiday resort would be named. Though Rose, of course, would become infamous.

But if Northam was a magical place for children such as Rose to grow up at this time, it was not so for their parents. For, when Northam men had returned home after the Second World War, it was to unemployment – except for the lucky few who found work at the shipbuilding works at nearby Appledore, or at Westward Ho! building amphibian landing craft. This meant poverty for many in the village, including the Letts family. Yet if Prime Minister Harold Macmillan's words, 'You've never had it so good,' grated on the nerves in this part of the country, the 1950s was still a time of free health treatment for all, and a new housing programme from which Rose's parents would benefit.

Rose's father, Bill Letts, had been a seafarer and naval man since being called up in 1943. An electronics engineer before enlisting, the Navy deployed his skills as a wireless operator on board aircraft carriers and at naval airfields across the country. Able Seaman FX 681316 had not long been married when he set sail for Australia, leaving his young wife and newborn baby behind.

Bill's petite, dark-haired wife, Daisy, was so beautiful she could have been a Hollywood movie star. She wasn't from the north Devon area as Bill was – or from Devon at all – but had met her husband while working in nearby Bideford at the start of the war. Bill had always been a serious young man who preferred his own company at the best of times, but after he met Lionel Green, a newcomer to the area from London, the two young men struck up a friendship. It was through Lionel that Bill was to meet his sweetheart, Daisy.

Rose's mother, born Daisy Fuller, originally came from

Chadwell Heath near Romford, which was still mostly fields with grazing sheep and cattle at the time. However, it was close to the East End of London, and moving to this tiny backwater of north Devon was quite a change for Daisy.

Rose West's Maternal Grandparents

As luck would have it, Daisy's parents were called Fred and Rose. Named by Daisy after her own mother, the young Rose would – many years hence – coincidentally marry another Fred; the couple's names becoming synonymous with evil. But this Fred, Fred Fuller, was a decent man. Originally from picturesque Grantchester in Cambridgeshire, Fred was an 'Old Contemptible' who had joined up in 1898, at aged 18, to serve as a professional soldier in the Queen's 2nd Essex Rifles. During his long and distinguished career, Fred had served both in the Boer War and at Mons, where he was decorated. He also met and married Rose (Woolnough), who lived close by his barracks at Warley.

Rose's Maternal Grandparents: The Fullers

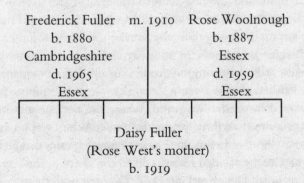

Frederick Fuller m. 1910 Rose Woolnough
b. 1880   b. 1887
Cambridgeshire   Essex
d. 1965   d. 1959
Essex   Essex

Daisy Fuller
(Rose West's mother)
b. 1919

This Rose and Fred would go on to have eight children: just as their namesakes, Rose and her husband Fred West, were to do many years later. When Fred Fuller retired from the services, he took a job as guard on a Sunlight Soap delivery van. And, just as he had when he was in the Army, he took home his pay packet to his wife each week rather than heading off to the pub as many men often did during the Depression of the 1920s and 1930s. Daisy remembers her father as a kind man who, every Friday after work, would pop into the shop while she and her siblings waited excitedly on the street corner until he returned with his pockets full of sweets for them.

Ironically, given that Daisy's father was used to a regimented way of life, it was not Fred but her mother Rose who was the strict disciplinarian, punishing the children if they stepped out of line. Rose senior was also often sick, and would spend long periods in hospital with 'sclerosis of the liver' during much of Daisy's childhood. The quiet and genteel Daisy left school at 14 to go out to work to relieve pressure on the family, knocking on doors until she found a live-in post. Eventually she obtained work as a domestic and barmaid in a pub in the cosmopolitan area of Brick Lane in the East End of London. In the 1920s and 1930s Brick Lane was a magnet for immigrants fleeing pogroms in Eastern Europe, and Bangladeshi seamen who brought their exotic foods and cooking skills to the area. It was here in 1936 that Daisy also witnessed Oswald Mosley's Black Shirts marching past, on their way to a rally to take the Fascist salute.

Working long hours for poor pay and with rowdy customers at times, Daisy began to look round for other employment. She found this with the Greens, a wealthy Jewish business family who lived in nearby Wanstead, where she became a domestic and nanny to their three young daughters. When war broke out and the Germans began their heavy bombing raids on the capital, the Greens decided to head off to the safety of the countryside: to north Devon, asking Daisy to come with them.

Bill was 20 at the time, and working in an electrical shop in Bideford. Always a hard worker, he earned extra cash at night by undertaking private wiring jobs for farmers and householders in the area — something he was frequently called on to do, as many dwellings in the north Devon area were only just becoming connected to the national electricity grid. When the Greens arrived in Bideford and needed their wiring fixing, Bill was called in. It wasn't long before Lionel Green noticed his shy pal's interest in the nanny, and played Cupid.

'Bill, meet Daisy! Daisy, Bill!'

As Bill and Daisy glanced coyly at one another, little could anyone have guessed that a child produced from their subsequent union would cause such unimaginable horror and tragedy.

Bill, though short at under five feet six inches, was a slight and dapper man who always wore a suit and tie, even when he was working. Whatever the weather, Bill was a familiar sight around the village in his formal attire. 'Can I get you a drink?' he asked Daisy, pulling a chair out for her. Daisy smiled. Unlike her more boisterous customers at the pub, Bill rarely touched alcohol, preferring fruit juice or having half a light ale at most; he also didn't smoke and shunned bad language. His polite though stiff manner, which smacked of a bygone era, struck a chord with Daisy as, like Bill, she had been brought up to be prim and proper, and was very ladylike in her ways. In Bill she'd found a man who wasn't interested in other women in the live-for-the-moment sexual freedoms that existed in wartime Britain, but one who was kind and caring: a 'true gent' as they'd say in the East End. At least, that's how Bill appeared to love-struck Daisy who, with little experience of life, thought all men were like her father . . .

Daisy's appeal for Bill was not difficult to see. A beautiful, exotic creature, rumoured locally to be Maltese, this quiet Essex girl was always respectful and homely, which attracted Bill as much as her looks. But, unbeknown to Daisy, she was Bill's rebound girl. There had been an earlier doomed romance, when Bill's girlfriend had moved away and married someone else. He'd taken the rejection badly and was a broken and disillusioned man – almost paranoid at times – until, that is, he met Daisy, and, after a while, proposed to her.

Daisy took Bill home to meet her parents at their new, larger home in Ilford. Soon after she was to become a war bride, 'making do and mending' with whatever materials she could lay her hands on during rationing in wartime Britain, to produce a bridal gown and veil. The young couple, who were not yet lovers, tied the knot on 18 April 1942, at St Mary's in Ilford, the service followed by a modest 'do' to celebrate. They were aged 21 and 23; and, although Daisy was the older of the two, some say her modest and childlike ways made her appear younger than her new husband. These 'babyish' ways were something that would later be said of one of her daughters, Rosie, when she grew up.

The happy couple stayed with Daisy's parents for the first year of marriage, then moved to their own place in the East End. They were about to spend their first Christmas together with their new baby, Patricia, when Bill's 'call-up' papers from the War Office dropped through the letterbox. Kissing his wife and baby goodbye, the young family man set off for HMS Gosling Fleet Air Arm, near Warrington, a Royal Naval training base for air mechanics, fitters and radio mechanics such as Bill.

Daisy was already pregnant with her next child, Joyce, who was born the following year at a hospital set up temporarily in the Northamptonshire countryside after the local maternity hospital in West Ham was bombed during the Blitz. Soon after the second little girl's birth in 1944, Daisy decided to take a leaf out of the Greens' book and took her little family to the safety of the north Devon countryside, moving in with Bill's parents in Northam. But, despite escaping the nightly poundings of air raids in London, she found a strange atmosphere at her in-laws'.

Rose West's Paternal Grandparents

Like Daisy's family, Bill's parents owned their own home. It was not as grand as the Fullers' place, but a pretty stone cottage nonetheless, set in the heart of the village, with steps up to the front door. Bertha Letts was well-respected locally though, like her daughter-in-law, Daisy, she too was not originally from the area. Bertha was the local district nurse and a familiar sight on her bike as she made her rounds in the village and nearby Bideford and Torrington, visiting the sick. Bill's father, William Letts, was also well known in the village where, always smartly turned out, he worked as a butler serving various rich women in the area. Or, at least, that's what he said he did, while rumours going round the village suggested that Bill's dad did something quite different for a living.

Rose's paternal grandmother, Bertha, was a member of the Barter family from Lymington, near the New Forest. As a young girl she had trained to become a nurse and, during the First World War, had bravely set off for the Somme to care for soldiers on the front line, coming face to face with all the horrific injuries that the fighting men had sustained. Rose's paternal grandfather, William Letts, was a Northam man born and bred. The son of a house painter, he was the youngest child and only boy, whose many sisters spoilt him as he grew up. At 19 years of age, William was called up to serve in the First World War. He joined the Royal Devon Yeomanry Guards, sailing off to fight with the Australians, possibly at the Dardanelles. On his return to England, William met Bertha while both were stationed at Plymouth. They married there towards the end of the war, settling first in Lymington and then, finally, at Bill's birthplace of Northam.

Rose's Paternal Grandparents: The Letts

William Letts	m. 1918	Bertha Barter
b. 1894		b. 1894
Devon		Hampshire
d. 1992		d. c.1960
Berkshire		Devon

William (Bill) Letts Junior
(Rose West's father)
b. 1921 Hampshire
d. 1979 Gloucestershire

As both William and Bertha came from large families, they were adamant that they did not want any children, with all the financial problems and struggle for space this could bring. Three years later, when Bill Letts Junior arrived, it was as a result of an accident and unwelcome news to them both. However, although they soon got used to the idea, Bertha now had a young son to care for, as well as a full-time career. On top of that, she kept the house as neat as a pin. It was so clean and tidy and ordered, in fact, that young Bill grew up hardly daring to breathe.

Later, this level of tidiness and organisation also proved difficult for Daisy to cope with when she moved in to her in-laws' house with babies Patsy and Joyce while Bill was away fighting at sea. Daisy felt she was walking on eggshells with her relatives, and the situation was not helped by the icy atmosphere that prevailed between Bertha and William as the latter's reputation as a ladies' man began to reach his wife's ears.

But while Daisy was finding life difficult at the Letts's cottage, Bill was discovering he actually enjoyed being away at sea and the routine that the services provided. As well as sailing off to places he'd never dreamt of going to before, including the Philippines and Australia, Bill enjoyed his new life so much that he decided to stay on at the end of the war. First he signed up for national service for six months, and when this ended, he became a volunteer. The Navy had little need for his wireless skills after the war, however, so Bill retrained as a steward and, as his records show, did very well at this.

The regular wage the Navy paid also influenced his decision to stay on, as Bill had a growing family to think about – Daisy had become pregnant again after his last home leave. Just before the birth of their third child, Glenys, in 1950, Bill and Daisy moved out to a rented cottage on Bone Hill where the remains of the many slaughtered Danes are laid to rest; an omen perhaps of Cromwell Street.

Rose's Childhood Family

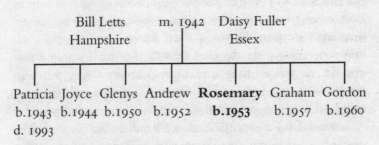

Bill Letts	m. 1942	Daisy Fuller
Hampshire		Essex

Patricia Joyce Glenys Andrew **Rosemary** Graham Gordon
b.1943 b.1944 b.1950 b.1952 **b.1953** b.1957 b.1960
d. 1993

Daisy possibly felt a huge sense of relief as she set out from her in-laws' cottage for the last time with the second-hand bits and pieces she'd collected for her family's new home. Not long after this, the couple took possession of a brand-new local authority house on a tiny estate tacked onto the village. This was 57 Morwenna Park Road: a three-bedroom semi which backed onto fields and which would be home to all seven children Daisy and Bill would go on to have, including the young Rosemary – or Rosie, as her family would affectionately call her. The estate, being out of the centre of the village, was socially as well as geographically distanced from the rest of Northam at the time, with its local authority housing and young, struggling families like the Letts'. But while some of those who lived in the village might have looked down on Morwenna families, these were decent, law-abiding people who had aspirations for their children, many of whom would do well in later years.

In the 1950s, the tiny estate would bustle each morning with young mums pushing Silver Cross prams across their doorsteps. The prams would bear the latest arrival, while the next in line sat on the pram seat and the other children clung onto the sides. The mothers would deliver the oldest children to Northam Primary School, then go on to shop at the greengrocer's and baker's in the village.

There was an air of optimism about this tiny estate, a sense of community and purpose: people might be poor, as one former resident said, but they were pulling together, and most fathers had found work by the 1950s. Two doors away from the Letts home, at number 61, were the Jubbs. Mr Jubb was the first man in the area to have a vacuum chimney-sweep business, which he operated from a van. The residents and children were intrigued by this newfangled idea, and more so seeing Mr Jubb on a weekday without his face and hands being blackened by soot as was normally the case. At number 53, two doors along from the Letts family on the other side, were the Gourdies. Mr Gourdie was the catering manager at the holiday camp less than a mile away at Westward Ho!, while the manager of the holiday camp, Mr Mitchell, lived a few doors down from him, at number 29, with his family. Further along from the Letts' were the Alfords, the talk of the estate when Mr Alford, an ex-Army man who had returned from serving abroad, brought back his beautiful Indian bride to settle there. Next to the Alfords were the Glovers, Mr Glover being a master baker in Westward Ho! Some of the families did exceptionally well in a short space of time, including the Hoppers, who within a few years moved to the centre of the village, where they set up in business selling woollen school uniforms and haberdashery.

On Saturday mornings there would be Uncle Mac on the radio, presenting *Children's Favourites* and playing Pearl Carr and Teddy Johnson, Sparky and 'The Runaway Train'; the following day families would listen to Perry Como singing 'Magic Moments' as they sat at the table waiting for the Sunday roast to be served up. On Sunday afternoons the only man in the street with a car at the time came out and cleaned it. Later the kids would marvel as he honked his horn while proceeding in stately procession down the road with his large wife beside him. At the weekends and after school, the streets would ring with the sound of kids' laughter as they played outside with bags of marbles and conkers baked in the oven, and chalked out hopscotch on the pavement. Most kids also went swimming at the Burrows beach with their older siblings, and to Sunday school at the Congregational Church, to give their parents a break. At the chapel, there would also be concerts and events laid on for the children by Reverend Green, whose wife would learn his Sunday morning sermon by heart and sit beside him as he preached to the congregation – mouthing, perfectly, every word of it.

There had also been a nearby prisoner-of-war camp, 'German ones, who were friendly to us,' Gill Job (pronounced Jobe) who grew up in Morwenna Park Road, remembers. Some of the men had their own families back in Germany, and went back as soon as they could after the war finished; others married local girls and stayed on.

It was place of wonder for children growing up, a former next-door neighbour of the Letts family said. 'Northam was then a small village with farms all around us so we had plenty to do – helping out collecting eggs, milking cows and harvesting time was fun. But potato picking was hard work, walking behind the tractor picking up all the potatoes and putting them into bags . . . I could never wait to get to the stables and, of course, to the beach. How lucky we were . . .'

Yet, for all the enjoyment other children had growing up here, there was one family whose children were never seen out playing: the Letts'. Dark-haired Patsy and blonde Joyce had to come straight home after school and play in the back garden, if they were let out at all. When other little girls knocked on the door to ask them out to play, the usually quiet and ladylike Daisy would yell at them to 'go away!' This soon began to raise a few eyebrows on the estate.

Once installed in her new home and able to do as she pleased without fear of offending her tidy in-laws, Daisy strangely still couldn't relax. With Bill away much of the time, she concentrated her efforts on keeping her two girls and new baby, Glenys, scrupulously clean. As a former neighbour remembered, '[Daisy] was very clean; she kept bathing the children all the time. He [Bill] must have got fed up with it – she was always bathing them.'

Although too poor to buy the girls new clothes very often, Daisy would patch up what they had, ensuring that they were always well dressed and that the two older girls were polite to anyone they should come into contact with. But, as people noticed, the girls rarely did come into contact with anyone outside school, other than when running errands to the shop for their mother, where they were said to be perhaps a little too well turned out and well behaved, like Stepford children.

Outward appearances had become increasingly important to Daisy who, at this time, would relish the compliments she was given about the children. 'Them were beautiful girls, and always beautiful turned out,' as a former neighbour remembered in her soft Devon burr, '. . . they were well fed and dressed lovely.' But, as another neighbour said, 'The kids had to play in the garden. They never had no life . . . never allowed out.'

But if the children weren't allowed to play or get dirty, all didn't seem quite right with Daisy either, who had become overly concerned with hygiene and the state of the house.

While Bill was at sea, Daisy would ensure the house was spotless, frequently scrubbing it from top to bottom. She may have busied herself in this way because she felt isolated in an area where she knew few people, but when the local women tried to engage her in friendly banter across the back gardens as they hung out the washing, she did not join in. Rather, she was subdued and nervy and referred to the neighbours formally, 'Good morning, Mr Lloyd' and 'Hello, Mrs Job'. That said, Daisy was shy, but it would be some time before the real reason for her aloofness would begin to emerge.

During these years, Daisy only saw Bill for intermittent periods of time when he came home on leave from his ship. The neighbours remembered him turning the corner at the top of the road, looking smart and handsome in his naval uniform, while cheeky kids ran alongside him, saluting him. But if Daisy was feeling isolated, she wouldn't have been fazed by managing the home and bringing up the children single-handedly when Bill was away, as her own father had been away serving in the Army during most of her childhood: she was used to it. There were also other women at Morwenna Park Road whose husbands were away. Mr Job was a master carpenter for the county of Devon, who only managed to come home once a month, and other husbands were still away in the services. Yet when Bill came home, a man described as quiet and charismatic by locals, Daisy didn't seem any happier. 'The dad, Bill, was charming. He was quiet and we all thought it was her really,' as a former neighbour, Gill Job, was to say.

There were signs too that Daisy was becoming anxious as her behaviour verged on neurotic. 'She came in crying to me mother one day, and I went round and helped her scrub the kitchen, because she wanted everything to be clean. It wasn't him. She was obsessed with it,' another neighbour, Mrs Cloke, was to say.

By 1951 Daisy was sinking into a depression and was finding it difficult to cope. Neighbours heard her yelling at Joyce and Patsy as she chased them with the copper stick. She was 'disturbed', as an ex-neighbour put it, whose concerned mother called in the local authority children's services. Perhaps as a result of this, and with Daisy's mental health declining, Bill was able to arrange for the two oldest children to be educated at a boarding school in neighbouring Cornwall. As Patsy, 8, and Joyce, 6, packed their bags, they were told they were going to a 'naval school'. What it was, in fact, was the Royal United Service Orphan Home for Girls at Narrowcliff in Newquay, which took in the orphaned daughters of service personnel and daughters of servicemen from 'difficult home circumstances' – where, for example, a parent was seriously ill. The children's home was run by a Miss Salmon and when Glenys reached the age of 6, she would go there too.

Although it was an open and happy environment at the home, where friends of the children could drop by to visit at any time, Patsy and Joyce would spend long periods of time there without ever seeing their mother. Daisy was possibly never well enough to visit them, although Bill, stationed at nearby naval bases in Plymouth and Cornwall, turned up to see the girls when he could.

Daisy now had only one child at home to care for, but, unfortunately, given her fragile state and the fact that she couldn't cope with the children she already had, she became pregnant again. The following year, in 1952, Daisy gave birth to their fourth child, a boy. But 'Dad', as Bill preferred to be called, was delighted to have a son at last. Moreover, with the baby's brown hair and fair skin, it looked the spit of himself – unlike the girls, who all favoured their mother. The happy parents decided to call the baby Andrew after his father Bill's second name.

Having been an only, often lonely, child, Bill had always relished the idea of having a large family, and was pleased as punch now that he had one. But six months after Andrew's birth, Daisy became ill again, and Bill felt he had no choice but to leave the Navy and the financial security it provided, to help his sick wife with the care of their children. He was discharged in September 1952 on compassionate grounds after nine years of service. This decision was one of *the* major factors to affect young Rose's life when she came along the following year, while doctors now felt Daisy was a suitable case for treatment.

3

The Treatment

IT WAS THE SPRING of 1953, and while the country was awash with street parties for the Coronation of Queen Elizabeth II, Daisy found little to celebrate as her depression deepened and she became increasingly anxious. So much so that she developed agoraphobia, not daring to leave the house or even open the door. Coming on so soon after having had a baby, this might today be put down to postnatal depression, but little was known about 'baby blues' at the time.

Bill had not been home long when his wife's nerves became so bad she had a breakdown, and was referred to a psychiatric hospital in nearby Bideford. Daisy was willing to try anything for her depression and when the psychiatrist suggested a course of electroconvulsive therapy (ECT), or electric shock treatment as it is known, she agreed. ECT is most notably known as the treatment given to Jack Nicholson's character, McMurphy, in *One Flew Over the Cuckoo's Nest* – except with Daisy, the 'electric hammer', as it is also called, was for real.

Daisy would have had her head shaved and been given a muscle relaxant; then, like Nicholson's character in the film, she would have been strapped to a hospital bed (to stop patients falling off when they convulse). After this, a number of large black electrodes are attached to the skull and she would have been given a piece of rubber or a spatula to bite on. A surge of electricity is then sent through the electrodes to the brain in an attempt to redress the chemical balance that regulates mood and to obliterate dark memories. Thankfully, once the power goes on, the patient blacks out. The shocks are accompanied by the smell of burning rubber, and the patient has convulsions like seizures on the bed. It was at the beginning of her course of treatment with the 'electric hammer' that Daisy fell pregnant with her next child: Rosemary.

ECT is a controversial treatment and, as the Royal College of Psychiatrists in London acknowledges, no one really knows how it works. However, although it can be effective in cases of severe depression, there are others who have suffered substantial memory loss and been left in a confused state afterwards, not always improving over time. Some patients reported feeling as if they were in a trance afterwards, or even zombie-like, and it has also been known to cause personality changes. As Laurence Olivier was to say of his wife, Vivien Leigh, she was 'not the same girl' after receiving ECT for her illness. Although this treatment is still available today, it is used less often and even banned in some European countries. It does, however, appear to have been popular in north Devon during the 1950s. A former neighbour and contemporary of Daisy's explained how she too had undergone ECT at this time, and believes she also suffered adverse effects from it.

In Daisy's case, her therapy was reviewed after her second session, when the psychiatrist voiced the opinion that her illness was far more serious than he'd at first believed. Bill was particularly sympathetic to his wife's mental health problems, and insisted she continue with her course of treatment, pregnant or not. Bill had worked with electricity since his training in his youth: he knew all about such matters; he'd even had a few shocks himself at work, and if a few volts helped her, so be it. Indeed, he might even have relished this idea as, while serving in the Navy, he had secretly administered shocks to the Wrens, laughing about his 'little prank' to his colleagues. Although no one back at home – and certainly not Daisy – knew about that.

33

Daisy's psychiatrist, in line with Bill's thoughts on the matter, decided to continue her treatment throughout the pregnancy, until the course was completed. This meant that as Rose lay silently growing in her mother's womb, so Daisy had more shocks blasted to her brain, sending convulsions through her body – the last one being just days before Rose was born.

There has been little research on the use of ECT with pregnant patients, and expert opinion is divided on it but, given the damage ECT can do to the patient, it seems unlikely the foetus would remain unaffected in every case. And when Rosie did finally arrive at the Highfield Maternity Hospital at Northam, her behaviour would soon give cause for concern amongst her own siblings.

Nonetheless, when Daisy finished her last ECT session and came home with a shaved head and clutching the new addition to the family in her arms, no one could miss what an exceptionally lovely baby Rosie was, with her olive skin, dark hair and soft brown eyes, just like her mother. People would remark on how beautiful the child was, and in Northam still do today. But to Rosie the world must have appeared a topsy-turvy kind of place where, as a toddler, she needed to hang her head upside-down to understand it, and as a baby rocked her head on the hood of the pram for hours on end.

'Stop that, Rosie!' her older siblings complained as she rhythmically bashed her head against the cot at night in the bedroom she shared with them. 'Stop it! We can't go to sleep!' They protested – though not too loudly for fear of waking 'Dad'.

Despite her rocking, Rosemary Pauline, as her proud parents named her, though shortening it to Rosie, was said to be a 'good baby' who rarely cried. However, while she was 'good' perhaps in terms of being less tiring for a mother with a demanding child, babies are not normally quiet for long: crying is the only way they can communicate their needs in their first few weeks and months of life, so this might be seen as a little worrying. As well as rarely crying, as Rosie got older she would continue to swing her head in front of her for long periods of time, inducing a trance-like state. At other times her large eyes were said to look vacant while life went on around her as she daydreamed, inhabiting a world of her own: Rosie's world.

The kinds of behaviour Rose exhibited can be indicative of learning difficulties. They might even have been linked to the ECT treatment her mother received at the time, which might not have had the safety standards of today, but again, no one knows for sure. Moreover, children, whether challenged intellectually or not (and we don't know that Rose was), are known to rock and swing their heads simply to obtain comfort from it or to relieve boredom, as in the case of neglected babies. Children also daydream or withdraw into themselves to escape the difficulties they face in their everyday lives, such as abuse or neglect. But it is unlikely that Rosie was neglected, as when her older siblings were at home, they were constantly around her; and when they weren't, Bill was there lending a hand. Rosie was also to be the baby of the family for another four years, with all the attention this brought her, until her brother Graham was born in 1957.

Neither the ECT treatment nor Bill being at home helped lift Daisy's depression for long. The washing line would be full of old army blankets flapping in the breeze as Daisy's cleaning obsession became ever more 'manic', as neighbours described it. Daisy at the time had army blankets on the front-room floor to keep the carpet clean, but would frequently wash the blankets to ensure they were also pristine. Alongside this, there was also a strong smell of bleach in the house.

Bill had not been home long, when he too appeared to be out of sorts. Local men who'd been demobbed some years earlier had the first pickings of the few jobs that existed in the area. Despite Bill's electronic skills and his naval records showing he was of good character, there was nothing for him. He was a man who had always provided for his family, and now he couldn't. And although he remained able to laugh and joke with people he met on the street, and was still very charming, at home he became listless and depressed.

Historically, there were often problems when men came home from the services. In the Navy, where discipline was rigid, there was also a strong pecking order. And, as the men were all stuck on a ship together for weeks on end, there was a lot of male bonding as the men depended on each other for their lives – it was an adrenalin-fuelled existence. That adrenalin wasn't there at home, and fathers like Bill found themselves at the bottom of the pecking order on their return, as their wives had become used to running the house on their own. Just as it took time for spouses to readjust to one another when they came home on leave, when the men returned permanently, domestic abuse was common, particularly amongst the unskilled. There was certainly domestic violence in some homes in the Northam area, and, Daisy's illness aside, the Letts too were finding it difficult to adjust. They had by now been married for over a decade, but had never really lived together – until now. Clearly it was going to take time to adjust.

Alongside this, without his uniform, Bill, like many ex-servicemen, would have felt a loss of self-esteem along with the respect it would have automatically commanded him. Bill, however, soon rectified this situation by inventing his *own* uniform: a black French beret worn at a jaunty angle, and a button-down, khaki raincoat with his ubiquitous suit and tie beneath – even in the hottest of weather. Everyone in the village would see Bill coming in his slightly bizarre, self-styled uniform – albeit that his leaky shoes were stuffed with newspaper as he tramped round the area looking for work.

Despite his skills, it was many years before Bill would find permanent work. The work he was able to find in between was a succession of short-term, low-paid jobs. When there wasn't even temporary work around, he and a friend, Ronnie Lloyd, set up a tent on the beach in the summer to sell Daisy and Mrs Lloyd's home-made cakes and sandwiches to holiday-makers. None of this would have helped Bill's view of himself, and it wasn't long before he began to talk incessantly about the happy times he'd had in the Navy. 'You should have seen the port when we laid anchor.' 'The sea was clear, we could have swum for miles.' With time on his hands, he continually complained to his wife, 'I should have stayed in the services. There's nothing here for me. I made a mistake.'

Of course Bill *had* sacrificed his career because of his wife's illness, but his constantly reminding her of it didn't help Daisy with her own problems. Besides which, Daisy was keeping quiet about the other mistake he'd made in the Navy, which the children wouldn't find out about until many years hence . . .

Bill's parents, still living close by, stepped in to try to help out the family when they could. But things had not become any easier between Daisy and Bill's mother, Bertha, over the years. Bertha had long since transferred her attentions from her husband to her only child. When the younger, attractive Daisy came along, replacing her in her son's affection, she, like the evil queen in *Snow White*, became jealous. Bertha found fault with her daughter-in-law whenever she could, criticising the way she looked after the children and spreading rumours about her in the village. And all these years later, she still disapproved of the beautiful Daisy.

Despite the bad blood between them and the fact that Daisy had hated living with her cold in-laws, she and Bill agreed to their eldest girl, Patsy, going to live there at different times during her childhood. Perhaps they had wanted to relieve some of the financial pressures at home, or the overcrowding problem there, now that baby Rosie was starting to walk. Thus, when Patsy wasn't away at the orphanage with her sister, the little girl spent most of her time at her grandparents', being taken on trips to the circus and generally indulged by them. Though Rose would have been too small to notice this, it not unnaturally made some of the younger children envious to see their sister being spoilt with gifts of teddy bears, watches and pocket money that they didn't have. Yet, how Patsy truly fared here we will never know, as she died many years ago. However, other children in Northam were told by their parents to keep away from 'old Mr Letts', who was not just selling his services as a gigolo to the wealthy widows who lived in big houses on the hill, but was also rumoured to be an unhealthy person for children to be around.

Even with Patsy moving in with her grandparents, things did not seem to be improving greatly at number 57 where, as soon as Bill went out, Daisy would be heard disciplining the children. As a former neighbour remembered, 'She did the hitting and the screaming at the kids. Making them tidy their rooms all the time. One morning she made them all go out and eat their breakfasts on the wall [at the front of the house]. She made a show of it.'

As the neighbour, a small child at the time, watched the Letts children enviously from across the road, she asked her mother: 'Mum? Can we have breakfast outside?'

'No,' her concerned mother replied, ushering her away from the scene. 'Go back in the house and sit up at the table.'

As the little girl retreated down her front path, she glanced back and noticed something different about Daisy. 'She was black and blue that day as they all sat there by the wall eating their bowls of cereal.'

While Bill was hitting Daisy, horrified neighbours also noticed Daisy being cruel to the older children, who were in their early teens at the time.

As a former neighbour remembered: 'When the girls arrived home from school she had them in the back yard checking their hair for nits. You could hear their screams next door. She'd go out and hose them down in the back yard – there was a high wall but you'd see her [Daisy] hosing them, and brushing their hair really hard. With all the washing and scrubbing she did, it's a wonder they had any skin left.'

On the rare occasion that Daisy allowed one of the girls out to play, her little friend, Gill Job, was startled by Daisy's reaction when they returned home afterwards.

'Joyce was thrashed when I took her out one day to the Burrows, on the beach. We'd catch horses and ride them there on the sand. You fell off (you just wore your knickers in those days) and would get sand and mud all over you. Joyce was running across the beach, laughing and screaming . . . like she'd never been able to let off steam before. She went home with sand and mud on her and was beaten black and blue. I wish to God I'd never taken Joyce with me that day after what happened.'

Few people, however, knew what went on inside the Letts' house, where outward appearances were everything. And if times were not so good for some in Prime Minister Macmillan's brave new world, Bill still had his pride. He had been brought up in a childhood home where everything had its place and there was a place for everything. This sense of order had been reinforced in the services, and it was he rather than Daisy who wanted everything to be shipshape and spotless, despite their having several young children. His home and family was the one area where he could exert some control over his life; where he had power – and he was going to use it. Just a speck of dust on the picture rail would lead to an irrational response, and in no time at all, Bill would fly into one of his terrifying rages where he'd lash out with his fists. Daisy had taken such terrible beatings she probably took the children outside to eat their breakfasts on the wall that day in an effort to shame Bill into stopping, while letting the world know what her 'charming' husband was really about.

Up until this point, Bill's friend Ronnie Lloyd was the only other person who had known the real reason why Daisy didn't speak to the neighbours during her husband's absences: Bill was controlling Daisy, even when he was thousands of miles away at sea. This quiet man was in fact paranoid that his beautiful wife was going to have an affair, as his other girlfriends had done. He'd accused her of being oversexed and beaten her into submission with his fists and a slipper behind closed doors. He'd told her who she could speak to and who she couldn't, and even went after the local grocer, telling him not to serve his wife if she came into the shop (though the shopkeeper and his wife ignored him). Bill expected Daisy to obey his rules for no other reason than he'd set them. If she broke them, he'd hit her; if she kept them, he hit her – behind closed doors where only Rosie and her siblings would see.

And, despite how it looked to the neighbours, Bill was actually the one fixated with cleanliness. He insisted on the girls' nails and hair being inspected regularly, and soaked the carpets in bleach to kill off any germs. He had developed obsessive-compulsive disorder (OCD) and wanted his own home even more pristine than his parents'. Fearing his wrath, Daisy constantly scrubbed the house and the children so as not to provoke him – though, of course, if he had a mind to it, nothing would stop him beating them. In the end, Daisy appears to have become so worn down by Bill that she simply threw in her lot with him – taking on board his OCD and other irrational behaviours as if they were her own, as she hit the children and constantly cleaned. It was a kind of *folie à deux*, or 'madness of two' which is sometimes also referred to as 'shared paranoia'. Put simply, it is where one partner takes on the irrational ideas and behaviours of the dominant – though ironically more disturbed – partner.

This wasn't the man Daisy thought she had married, a kind man like her father; but was instead a monster who changed from Jekyll to Hyde in a flash. And as the neighbours might have said – had they known – Bill had quite simply driven Daisy right round the bend. While Rosie and her siblings had two mentally ill parents whose behaviour shaped their childhood and psychological development.

4

Rosie Learns Her Lessons

IF ROSIE WAS A quiet baby, she was also a well-behaved child who liked to sit and play with her dolls rather than join in with the games of her more boisterous siblings. It hadn't been for the want of trying, but as Rosie grew up she found it difficult to grasp things. 'It was frustrating trying to teach her anything and you had to show her several times. You'd be fed up by then,' her brother Andy said. 'My parents shouted at her to try to make it sink in.'

The little girl with long dark hair right down to her waist would irritate her siblings. 'Come on, Rosie! Keep up! Keep up!' they'd call to her as they hurried to get to school or run an errand, but to no avail, as Rosie always lagged behind. And soon, kids being what they are, they nicknamed her Dozy Rosie – which was the name that her father both encouraged and played into . . .

But although Rose struggled to keep up physically and intellectually, her contemporaries remember her as being polite and always doing as she was told. There were others, however – neighbours and peers – who barely remembered her at all, as she was so quiet as to be almost invisible. Rose probably learnt this as a way of coping, for when Bill was at home the house was deathly quiet, and meals would be taken in silence. If the children so much as wriggled in their chairs or dared start eating before their father, Bill's face would contort into a terrifying expression before he lashed out at them verbally and with his fists. But, as Andy Letts said of his younger sister Rosie, 'She was so quiet and obedient that Dad didn't notice her to tell her off.' Instead she would sit quietly doing her sewing or knitting, which her mother had taught her.

The family were constantly walking on eggshells around Bill, even quite literally when he smashed all the eggs on the floor in front of his hungry family: the only food they had that day. He would also spoil all the food they had by pouring salt into it and, on one occasion, put soap in the gas cooker so that Daisy couldn't cook hot food for herself and the children. As soon as Bill stormed out, Daisy rushed round to the neighbours, sobbing. Mrs Cloke went round to help her clean it out and to clean up the kitchen, where Bill had tipped the contents of the dustbin all over the floor.

As Bill continued to wreak havoc on his family, Daisy was desperate to take the children and leave him, but with no women's refuges at the time, and her mother seriously ill, she simply had nowhere to go. Daisy was also too ashamed to tell her family the truth about Bill. And as he was such a well-versed 'street angel, house devil', who would believe her anyway when everyone thought *she* was the problem? But as time went on, opinion began to change as Bill's paranoia and irrational outbursts became impossible to hide even from the neighbours. Bill had returned home early from work one day to find Daisy innocently exchanging the time of day with other women outside the house. Flying into a rage, he punched Daisy in the face, grabbed her by the hair and dragged her back into the house, where he continued beating her. The neighbours were so shocked that they called the police. But times were such that abuse in the home was neither uncommon nor always taken seriously; indeed, a small group of children, who watched the incident from further along the road, had seen it in their own homes often enough too.

The three oldest girls had breaks from home at the orphanage, where Daisy no doubt hoped they might have a safe and better life. During sporadic periods when she wasn't depressed, Daisy did try her best to help the children lead a normal life – to enjoy the kind of childhood she'd had herself. On rare occasions, this included allowing friends of the children to come round to play. But even then she would be on edge, for Daisy knew if Bill found out about it, he would 'discipline' her and the children. Rita New, then Williams, a childhood friend of oldest girl Patsy, remembers: 'Mrs Letts was a very kind lady; she was lovely, and even though they were poor she made me Spam sandwiches for my tea with the girls. But as soon as the dad was about to come home from work, I had to go home.'

Daisy felt knots in her stomach and her teeth began to chatter as the time approached for Bill to return, which pre-school Rosie would have picked up on. The children also lived in fear of their father and, as well as abiding by his strict rules, had to undertake duties he set them. These 'duties' were household chores, which he expected the school-age children to do both before and after lessons each day. If the children didn't wake up on time, Bill threw a bucket of icy water over them as they slept in the bed beside young Rosie. And if the chores weren't done to Bill's satisfaction – if he found even so much as a grease mark on the windowsill – he would make them clean the entire house from top to bottom all over again.

From mopping the bathroom floor to scouring the kitchen clean, this pattern of existence was like being on board ship. And even those children too small to clean had to help with the washing and ironing. 'You didn't dare argue with him,' as Andy said. 'One look from him would send the fear of God through you.' As Daisy and the older children tried to ensure everything was 'shipshape' so as not to provoke Bill, Rosie learnt a valuable lesson early on: to be obedient and to keep her head down to survive.

To Rosie and her siblings who didn't go away to school and therefore knew no different, nothing Bill did was extraordinary;

to them it was normal, while to most outsiders 'Dad' was still seen as the smart and charming man in the beret. And if others thought he was charming, then it validated that view: it must be right.

In early 1959, Rosie, never having been read a bedtime story, set off for her first day at Northam Primary School, armed only with this view of life, and where she was to remain as quiet and eager to please as she was at home. In class Rosie was said to sit and stare at the blackboard for hours; her voice and language was still baby-like, and she continued to suck her thumb long after the time children usually stop, obviously still needing the comfort it gave her.

Rosie did not do well academically and was held down a year at the school. This is not necessarily a measure of her intelligence, for although Rose lacked maturity, children from troubled backgrounds often have problems concentrating at school as it has little or no meaning in their struggle for survival. Practice at the school was such that less able pupils were made to stand in the corner, wearing a dunce's cap. Rose was one of those children. Even given the era, it was neither a usual nor acceptable form of punishment for a child. The school already had a poor record for the 11+ exam, and was subject to local speculation – it was rumoured that a particular teacher liked to touch the girls there if he could. A child with learning difficulties was also said to have been caned there before Rosie arrived, although the slipper was the usual form of punishment for all the pupils.

However, Rosie continued to be 'polite', 'steady' and 'sensible' with her teachers for the most part – slipping under the radar here, too, while her inability to join in with her peer group left her isolated and open to being teased. Little wonder that Rosie would either stay off school or, when she went, preferred to play with children younger than herself, or played alone at break-time: in Rosie's world.

Yet, although being slow at her lessons, Rose was later able to write very well, and particularly since being in prison. Her letter as a young teenager to Fred – 'Last night made me realise we are two people, not two soft chairs to be sat on . . .' – even shows a gift for words.

When Rosie's baby brother Graham came along, the little girl at last found she had a playmate – even if it was at home. 'Baby! Mummy! Baby!' she yelped with glee as Daisy let her help bathe and feed him. She was to do the same when her youngest brother, Gordon, arrived three years later in 1960, when Rosie was almost seven. A few years later, this behaviour would develop into something shockingly inappropriate and disturbing, suggesting that Rosie's boundaries had become seriously blurred along the way.

It is deeply ironic that Rose would demonstrate such a strong maternal instinct so young. It is possible that she enjoyed spending her free time with her younger siblings because they were small and helpless and could neither challenge her nor make her feel foolish. Significantly, Rose would later lose interest in her *own* babies as soon as they grew a little older and developed wills of their own. Being held back a year at school also gave Rosie the opportunity to discover the power she had over younger children. On one occasion she was said to have gone home with a gang of younger children from her class, pouring them imaginary cups of tea on the grass verge outside her house.

If things were beginning to pick up for Rosie at this time, by the mid to late 1950s they were also improving for the rest of the family, when Bill found full-time work at last, at Bernard Smith's TV repair shop in nearby Barnstaple. With his background in electronic engineering, the job was ideal for Bill, who serviced the televisions and went round to people's homes to install them. The family had a decent income at last, and Bill was given a works' van to drive around in. As television was such a new and glamorous phenomenon at the time, it also gave Bill status in the village. This was important to Bill, who liked to brag of his achievements, to mark himself out as superior to others in the village. That said, the neighbours had already begun to notice all was not quite right with Bill, who at times seemed almost delusional.

Having taken to digging potholes in his back garden for no apparent reason after work, he then began digging a trench to create a ha-ha. These are the deep ditches commonly found at stately homes, which divide the formal gardens from the rest of the grounds – but Bill was putting one in the tiny front garden of his council house. As a former neighbour remembered, 'He had to fill the ditch in eventually, as there was mud everywhere. But he never did the back garden where they [the kids] played, it was a mess.'

But if Bill had delusions of grandeur, he could still charm the ladies, and he is alleged to have had an affair with the wife of a respected small businessman while on his rounds in the area. Bill's relationship with his own wife continued after the affair petered out, although Daisy might well have wished that her husband had run off with another woman; for, as she later told her family, she had by now come to hate Bill. And her feelings towards him would not change, even after his death.

Bill, on the other hand, was unconcerned about Daisy, although he did harbour a soft spot closer to home . . .

5

Daddy's Girl

THE EXPERIENCE OF EVERY child growing up in the same household is different, and this was the case with the Letts children. As Rosie's older brother, Andy, was growing up, his father was extremely cruel to him. Bill saw his first-born son as competition: a threat to his own masculinity in a house hitherto full of women, so that no matter what Andy did to try to please Bill or to seek his approval, he never could. Andy, like Rose, had been brought up with his father at home from day one after his birth. And with no other experience of life at this time other than at Morwenna Park Road, Andy spent many years blaming himself for his father's violent outbursts, believing that he had to be a better son to make things right. The younger boys, Graham and Gordon, when they came along, were also savagely beaten by their father, and Bill also attacked Joyce and Patsy. But for Rosie and her sister Glenys, three years her senior, the story was different.

While Daisy did whatever she could to stop Bill beating Andy if the chores weren't up to scratch, Rosie and Glenys were often spared doing them. Glenys was away at 'naval school' between the age of 6 and 8, together with her big sisters, but when she came home, Bill allowed her to sit in the bedroom reading her comics while the other children did the work around the house. Bill knew Glenys was bright and she was looked on as the brains of the family, later going to night school and working at GCHQ, the Government Communications Headquarters in

48

Cheltenham. Joyce's role was that of the 'little mother' of the house, a mini-Daisy doing the washing and ironing and helping with the children, while Patsy went to live with their grandparents. Soon after Rosie started school, she too was given her share of the chores to get on with. But Rosie was as slow to do these as everything else, and whined in her babyish voice (which she retained as an adult). To spare her their father's wrath when he got home, the other children did her chores for her. But then, to her siblings' amazement, Bill began allowing her to duck out of doing them altogether.

He also began turning a blind eye to her breaking the rules at the dinner table, where she would play with her food while her siblings had to finish all theirs. But what Rosie perhaps lacked in conventional intelligence, she was more than making up for with intelligence of another kind. As her older brother was to say, 'Rosie was very clever as a young child in learning how to manipulate Dad.' Her inability to do things 'right' and her childish ways would both charm and amuse Bill. 'He felt sorry for her,' Andy explained, 'and would let her off.'

Having realised his youngest daughter was vulnerable, he took her under his wing. But unbeknown to the family, there was another, darker, side to Bill's protective and softening attitude towards her. For it is here that Bill is believed to have begun secretly grooming his little girl in his own sexual desires, and by satisfying his demands, Rosie soon learnt that her home life could be happier than that of her siblings.

Thus, while Bill openly referred to Rosie as being 'as thick as two short planks' and laughed at her shortcomings, he was in fact encouraging her in the role of Dozy Rosie so that he could exploit her. And at the same time that he was cultivating Rosie, he was still torturing his wife and children. Not only did Rosie live with this on a daily basis, absorbing it as nothing more than normal family behaviour, it is here she also learned another important lesson in life: that if her mother couldn't shield them from their violent father, then older men such as her father could be her protector: that she could charm and 'please' them, as she did Bill, to ensure her survival. It was a skewed way of thinking, but completely logical given her circumstances. Although Bill never attempted to abuse Glenys in any way, Rose had become known in the family as 'Daddy's Girl'. Yet this was a smoke-screen, for if anyone was Bill's favourite it was Glenys.

While children seek out the best way to survive, fathers who abuse tend to focus on their more vulnerable child or children. Glenys was bright and feisty and therefore more of a risk to Bill in that she might raise the alarm about him outside the family home, and was also more likely to be believed. In Rosie he had a child who was immature for her age, and who was already regarded as 'disturbed' by at least one of her siblings. It was not, therefore, a difficult choice for Bill to make. But while some fathers use fear and intimidation to groom their children, it is likely that Bill played the card of the loving father. Geoffrey Wansell says in his book, *An Evil Love*, that the version of parental love Rosie received at her father's knee was 'distorted', 'perverted and brutal' but, if this was the case, the little girl didn't know it – to her it would have been customary. Bill is also likely to have made Rosie believe she was 'special', while their relationship, as Christopher Berry-Dee and Steven Morris suggest in *Born Killers*, gradually became 'intimate until the point of inappropriateness until it became fully sexual', although this was possibly not for some years hence.

And as Bill continued to groom Rosie, she began to grow up discovering the power she had over older men, whom she would later use to protect her. And, as she watched her father beat her siblings, in Bill she had a role model for Fred West; thus Rose was a 'Daddy's Girl' of a different sort.

Serial Killers and Favouritism

'We were all frightened to death of me Dad. He were like a monster ... we'd all sit there in fear,' Carl Sutcliffe, the Yorkshire Ripper's younger brother, was to say, although it could easily have been Andy Letts talking about his father, Bill.* However, in cases where a budding male serial killer is brought up by both parents, they often appear to be the mother's favourite as she tries to protect their 'weak' son from a bullying father.

Peter Sutcliffe was the oldest of six children who spent the first few days of his life in an incubator. A sensitive and sickly boy who liked art and music, his father mocked him as being weak and a 'Mummy's boy' – unlike his stronger younger brother Mick. Bullied by his father, Sutcliffe not unnaturally clung to his mother's skirts as a child. And like Daisy, while Kathleen Sutcliffe did not have the means to leave her cruel husband, she did whatever she could to protect her eldest son from him. Peter, in return, idolised his mother and called her 'the angel'. He even changed his name to Coonan, his mother's maiden name in recent years. As he grew up, Sutcliffe came to believe there were only two types of women in the world: angels and whores. While his wife was also an 'angel', other women met in pubs and on the street were 'whores', who he said he was on a mission to kill. In overcompensating for a bullying father, Sutcliffe's mother raised a narcissistic, cruel and self-serving son.

Dr Harold Shipman, who killed hundreds of patients over several decades, was also his mother's favourite. Called Fred within the family, he was brought up in a council house in Nottingham. His father was a lorry driver and his mother, Vera, a housewife with aspirations for her oldest boy, who was showing promise at school. Vera invested a great deal of time and effort

* As told to Gordon Burn in *Somebody's Husband, Somebody's Son* (1984).

in her son during his formative years, instilling in him a belief that he was different to others, even his own siblings: that he was superior to them. Vera had been illegitimate and bore the stigma of this at the time. She had also worked in menial jobs and wanted better for her son – possibly so that she could bask in reflected glory. She told Harold he was destined for greater things, a position in life such as a doctor, where people would look up to him. Just like Bertha Letts with her young son Bill, Vera Shipman made sure her boy was always smartly turned out in formal attire, including a tie, wherever he went. His style of dress and his haughty attitude made him unpopular with his peers at school. Harold also found college difficult, particularly socially because he had no idea how to mix with people and was, for the most part, a loner. Although his mother didn't live to see her boy become a doctor, Shipman carried with him the supercilious, sneering attitude he'd developed as a child, talking down to his patients and colleagues.

Myra Hindley had a bullying father who beat her mother, but from an early age she lived with her grandmother, Ellen Maybury, in Manchester, who was said to be 'devoted' to her young granddaughter. In the US, Charlene Gallego, who killed a number of young girls with her husband Gerald, was another 'Daddy's girl'. Charlene's wealthy father doted on her, spoiling her with presents and money and believing she could do no wrong. With Rose, the dynamic of being 'Daddy's girl' meant she was protected from physical violence by the dominant, violent parent – although this was in exchange for something equally abusive. Rosie's experiences were actually closest to those of another Mummy's boy and eldest child: a one Frederick West. Or Freddie, as his parents affectionately called him.

In this case, Freddie's father, like Sutcliffe's, was a bully and sexually aggressive. Walter West frequently boasted of his sexual exploits to his son and forced himself on young girls in the fields in front of the boy. Walter had wanted a son, but as soon as

Freddie began to grow up, he became jealous of him as his wife doted on the boy. As Fred's younger brother Doug was to say, Freddie was 'Mammy's blue-eyed boy' who could do no wrong. She took her oldest son's word over his younger siblings' and her husband's, and stuck up for the boy even when she knew he was in the wrong. In return, Freddie worshipped his mother – just as Sutcliffe had worshipped his mother, who he called 'the angel', and Shipman, who had also, as a young teenager, nursed his beloved mother until her death from cancer.

Although Rosie escaped her father's beatings, Freddie did not get off these any more lightly from his parents, particularly his mother, who would administer the beatings with a thick leather belt. Yet he was still her favourite and if anyone picked on him, including the teachers at the village school, she would race after them and give them 'what for'. Being Mrs West's 'favourite boy', however, didn't just mean protecting him, but something more sinister . . .

But there is another Mummy's boy integral to this story: Rosie's own father, Bill, who, unbeknown to Daisy and the family, had a secret that he was keeping all to himself and which Rosie and the family would not find out about until twenty years later, after his death . . .

6

There's Something About Bill

IRONICALLY, OR PERHAPS NOT, Bill shared some similarities with the profile of male serial killers. Like the Yorkshire Ripper, he too had been a weak, sickly child who was cosseted by his mother as she tried to protect him from a bullying and violent father. His father, William, had not wanted him; but just as soon as he came to accept him, he lost interest again when Bill began developing a will of his own (as Rose was to do with her own children).

William's wife Bertha was a whist player and would make a point of going out two or three evenings a week to see friends and play a few rounds, leaving William to look after his son. She hoped to get the two to bond. William, however, was cold towards the boy, and Bertha would come home to find her small son alone and neglected. Later, when William bothered to speak to his son at all, he never stopped telling the boy, 'You were an accident, we didn't want you.'

Just before Bill was due to start school, he contracted rheumatic fever, a disease that killed many children at the time. The illness is characterised by a high temperature, painful joints and severe mood changes. There is also the possibility that a long-term heart condition can develop from the scarring, creating problems later in life. Bertha was beside herself as her son lay gravely ill but, using all her professional skills, nursed the boy back to health. Bill would, however, remain a weak and sickly boy, and Bertha became overprotective towards him, mollycoddling him.

But while Bill became the focus of Bertha's attention, the cracks in her marriage began to deepen. Rheumatic fever in the 1920s and 1930s was often associated with poverty and malnutrition. Yet the Letts' home wasn't an unskilled working-class household, although money had been in short supply there for some years. The problem was William, who had taken building work for a short while after his return from the Great War, but soon lost interest. Bertha had long since realised that if the family were to have any income, it would have to be she that earned it. And while she worked and looked after the house and their little boy, she transferred any remaining affection she had for William to Bill, indulging the child whenever she could.

As a former neighbour said, 'Bill was spoilt . . . She [Bertha] took him to school and met him after, and always took his cap off before he went in the classroom and combed his hair, and the same when he went home in the evening.'

Bertha wrapped up her frail son to protect him from the cold north Devon winters, and in the little spare time she had, she knitted Bill long woollen stockings for his thin little legs. Because of Bill's sickness, he started school long after his peers in the village, but when he did finally attend Northam Primary, Bertha insisted he wear the long knitted stockings beneath his short trousers. This made him a target for the other schoolchildren who, like his own father, called Bill a 'cissy'. 'We all thought it was very queer,' one of his friends, Ronnie Lloyd, was to say many years later. Bill hadn't long been at the school when the other children started to bully him. As soon as Bertha found out she was straight down the school, sorting out the bullies herself (just as Freddie West's mother would do years later).

The situation wasn't helped by Bertha taking Bill to school and fetching him, even when he was 11, instead of letting him walk the short distance by himself or with his classmates.

Consequently, young Bill didn't possess the social skills to enable him to mix with other children at school, and he had no friends outside it because his parents simply would not allow it. Instead, he was stuck at home in a sterile environment with his morose father while Bertha was out doing her rounds.

William had narcissist personality traits – he was attention-seeking, envious, self-centred and lacked empathy. Having been brought up with older sisters attending to his every whim, he now found himself playing second fiddle to his son and didn't like it. When he eventually turned his hand to paid work as a butler-cum-gigolo, it was as much about receiving attention from women as it was about money or sex. His new 'job', however, only served to intensify the frosty silence in the house between himself and Bertha, which Bill had to endure while growing up. Later, when Bill married Daisy, he'd wanted to avoid the mistakes his parents had made, but he simply had no idea how to go about it.

As Bill grew into a teenager, the strange young man was not popular around the Northam area and had few friends. His strict and controlling father set him a time by which he had to be home each evening. If he missed the deadline by even a minute, his father would thrash him and lock him out, forcing Bill to sleep in the shed. It was the same behaviour Bill would later inflict on his own children, as the bullied became the bully. Because of the toxic parenting he'd received, he would also have harboured a lot of anger, which he would unleash unfairly on his wife and children.

Unlike his father, however, Bill was a hard worker, and Bertha encouraged her son to get a skill so that he would not have to rely on unskilled, low-paid work. Bill found training and employment in an electrical shop in the nearby town of Bideford, and then moved on to the Bristol Airport Company, where he worked as a radio engineer. It was around this time that it first became apparent that all was not well with Bill, who began to think his workmates were all 'ganging up' on him. He started to become aloof and distrustful of people and was always on edge. His odd manner did nothing to endear him to his colleagues, and even less to the opposite sex, whose rejection of him before Daisy only confirmed his bitter view of the world.

Later, he appeared to have delusions of grandeur when he attempted to build the ha-ha, believed people were against him, became preoccupied with violence, and suspected Daisy of having affairs – these are all symptomatic of paranoid schizophrenia. Bill was also a sadist, who enjoyed inflicting pain and humiliation on his family, for when he threw away the children's food and tossed boiling water over his wife, he would be grinning with pleasure at 'teaching them a lesson'. As Daisy told writer Howard Sounes:* '. . . He [Bill] seemed to enjoy making you unhappy.' But what Daisy didn't know until she read his medical records many years later, after his death, was that Bill had a secret he had managed to keep even from the Navy. As a young man, he had been diagnosed with paranoid schizophrenia and had suffered 'severe psychotic' episodes ever since.

His illness, however, appears to have remained untreated for most of his adult life with all the devastating effects this had on his family, including his youngest daughter, Rosie. As a former neighbour said, 'The family had a terrible life with Bill. He was a very violent and cruel man. He would beat his wife all the time and make a mess in the house so that she [Daisy] and the children would have to clear it up.'

Clearly although appearances were important to Daisy, she could no longer hide what was going on behind closed doors. Bill's cruel streak was also evident when he began working at Bernard Smith's TV repair shop in Barnstaple in the late 1950s. A former engineer remembered working alongside him in the service department, where Bill would brag to his colleagues

* In *Fred & Rose* (1995) by Howard Sounes

about his time in the Navy, recalling with relish how he played tricks on the Wrens by giving them electric shocks – just as he enjoyed Daisy being given electric-shock therapy. And it didn't stop there as whenever a new apprentice joined the service department, Bill would give them a shock with an electrical insulation tester known as the 'Megger': a device delivering some 400 volts. The engineers did not all share his enthusiasm for his cruel pranks or his warped sense of humour, but Bill would find it immensely funny, guffawing with delight at the other person's pain. This sadistic behaviour also smacks of the Yorkshire Ripper, who would laugh manically at the expense of others as he played grisly pranks on them. This included using human skulls to frighten schoolgirls with as they passed by the graveyard where he worked in Bingley, and grinning with pleasure as he threw a 10-year-old girl down the stairs. But Bill wasn't a killer. Or was he . . . ?

Bill did, however, have a few good days where he would happily plan for events such as family birthdays and anniversaries, but Daisy became so disturbed by her husband's behaviour, she began to think it was all to do with the moon. If the moon was full, Daisy told herself, 'I have to be careful.' There is no doubt that Bill's mental health affected Daisy's, and of course that of the children too. Had Daisy known about Bill's diagnosis, she could have sought help, or even had him sectioned when he had a psychotic episode. This would then have given the medical profession the chance to treat him and allowed the family some peace. Instead, Rosie and her siblings grew up with this behaviour as the norm and, in the case of Andy Letts, labouring under the misconception that they were somehow to blame for it.

Although Bill's family were not aware of his illness, children in the area would notice his odd behaviour and call out 'schizo' as they passed him on the street, little realising just how close to the truth this was. This bears striking similarities to Peter

Sutcliffe's father, John, who also had a flamboyant style of dress and peculiar ways. When local kids met him in the streets of Bingley they would shout the same thing, 'Oi, schizo!', and run away laughing.

Adults around Morwenna were also developing their own ideas about why the Letts children were never seen out playing. As a neighbour said, 'My mum worried all the time about us [being out] because of the tide, but their parents worried about what they'd say [was going on indoors].' The neighbours heard the children's cries and called in social services, but were shocked when, apart from the girls being sent away to a children's home for a while, nothing changed. And if the neighbours complained to Bill about it, he would simply close the windows, lock the doors and get out the copper stick.

When Daisy was well enough, she would take the children for long walks across the Burrows country park, to the sheltered beaches of Northam, Westward Ho! and Appledore. Here they could escape their psychotic father and play to their hearts' content: looking for starfish in the rock pools, paddling and making sandcastles, until it was time to go home again when Daisy would ensure they were cleaned up first. Daisy was still desperate to leave Bill, and promised Patsy she would just as soon as the younger children had grown up. But every year Bill made sure there was another baby on the way to keep her there, although Daisy was to have several miscarriages.

When the children got older, 8-year-old Andy or one of his big sisters would push the well-worn pram over the Burrows with Gordon – the latest Letts arrival – inside. Three-year-old Graham would sit on the pram seat at the front, while Lassie, Glenys's collie, ran along beside this – briefly – happy little bunch. The children would pass an aged donkey in a field on their journey, which they would make a fuss of and play games of trying to guess its age. Rosie, however, never went on any of these trips but stayed at home with her mother, who would teach her knitting and crochet and later dressmaking – which Rose would excel at and use as a means of enticing a young victim to her bedroom in Cromwell Street many years later. Otherwise, little 7-year-old Rosie would be at home, alone with her father.

When Bill wasn't trying to electrocute his workmates, he would take Patsy and Joyce out in the work's van. One of the young apprentices at Smith's was keen on Patsy, but Bill warned him off her, telling him that his family were of the 'Catholic persuasion'. This was one of Bill's many lies: the Letts' were not raised as Catholics and didn't go to church at all at this time. It was no coincidence that this was when Daisy had just had another baby, and clearly Bill had his own ideas for Patsy.

When the 15-year-old got out of the bath one day, her father followed her into her bedroom where he pushed her onto the bed and tried to remove her bathrobe. Patsy screamed as he tried to touch her and pushed him away. She then rushed out to the landing, where Bill caught up with her and hurled the young girl down the stairs. Her injuries were such that she had to attend the Casualty department at the local Barnstaple hospital. After making a second attempt to molest Patsy, Bill beat her when she resisted. Patsy fled Northam soon after this, joining the Wrens with the help of her friend's father, Mr Sander Job, who gave her a reference. With Patsy gone, Bill bullied his next daughter, Joyce. On a trip out in the van, he took her to a pub. Bill was barely a drinker himself, but tried to ply the 14-year-old with gin masked with orange juice. Joyce had always stood up to her father, which didn't go down well with Bill, who would hit her.

Soon afterwards, Daisy and the younger children helped Joyce move her bed across to her friend, Diane Glover's house. Diane was two years younger than Joyce and both girls attended secondary school in Bideford at the time. The younger girl remembered sharing her bedroom for several weeks with Joyce, who said her father 'had turned strange', and that she needed to get away from him. This begs the question: did Daisy know that Bill had been physically abusive to both the older girls and had tried to sexually abuse Patsy? And if so, did she also have any doubts or concerns about his special 'bond' with their youngest daughter?

Joyce began work in Bideford soon afterwards and moved back home, but when her father hit her again, she went to stay with another friend. Glenys was the next daughter in line, but Bill did not turn his attentions to her. As a small child she could happily sit on her father's lap without him ever touching her inappropriately, or hitting her. Although the exact nature of Bill's relationship with his youngest daughter is unclear at this point, he had actually begun to look for opportunities elsewhere to satisfy his lust for young girls.

The Rock & Roll Club

Bill had only been in his job at Smith's for a year or so when, having been caught using the works van to go on day trips to Plymouth, he was sacked. Bill found another job soon after, working for television repairers, Squires in Bideford, but he quickly lost this job too and money became scarce once again. Some time before the last child, Gordon, was born in 1960, Bill obtained a part-time evening job as a caretaker in the Order of Buffalo Hall behind the Kingsley Inn public house in Northam. Ironically, given Bill's track record with his own children, he set up a youth club in the hall with his friend, Ronnie Lloyd. The two men played their favourite rock-and-roll records on Bill's tape recorder and amplifiers. From Eddie Cochran and Gene Vincent through to Buddy Holly and Elvis, the recordings were all in mono. There was very little for teenagers to do in the village at the time, and these weekly rock-and-roll sessions soon became popular, even though only fizzy pop and crisps were allowed. As a local lady who attended the club as a young girl remembered, 'Bill was always saying to the teenagers, "You're not allowed to drink or misbehave." He wouldn't have any of it.' Even so, he didn't let his own teenage daughters attend it.

Several months later, Bill fell behind with the rent on his council house. Rumour had it he had debts from a café and shop he'd once run with a friend in Redruth during his time at a naval airbase. He was also said to be spending what little income he had on himself, and buying modern recording equipment which he'd invite Joyce and her friends to sing into in the scullery. But whether Bill couldn't or wouldn't pay the rent, he began making claims to the council that his house was poorly maintained. When council officials called to see for themselves, Bill bolted the door and refused to let them in. At the same time, the youth club closed down amidst rumours in the village . . .

7

Plymouth Ahoy!

I N THE COLD WINTER of February 1962, the family got up in the middle of the night, packed the few personal belongings they had and set off for their new home in the large, sprawling city of Plymouth, in south Devon. As Bill could not afford to hire a removal van, the family had to leave most of their furniture and belongings behind. Their leaving was not a surprise to everyone who passed number 57 in the following days, as one of the girls had told her friend Rita that the family were about to do a 'moonlight flit'. But still it came as a shock to most of the neighbours at Morwenna as the Letts family had lived there for over a decade.

Bill and Daisy told the children they were moving as there was no work in north Devon. This was partly true, but as well as owing rent on the house, there was another reason. As another neighbour said, 'Social services stepped in and stopped the youth club, then they flitted off', after rumours of Bill's penchant for young girls began to circulate. Once more Bill appears to have been careful about the girls he selected, for both Rita Williams and Diane Glover, who lived with their parents in the same street as the family, recalled never having any problems with him or even being aware of any abuse going on.

During his time at the repair shop, Bill had been making secret trips to Plymouth where, with his naval background, he'd found full-time work on ships' radar at the naval dockyard in Devonport. This, though, as with most things connected to Bill, was not quite as important as he liked to make it sound and actually amounted to his working in the stores. But it was a job, nonetheless, and one which would provide for his large family, Bill having found accommodation for them in an area close to his works.

If the family had been cramped in their three-bedroomed semi at Northam, they were now having to squeeze into a confined attic flat that boasted a tiny kitchen-cum-dining area, an even smaller middle room where they could watch TV, and an outside toilet serving the two families living there. Joyce came with them, but the flat only had two bedrooms, which meant the six growing girls and boys still had to share bedrooms and beds. Soon, however, Bill hit Joyce again, attacking her on the stairs and blacking her eye. Joyce ran into the Scoblings' flat below, shoeless and sobbing. Later that day, the 15-year-old returned from work to find her belongings on the doorstep and Daisy (possibly at Bill's behest) telling her to leave.

To escape their claustrophobic environment, the older of the five remaining children were allowed more freedom. As Andy recollected, 'We were always out as we were too crowded.' He and Rosie would play in the long yard at the back of the house with a pet rabbit that one of the children had acquired. As he got older, Andy found he was able to wander off without being missed, and would lose himself in the city and the wastelands where houses had once stood before the heavy bombing raids on the city during the war. Rosie, though, still had to stay close by, in the yard or the flat.

Although moving from the close-knit village she had grown up in to a large city may have seemed strange to Rosie at first, it was not the upheaval it might have been as she did not have any friends in Northam to miss. At Benbow Street, however, she made her first little friend – the daughter of the family who owned the house and lived in the lower part of it: Joan Scobling. Joan was a year older than Rose and, if Joan wasn't there, there were always plenty of other children at hand to play with. As a former neighbour, Mrs Blake, said, 'I can remember the children – with the Scoblings and the Letts, there seemed to be dozens of them around.'

In reality, though, as Joan recalled in the *Plymouth Evening Herald** at the time of Rose's trial, 'It was very, very rare that Rosemary was let out to play, and she seemed quite happy to stay in after school and help her mother with the chores.' Rosie was also remembered as a 'good little girl' and 'obedient', with no signs of the monster she was to become just a few years later. On occasion she was allowed to help the old lady next door with her laundry in return for some biscuits. Rosie delighted in pretending to be a housewife and, although still only 8, she was a dab hand at the ironing by now (which she'd make her own children do from a very young age).

Since arriving in Plymouth in early 1962, Rosie 8, Andy, 9, and Graham, 5, had been enrolled at the local school in Devonport. The school was on the High Street and had suffered heavy bombing during the war. A new school opened that same year as part of the regeneration programme in the area, and the Letts children, along with the rest of their classmates, moved to the Morice Town Primary in September. Despite this, little else had changed for the Letts children for, as one of their neighbours in Plymouth recalled in the press at the time of the trial, while Rose 'wasn't academically very bright', she and her siblings were always turned out as 'clean as new pins'. What the new neighbours probably didn't realise was that the children's smart clothes often hid bruises, as Daisy instructed Bill to only hit them where it wouldn't show – although with the older girls gone, this applied to the boys rather than to Glenys and Rosie.

When the story of the House of Horrors first broke, the family who'd lived in the flat below them at Benbow Street

* *Plymouth Evening Herald*, 22 November 1995

remembered the Letts 'for their cleanliness – it was almost an obsession with Rosemary's mother', Joan Scobling was to say. Daisy's depression had also returned around this time and Bill's OCD was still very much hers. She had become particularly worried about the shared toilet and she scrubbed it with bleach at least four times a day (which was something Rose would make her own children do some years later).

Andy recalled how his big sister Joyce was 'lovely' and 'always brought us little treats' when he and his siblings were small. She'd come back to Benbow Street that Christmas with a hamper for her little brothers and sisters, bought with money she'd saved each week from her job. She'd been forced to take refuge with her friend's parents in Northam after Bill's last attack, but travelling back to Plymouth, she was heartbroken when her mother shut the door in her face. Glenys, on the other hand, still seemed able to get away with more as far as Bill was concerned. The neighbour's cousin, Brian Scobling, who lived next door, recalled how he'd had a crush on Glenys: 'I remember I asked Glenys for a kiss. I suppose we were about 13 or 14 years old, and she was my first girlfriend.'*

If Bill knew about Glenys's friendship with Brian, his response was very different from when the young engineer at Smith's in Barnstaple had showed an interest in his oldest girl, Patsy. While Glenys had her little pal next door, and Andy would lose himself in the city, Rosie – when she wasn't spending the rare occasion playing with Joan – was left isolated once more with only her mother and baby brothers for company. And when Daisy took the little boys out, Rosie would possibly once more be left alone in the flat with her father.

Since moving to Plymouth, Rosie had begun to suffer nightmares. She was being bullied at her new school, and would run home in tears. A former school pal in Plymouth recalled later

* *Plymouth Evening Herald*, 22 November 1995

how vulnerable she'd been. The little girl was also exhibiting other disturbed behaviour at this time: she came home from school and cut up the bedclothes she shared with her brothers and sisters to make clothes for her dolls. And, as can be symptomatic of 'troubled' children, Rosie frequently told lies. These were not practical lies to get her out of trouble, or even childish boasts, but were transparent and pointless. 'She said stupid things,' as her brother was to say.

Most children grow out of lying as they get older, but the little girl from Benbow Street with the long plaits in her hair would go on to become a pathological liar, i.e., lying to get her own way with no concern for anyone else. But as her little friend, Joan, was to tell the press at the time of her trial, 'I find it all totally unbelievable. If someone had told me Rosemary had become a nun, I would have found it easier to believe.'

In early January 1964, when Rosie was 10, her father learned his lungs were diseased from working with hazardous materials in the docks and he would have to leave his job. With the baby of the family, Gordon, only just enrolled at Morice Town Primary School, it was a matter of days before the family suddenly upped sticks and moved again.

Bill was, if nothing else, a hard worker – and found full-time work almost immediately in another part of the country. He had always boasted he could turn his hand to anything to earn a living, and in truth he did: from electrical engineer and wireless operator to steward, TV repair man and cook. However, despite Bill's unhealthy interest in young girls, his next job was in the kitchens of a children's home near Chipping Camden, on the Gloucestershire and Warwickshire border. The job came with a rambling, detached Victorian house in the nearby village of Mickleton. The house was 'dark and cold, like a fridge, even in the summer', Andy was to say, but it had long gardens and an orchard where the children loved to play and watch the swallows nesting, their only respite from the violence and shouting.

Rosie and her brothers went to school in the picturesque Cotswold village of Moreton-in-Marsh but, nine months later, just before the start of the new school year, Bill either lost his job or decided to move on again. The freedom and space which Rosie and her siblings had enjoyed for the first time in their lives at the old house was now gone as they moved back into cramped lodgings while Bill looked for another job and alternative accommodation.

In the latter part of 1964, Bill found work with an electronics firm in the pretty village of Bishop's Cleeve, on the outskirts of Cheltenham. Like the housing provided around Dagenham for the Ford car workers, the village boasted solid, red-brick housing built to accommodate the workers at the new industries in the area, including Smith's Aerospace, the local defence company that Bill now worked for. This meant another two changes of school for Rosie and her siblings, while the family remained in rooms above a coach builder's, Leo Tudor's, in Cheltenham, until they were allocated a house on the Smith's Estate. The few bits of furniture they'd accrued since leaving Northam then arrived out of storage.

Their new house was a modest semi occupying a corner plot in Tobyfield Road. With Bill's improved pay and conditions at Smith's, it seemed as if things were at last looking up for the family. But, of course, this could never be, as they had taken the same toxic problems with them. Added to which, everything about the family was built on secrets and lies. The girls who went to 'naval school' had no idea it was in fact a children's home, the younger siblings had no idea why their older sisters had to leave home; nor did the extended family realise that Bill's new job working on flight simulators was actually not so much 'hush-hush' as rather lowly. Bill's disappearance during his naval career, when he'd lived in Australia with another woman, remains to this day shrouded in mystery for some family members – even though he was gone for two years. His father having had an affair closer to home also seemed to have slipped under the radar.

Bill's own parents also kept secrets, for had they known about their son's psychotic illness, which, as Bertha was a nurse, they surely did, they hadn't told Daisy about it. In the family's new house at Bishop's Cleeve, as with the others, the truth was fragmented and compartmentalised between the parents and children, so that no one really knew what was going on right under their noses. The only one who had a complete picture in fact was 'Dad', whose moods continued to lurch from manic laughter to brooding silences and delusions until, like a pressure cooker without an air vent, he blew his lid. And while Rosie, in her formative years, would have grown up believing her father's behaviour was normal, she was being coached by Bill to share secrets with him that no child should.

This, then, was Rosie and the family's fresh start. While some twenty or so miles down the road in a village on the other side of the Forest of Dean lived a man twelve years her senior, who would be both Rosie's prince and her saviour: the young Freddie West. Or 'Weird Freddie', as he was known to his peers. But it would be another five years until they would meet and six years before she would kill for the first time, alone and unaided.

PART II

House of Cards: The Early Teen Years

8

'The Times They Are A-Changing . . .'

Bishop's Cleeve, near Cheltenham, Gloucestershire, 1964

B Y THE SPRING OF that year, Harold Wilson's Labour govern-ment had swept into power and the swinging sixties were well under way, with music from Dylan to the Beatles, Red Bus films, Mary Quant, Carnaby Street and the Pill. Jobs were also readily available and if you didn't like the one you were in, you could be in another by the next morning. During the autumn of 1964, Rosie turned 11 and the Letts were settling into their Gloucestershire home, where this new dawn wasn't wasted on Bill, who grasped at the opportunities it offered.

Having just started his new job at Smith's Aerospace, Bill went out and bought himself a briefcase and brand-new car. Already 'fanatical' about wearing a suit and tie every day, he began swan-ning around the village 'like he was a managing director of a company', as one of the family remembered. Bill was now earning about £30 a week. This was decent money at the time, although Daisy still wore the same old red winter coat she'd had ever since they'd been married. This wasn't something that concerned Bill; after all, he handed over his pay packet to his wife every week. But, as Daisy said, she was always the one with the 'worry' for the family budget, and if Bill had spent more than they could afford, she and the kids would be the ones that suffered as usual.

Rosie, following in Andrew and Glenys's footsteps, began Cleeve secondary school the next autumn. All three needed new uniforms again – navy blue this time – which Daisy scrimped and saved to provide, ensuring the children were well turned out as usual. While Daisy was left to juggle the household budget, items Bill purchased such as the briefcase, hi-tech stereos and a smart new car were not necessary to his job, but all part of his delusions of grandeur: symptoms of his illness. Bill didn't even have a driving licence and would never possess one, not even when, a few years later, he began taking Rosie out to the countryside to give her 'driving lessons'.

By this time, the two oldest girls, Patsy and Joyce, were making their own way in the world and had no contact with the family. Pat went to Australia with her new husband and Joyce was starting a family and training as a nurse. The five children who were still at home: Glenys, 14, Andy, 13, Rosie, 11, Graham, 7, and Gordon, 5, were crammed into two bedrooms in what was essentially a compact semi at 96 Tobyfield Road.

Once more, 11-year-old Rosie was the new kid on the block. She had begun overeating just before the family left Northam, and was a little plump by now. Overeating is often a way of trying to cope with stress and negative feelings, and it was something Rose would also do in later years. Rosie didn't find life at her new school any better than she had at her former schools, where she did not shine academically and found it almost impossible to make friends. With her puppy-fat and babyish ways, the young girl cut a solitary figure in the playground. One of her former peers at school remembered her as 'a social outcast', while the boy who had sat by her in class said she was so quiet that he barely remembered her. With no pals to play with, Rosie spent her spare time with her pet hamsters. She and her siblings would also fuss over Andy's dog, Ben, whose glossy coat was maintained by the raw eggs the dog loved to eat.

On one particular day, Ben had leapt over the fence and returned with a box of eggs the milkman had left on a neighbour's doorstep. As Daisy struggled to free the egg box from the reluctant dog's mouth, Rosie and her siblings burst into laughter. Eventually winning the tug of war, Daisy insisted the giggling children returned the box, complete with the teeth marks in it, to its rightful owner. But happy times such as this were few and far between, and certainly did not happen if Bill was at home – although he was never cruel to the dog, or any other animals they had, reserving this for his family.

While Rosie had no friends, her older brother Andy was also bullied at their new school. He became popular, however, as he was good at sports, particularly long-distance running. But just as Daisy had not visited her older three daughters at the children's homes, neither did she come to see Andy at sports day or Rosie and her siblings in anything they did at school. Daisy possibly didn't attend the children's school events early on because of her illness, but as one of the older girls was to say many years later, their mother didn't know how to nurture. Certainly there were no books in the house and the children were never read a bedtime story. Daisy also found it hard to comfort and support the children, particularly the girls as they grew older. This was possibly due to Daisy's own mother, Rose, who throughout Daisy's childhood had suffered from sclerosis of the liver, which is often associated with alcoholism. Rumour had it in the family that Daisy had actually gone into care as a child for a period of time, and that she'd received mysterious burns to her body. Having a seriously ill parent can in any case cause a young child to suffer from anxiety and depression. And with her mother being frequently hospitalised, Daisy's maternal role model was at best absent. This, coupled with Bill's own paternal role model, did not bode well for Rosie and her siblings.

If little had changed for Rosie at Bishop's Cleeve, neither had it for her less favoured siblings, who were still expected to rush home from school each day to perform a list of chores. The chores now took precedence over any homework they might have been set and put paid to the possibility of a social life, had they been allowed one. The only difference between the old life and the new was that some of the children were now growing into cowed and resentful young adults, while the bond between Bill and his youngest daughter would soon show signs of having intensified. Alongside this, Bill was finding new ways to bully and torture his family.

As his eldest son, Andrew, said: 'He would take pleasure in punching me in the stomach.' There were times, in fact, when Andy believes that if his mother had not stepped in, Bill would have killed him. 'Once he started beating you he couldn't stop, he just kept on going.' And he didn't just reserve such beatings for the older children. Graham, too, as a young boy had had his head smashed against a stone wall by his father. When Daisy intervened, it fed straight into Bill's paranoia that everyone was against him and he would turn on Daisy. As well as his fists, Bill also began using anything that came to hand, including an axe handle and a knife – cutting and jabbing at Andy with it when he took longer about getting his breakfast cereal than Bill wanted him to. Andy had just started an apprenticeship at Smith's, and the distressed boy plucked up the courage to go into the local police station to report the attack, his face and hands covered in blood. After telling the police the whole sorry story of life behind closed doors at Tobyfield Road, they decided not to take it any further and, once again, an opportunity to help the Letts children was missed. Only a few short years earlier, Patsy had been treated at two different hospitals for the injuries received after Bill had attacked her. She had been aged 14 at the time of the first attack, but there had been no police or children's services investigation into the assault.

These incidents gave clear signals to the Letts children – if any were needed – that there was no help out there, even when they asked for it. In a letter written to a pen pal from prison in 2005, Rosie says, 'My parents were sick people who should never have had children in the first place. They were control freaks and at their hands we suffered mental, physical and sexual abuse . . . No one cared for us EVER!"* She might as well have said 'nobody helped us either'. Ironically Andy, who was closest to Rose in age, and who often bore the brunt of his father's beatings, came to abhor violence, while Rosie, who mostly escaped his rages, came to be violent herself. Andy was better equipped to process and reject this kind of behaviour, while Rosie, as Brian Masters suggests in his book, 'She Must Have Known', saw her father's conduct 'as worthy of emulation, but had not the intelligence or subtlety to appraise its likely effect.'

Andy had also seen another version of family life at his girl-friend's house in Cheltenham, where he began to stay for periods of time. He had met Jackie Hughes while staying with his sister Glenys, who lived next door to her in Union Street. Having spent time with the Hughes family, he found family life there very different to his own at Tobyfield Road. It took him some while to adjust to the freedoms there, and he was astonished that the children could laugh openly and even chat over the meal table without fear of being beaten. 'I couldn't understand it,' Andy said. 'I didn't get it at all.'

There is of course, another dimension to this, While Daisy tried her best to protect Andy from Bill, she had failed to notice Bill's dark and insidious abuse of their daughter. Having realised there was no help coming from outside for herself and her siblings, this would have had the effect of reinforcing Rosie's position of siding with the strongest parent, and of acquiescing in Bill's grooming of her to ensure her survival.

The only time there was any respite from Bill was when Grandad Letts came to stay. Since Bertha had died shortly before Bill took off for Plymouth, William would often turn up to visit his son and family in their new home. The children would watch open-mouthed as Bill redirected his violent outbursts from Daisy

* Published in the *News of the World*, 28 September 2008

and themselves to William. As far as Bill was concerned, it was 'payback time' for the cruelty he'd suffered at his father's hand. He would hit the old man on the back of the legs and scream abuse into his face, berating him for owing him money which he would borrow off Bill and never pay back. (Bill would later do the exact same thing with his oldest son.) But, despite Bill's treatment of him, Grandad Letts continued to visit. He even set up home with the family for a while where he insisted the place was kept meticulously clean and tidy, just as he had with Bertha, and which his son Bill insisted on with his own family: an OCD legacy, as it were.

Rosie Fights Back

A little before Rosie reached her teens, she'd become 'hefty', as a family member recalled. She had also quite literally begun throwing her weight around as she turned on her tormentors at school. And such was her revenge that she became known on the Smith's Estate as someone best avoided. 'A swipe from Rose and nobody messed again,' Graham was to say of his sister. Not only did she lash out at the girls, but she also gave the boys a good hiding as well. As boys are usually smaller than girls at this age, it was perhaps not quite so remarkable, but sticking up for herself and gaining a reputation for being 'hard' would have given her a feeling of power and being in control: something she'd never experienced before.

Most people who are abused as children do not, of course, go on to kill. Criminologist Lonnie Athens in the US developed a theory to try to explain this: he believes that excessively violent people are socialised to become that way. (He used men, but his theory works for women too.) The first stage is where the child is dominated by a violent parent and sees their mother or siblings being frequently beaten and humiliated. They then go through a belligerent stage and, noticing violence is used to resolve arguments, decide to try it out for themselves the next time they are provoked. They then learn by hitting others that the victim both fears and respects them. This gives them a sense of power, as Rose was beginning to realise. Rose, however, was not retaliating in a major way. It would be some years before she would be 'coached' to gravely hurt someone, which is a critical stage, as the young person may then move onto the next, dangerous, stage of being ready to use extreme violence to settle all arguments with no or only minimal provocation.

For now, however, Rosie was enjoying 'getting her own back', just as her own father was 'enjoying' this with William. But she was not entirely self-centred or sadistic like Bill; or yet a bully like him. She was a young girl who, aside from sewing and playing with her hamsters, used her new-found powers to protect her younger brothers, going after anyone who hit Graham and Gordon and delivering them a powerful whack.

Around the time that Rosie began to fight back, William Letts decided to settle permanently in Bishop's Cleeve, buying a caravan on one of the static sites in the village with the money from the sale of his cottage. Though why William should want to live so close to his son in the face of such hostility from him might seem baffling, the likely reasons for this when they began to emerge after Rosie's trial would shock any ordinary person. Except perhaps Bill.

9

Acting Out

Bishop's Cleeve, near Cheltenham, Gloucestershire, 1967

IT WAS 1967 AND the Summer of Love. Rosie was 13 and enjoying the hot weather as 'Let's Go to San Francisco' played on the radio, followed by one of her favourites, Glen Campbell singing 'By the Time I Get to Phoenix'. During the school holidays, the young teenager also liked to help her mother with the boys' care, and began masturbating her 7-year-old brother, Gordon, as she towel-dried him when he got out of the bath.

Daisy had got herself a job in the canteen at Whitbread's brewery in the village. The job started in the afternoon and went on until late evening. It was Daisy's first taste of independence since she'd married Bill, and at last she had some spending money in her hand at the end of each week. Glenys had finished school and moved out by this time, and Andy was working in Cheltenham and staying over at his girlfriend's house. Bill was rarely home in the evenings as Smith's Aerospace had a social club where he would go after work to unwind, having his usual half of light and playing a few rounds of pool. This meant Daisy had to rely on Rose to get the little boys – Graham, 10, and Gordon, 7 – their tea when they came home from school. Rose also had to get them to bed on time and then babysit them.

In theory, playing the housewife and little mother was the role Rosie most enjoyed; it made her feel grown-up, as her brother Andy was to say. But, in practice, left alone at night with her brothers, she foisted the list of chores she herself was now expected to do onto them. Graham and Gordon, however, happily undertook the vacuuming and cleaning; they looked up to their big sister, who had become their protector. This was not just from the local children, but from their father too, as she tried to shield them from Bill. But at 13, Rose was just a child herself, and began taking herself off to the village each evening, leaving her brothers to their own devices and the house in chaos. Soon the boys began to wander down to the centre of the village too. And, from having absolutely no freedom, the three youngest now had time on their hands to do as they pleased – and they became feral. Rose started to hang out by the shops where she took up smoking to look older, and chatted and laughed with bus drivers and local boys. Her little brothers, meanwhile, behaved like jackdaws, pilfering whatever small goods took their fancy to sell on and buy alcohol with.

All that Rosie had learnt at her father's knee was now becoming alarmingly apparent. She had begun by masturbating her brothers and would soon progress to exhibiting other kinds of sexual deviancy. Yet, ironically, the mention of sex was completely taboo in the Letts' home. Bill had been nicknamed 'The Sunday School Teacher' by his teenage children, as he quickly turned off the television if the merest hint of anything sexual came on screen. By the same token, neither he nor Daisy explained the facts of life to the children. Grandmother Bertha had been left to tell Joyce and Pat about sex as she was a nurse; this was then passed down to Rosie before she reached puberty. Yet, for all this coyness around the facts of life, sex was secretly and illegally practised regularly within the Letts household. Although less so in a normal marital way as since the birth of Gordon in 1960, when Rose was six, relations had pretty much ceased between Daisy and Bill.

Rosie began practising her sexuality on her brothers, where she would parade around the house naked after a bath. Bill had tried to accost Patsy after a bath, so perhaps he had done the same with Rosie and met with less resistance as he'd been grooming her for years. Indeed, Rosie appears to have been used to being naked around her father. On one occasion she'd stripped off and stood naked in front of him, telling him about all the children she was going to have one day. When she became bored by her sexual explorations with her brothers, and possibly even Bill, she began testing her powers further afield, with boys from the village, asking them round when her parents were out, or going to their houses, where she would invite them to touch her. This was not the behaviour of a normal 13-year-old girl; this was a girl who had been highly sexualised and who was sexually precocious as a result.

In the past, Andy had taken the youngest boy, Gordon, for long walks with the dog over the fields to escape their brutal father. But during the periods that he was living away from home, he could do little to help. The only one showing the little boys any affection at this time was big sister Rosie, who, when she returned home at night, would climb into bed with them. The three of them would then huddle together for comfort: a tight-knit little band with Rosie as leader.

Because of a lack of space, the Letts siblings of both genders had, at various times, shared bedrooms and beds with each other. When Rosie first began to share a bed with Graham, she masturbated him in the morning and again late at night, graduating to having full sex with him when he was twelve. This continued up until Rosie left home. Graham had thought this was just sisterly affection and, having frequently been beaten senseless by his father, was grateful of any little bit of warmth shown to him. Gordon possibly also found comfort in it too.

Rosie, however, hadn't become sexually active by accident, and was showing all the signs of being highly practised in such matters. In satisfying Bill's demands as a young girl, he would typically have made her feel this was to do with love and affection. Emotionally, this meant she had grown up with what experts call 'blurred boundaries'. In abusing her brothers, she was probably showing them the same form of 'love' and 'caring' she had learnt from her father. Even so, Rosie knew this was wrong for, as Graham was later to say, 'She knew I wasn't going to say anything.' This indicates that Bill, like many fathers who abuse their children, had warned or frightened his little girl into keeping the abuse their 'little secret'.

A Mysterious Case

In January 1968, just after Rose had turned 14, a young girl disappeared as she waited at a bus stop on Bristol Road, Gloucester. This was Mary Bastholm, a 15-year-old waitress, who had been on her way to play a board game with her boyfriend. To this day her body has never been found, but pieces of the Monopoly set: hotels, paper money and icons such as the iron and top hat, were found strewn in the snow where she waited. There had been two rapes in the same area shortly before this incident, so Gloucester police set up a vast search using tracker dogs and helicopters, but still found no trace of Mary. Andy, who was almost 16 at the time, used the same bus route home to Bishop's Cleeve as the young girl. He was on the bus when the police came on board appealing for information. When Andy arrived home that evening and told his parents what had taken place, Bill immediately warned Rosie to be wary of 'strange men' – yet the 'strange man' was within, and the damage already done. And although Rose had no idea of it then, Mary's disappearance was to have a significant bearing on her future life. It is now believed that Frederick West was responsible for abducting the young girl.

★   ★   ★

Life carried on as normal at Tobyfield Road where, just a year earlier, Bill and Daisy had celebrated their silver wedding anniversary. Having reached the state of twenty-five years of wedded bliss by default, they then handed on their warped and dysfunctional model for marriage to Rosie and the rest of their children. Daisy may have hoped her husband would mellow with time, but while his violent, paranoid schizophrenia remained untreated, this could never happen. The only respite the family had from Bill was when he bought a tent the size of a marquee, which took up the whole garden when he put it out to air. He then packed up the tent and a sleeping bag in the boot of the car and set off for the weekend – as he would frequently do in the summer. Where he went and what he did, no one was ever quite sure, but they were all probably glad of the break.

By now Daisy's family had raised concerns over Bill's heavy-handedness with the children. Bill did not let this pass, and when Daisy's younger sister, Eileen, came to stay the following year, he took great pleasure in making life as uncomfortable as possible for his sister-in-law, removing the living-room door to make sure she got a nasty draught as she slept on the settee. Andy was so embarrassed by his father's behaviour that he offered her his bedroom in exchange for the settee; compared to what he was used to at times, this was still luxury.

Andy was, at seven stone, far too small for his frame: 'undernourished', as a former neighbour was to say of all the children, except Rose. While training as an apprentice, and even while he was still at Cleeve School, he'd often slept in fields and under hedgerows in preference to going home to face another pasting. Bill knew his son hated violence and, mistaking it for cowardice, hit him all the more, but was shocked when Andy finally snapped and punched him back as hard as he could. And in the usual Letts tradition, Andy then found his clothes and belongings on the doorstep that night when he returned home from work. Andy would still go back to live at Tobyfield Road for short periods of time during his teens, unable to refuse his mother's requests to come home when she turned up at his bedsit sporting bruises at various times. But, in a response typical of bullies, Bill never hit Andy again – although his attentions were now focused elsewhere.

At the time of her trial, Rosie spoke of how she'd 'lost her virginity' at 14, and it is likely that at this point Bill raped her. She would also tell her children how their granddad had hurt her at this age, although never saying more than this. Later she would refer to the abuse in terms of dark shadowy figures in hats and other grotesque imagery. While Rose's relationship with Bill would grow into something sinister and unholy as she got older, for now the young teenager would do whatever it took to placate Bill and comfort Graham, 10, and Gordon, 8, the only way she knew how: by abusing them. Although it is unlikely that Daisy had any knowledge of Bill's abuse of their youngest daughter, when she had scrimped and saved enough to buy Rosie a set of new grown-up underwear, the young girl sat on the bed with a pair of scissors and proceeded to chop them all up. This may have been a cry for help to her mother or, more likely, an act of contempt, but it was certainly a clear sign – if one were needed – of a disturbed young girl.

Daisy had maintained for many years that she would leave Bill just as soon as the youngest children reached their teens. And, as that time began to approach, the normally downtrodden Daisy became stronger and more confident. The change in her had begun since she'd started going out to work, and with Bill out of the house more often anyway, she never suffered from severe depression again. But when she finally gathered the strength and courage to leave Bill the following year, she and the family would be shocked by Rosie's reaction to it.

10

Birthday Surprise

Cheltenham, Gloucestershire, 1969

I T WAS FEBRUARY; ROSIE had just turned 15 and was coming up to leaving Cleeve secondary school. The young girl loved baking and rushed home to help her mother with the birthday cake she was making for her dad's birthday. Today her father was 48 and her mother was trying to make the best of it. Daisy had tried to separate from Bill in the past, even going down the official route of applying for an injunction on the basis of his violence to make sure he never came near her or the children again. But this hadn't worked either, as Bill was manipulative and there was little public understanding or sympathy as regards mental-health issues at the time. Bill told the court all about his wife's depression and the electric-shock therapy she'd received for it, and the case simply collapsed. Ironically, had Daisy known about Bill's own psychiatric problems, the outcome might have been different. As it was, the police had not intervened when Andy had asked for help and the authorities had not taken notice when neighbours heard the children's screams and raised the alarm. Numerous failures had conspired to keep the family together, and now they were going to celebrate 'Dad's' birthday together – except that Daisy had run out of the ingredients she needed. Still in her school uniform, Rose popped to the shop for her mum, and picked up the extra supplies. The shop was just fifty yards from her home, beside the Swallow pub – a 1960s-built establishment, and the only pub on the estate.

Daisy and the children always spent their time in the kitchen, even when it wasn't Bill's birthday. They used the side door to it rather than go through the front of the house and risk disturbing Bill as he watched television. When Bill went to bed, the television set went off and stayed off. When it was on, the children would rarely want to watch it with their father, as they were expected to sit as quiet as church mice beside him. As Andy's girlfriend Jackie said, 'I used to find it strange that Andy would tell me to open the sweet wrapper quietly when we sat watching TV with his dad. I didn't like that, I wasn't used to that. We used to joke and laugh around when my dad was watching telly. When I went round Andy's house after that, I used to stay with Daisy in the kitchen. She was always there.'

On this particular day, Rosie had only been gone to the shops a matter of minutes when Bill returned home from work. The moon must have been full again as far as Daisy was concerned, as before she'd even had a chance to say 'Happy Birthday', Bill had ripped the bowl from her arms and tossed it at the wall, and flung Daisy behind it. After battering his wife, he then turned his attentions to the house. Rosie returned with the margarine to find the place wrecked, blood and cake mix everywhere, and Daisy packing their bags, resolving this was the end.

Glenys, a petite blonde, was 18 and heavily pregnant with her first child when her mother, black and blue from the beating, arrived on her doorstep with Rosie, Graham and Gordon in tow. It was a tight squeeze at the rented terrace in Union Street, but to her credit – and that of her young husband, Jim Tyler – they made room for them all. Bill, however, was noticeably absent; he neither chased after his family, nor seemed at all concerned about his sons having to change schools yet again. Rather, he sat back and luxuriated in having the house all to himself.

Rosie tried to do her bit to help out at Union Street,

donning a pair of Marigolds and cleaning the windows. She was supposed to be attending school in Cleeve, but was in her last term, so finding a job and earning some cash had suddenly become more important to her. Her sister Glenys had only recently married Jim, a tall, personable young man who was something of an entrepreneur. By trade Jim was a car mechanic and worked at the Audi garage in Cheltenham, but he and Glenys also ran a roadside refreshment business up at the village of Seven Springs on the Cirencester Road. Jim would tow their Sprite Major caravan to an area of wasteland by the gravel pits each morning, where he would set it up and then set off to work. Glenys would then spend her days serving the customers that stopped off there: from lorry drivers and travelling salesmen, to the gas-pipe fitters connecting natural gas from one side of the Cotswolds to the other. In the evening, 18-year-old Glenys would go home and do the books for the business.

As Glenys was only weeks off giving birth and Rosie needed a job, it seemed the ideal solution all round for Rosie to run the refreshment bar while her sister took maternity leave in March of that year. Rosie happily agreed to the proposition, but serving mugs of tea from a snack bar wouldn't stay top of her list of priorities for long. On occasion, when Jim was test-driving a car he'd just serviced, he would use the opportunity to replenish the snack bar with supplies. But each time he did so when Rosie was in charge, he would find the caravan hatch closed and Rosie emerging from the cab of a parked-up lorry with her clothes unbuttoned and her hair dishevelled. Jim referred to his ex-sister-in-law as being a 'hot-arsed little sod'. Rosie was clearly beginning to test her powers out on older men rather than mere boys from the village. During another of Jim's drives there, he found her clambering out of a car full of gas fitters on the pretext that the men had just run her down to the shops because she'd run out of hot dogs. As crime writer

Carol Anne Davis suggests in her book *Women Who Kill*, the few compliments these men paid her in return for sex were probably 'the kindest words she'd ever known and the casual sex was the closest she'd ever gotten to love.'

Rose had only just turned 15 at this time, and in her schoolgirl socks and with her baby-like voice, she appeared even younger: either way, having sex with her was an offence. Despite this, or perhaps because of it, a steady stream of vehicles parked up by the caravan each day, while the snack-bar sign permanently read: *Closed*. Rosie boasted that profits had gone up since she'd been working there, but it was more likely that when Glenys next did the books, she found profits had taken a nose-dive.

The family were overcrowded in the tiny Union Street terrace, but free at last from Bill's unpredictable behaviour and violent outbursts, they were likely to have been suffering from post-traumatic stress at this time.* Rose, on the other hand, who had developed her own way of 'coping' with her father, began looking for another protector. As well as seeing older men after work, with Glenys in hospital, her brother-in-law, six years her senior, became fair game. Woken in the night by the sound of crying, Jim crept down to her room to investigate, where he found Rosie in bed rocking and sucking her thumb, just as she'd done as a young child. Putting a comforting arm around her, he asked her what was the matter. Rosie regaled him with a story of unrequited love between herself and an older man who visited the snack bar. She also told him how lucky her sister was to have

* This can occur after witnessing or being involved in horrific events such as a serious road accident, terrorist attack or violent personal or sexual assaults. It can also occur in situations where a person feels extreme fear, horror or helplessness. It causes symptoms such as sweating, shaking, dizziness and stomach upsets. Andy Letts was known to faint as a child and Gordon still has blackouts. Post-traumatic stress disorder (PTSD) can also lead to depression, anxiety, phobias, and drug and/or alcohol misuse.

found a man such as himself, running her hand along the inside of his thigh as she did so – at which point Jim jumped up and made his excuses.

There is another version of this story. Some members of the family believe Daisy came home and caught the pair in bed together, leading to a fight between Glenys and Rosie. Soon after, Daisy and the younger children moved out. At her trial, Rosie said she'd returned home from work one day to find her mother and brothers had packed up and gone. She'd asked Glenys where they'd gone, but her sister had been instructed not to tell her. Rosie said she could not believe her mother had abandoned her and, at her trial, said it had left her psychologically scarred. She had left home in support of her mother when Bill had attacked her, and now Daisy had betrayed her and she felt unable to forgive her for many years. Andy Letts refutes this story. He recalled his mother buying a copy of *The Lady* and a week or two later finding a job in the countryside, with a tied cottage for herself and all the younger children. Rosie, however, hadn't wanted to go with them. 'Mum begged her to go to Teddington, but Rosie said she was going home to live with Dad,' says Andy, 'we just couldn't believe it. After all of the violence, and everything, she wanted to go back. She wouldn't listen to Mum.'

The family were nonplussed at her behaviour, but at the time Rosie was staying out late with the different men she was seeing, and moving to a rural location may not have seemed ideal to her. But neither did she rush back to her father, who she knew would try to restrict her going out, preferring instead to wander the streets where, according to her former brother-in-law, 'the police picked her up for street-walking in Cheltenham. She was only 15.'

If it is true that the police believed she was working as a prostitute, nothing came of it, although she was probably picking up men in order to find a place to stay, offering them sex in return for a bed for the night. One Sunday evening, as she walked the streets with her holdall, she was offered a lift by an older man she'd briefly met at her sister's house. The man had a soft, lilting Irish accent and red hair. He told her she shouldn't be wandering around the town on her own at that time of night, and said if she had nowhere to go, he'd have to report it to the police. He offered her a cup of tea at his flat and, because he knew her brother-in-law, she accepted. Back at his flat, Rosie then had sex with the man who, at 30, was twice her age. But he was 'kind to her' and offered her a place to stay in return for rent when she got a job – and probably also sex. Soon after, Rose found work at Sketchley dry cleaners and from there moved on to train as a seamstress at the County Clothes shop on the Promenade in Cheltenham.

The boys, meanwhile, had moved with their mum to Hitchman's chicken farm at Teddington – a village near Tewkesbury in Gloucestershire. The cottage that came with the job was normally for a husband and wife: the wife looked after the farmer's house while the husband worked on the farm. In this case, while Daisy settled into her post as a housekeeper at Mr Hitchman's, 16-year-old Andy had to give up his job at Smith's to help the farmer – both mother and son working to keep a roof over all their heads. The move also meant Graham and Gordon had to change schools again. But despite the drawbacks, the countryside around Teddington offered Daisy and the boys a peaceful retreat from Bill.

The farm cut across a sizeable acreage of land, with long rows of wooden huts with mesh runs attached for the hens to roam around in and lay their eggs. As well as the hens, there were horses and other kinds of livestock. By now, it was the early summer, and Gordon and Graham would play in the fields around the farm and collect the eggs from the runs at different times of the day. Andy was set to work haymaking and painting the long rows of wooden hen houses spanning one entire field.

At first he loved being on the farm, where he watched the new chickens hatch, until the farmer wrung the necks of all the male chickens. Living in a rural idyll, he realised, was not quite all it appeared to be – just like his father's 'charming' persona with strangers.

Rosie had still not returned home by this time, but turned up out of the blue to visit her mother and brothers, bringing her new boyfriend along with her, a soldier from the local army barracks. According to Gordon Burn in his 1998 book on the Wests, *Happy Like Murderers*, she brought other men there too, having sex with them in the fields around Teddington, followed by a drink in the local pub, before setting off home again – wherever that was. Rosie's whole life, it seemed, had become about sex.

Since Rosie's first brush with the law, or possibly as a result of a tip-off from Bill, the police had begun keeping an eye on her. She was now working at a baker's-cum-teashop in Cheltenham, where, for several weeks, a policeman would wait outside until she left for the day, then take her in for questioning. The police knew she was seeing a lot of older men and were particularly interested in the one whose flat she went back to each night. They wanted to know whether an offence had been committed as she was still under age. By now Rosie's use of language had become 'choice'. This is ironic given that her parents didn't swear, let alone use the 'c' word, as Rose now did and would continue to do, even at her arrest some twenty-five years later. In the event, the police did not charge the older man from whom she rented the flat, but neither did Rose stay away from him or any of the others as she promised the police she would. And so a police constable continued to wait outside the baker's until Rosie finally gave in and returned home.

Although Daisy continued to ask Rosie to move in with her and the boys at Teddington, the 15-year-old preferred to stay with her father. A chicken farm in a remote village might not, of course, be an ideal place for any young girl to live who'd rather be out enjoying life. However, despite the family's astonishment at Rosie going back to live with her violent father, it was not quite the extraordinary decision it might at first appear. Rosie, after all, did not have the same relationship with Bill as the other children – or even her mother – had. She was not frightened of Bill, and knew how to keep him happy. Recognising she shared a special bond with her father, they had even seen her take his side during one of his violent outbursts against other family members. What they didn't realise, however, was that this 'bond' was based on abuse; nor could they have guessed that Rosie and Bill's 'relationship' would continue right up to his death. Her warped and brutal experiences with Bill as a child had forged her template at a young age and would mean that once she met the older 'Weird Freddie' West, she would neither find his behaviour abhorrent nor particularly strange, but would have felt comfortable with him, even excited by him, when most other young girls would have run a mile.

To understand Rosie's relationship with Fred West, it is necessary to look at his background, and how the two would have been drawn together.

11

A Country Boy

Herefordshire, 1942

MUCH MARCLE IS A pastoral idyll in Herefordshire that remains almost untouched by time. Bounded by the Malvern Hills on one side and the Forest of Dean on the other, it is equidistant from Ross-on-Wye to the west and the city of Gloucester to the east. During the 1940s, Much Marcle was as insular and inward-looking a village as any that might have been found in the Fens of East Anglia or remote areas of north Devon at the time, not unlike Rosie's childhood home of Northam. The poet John Masefield described the area as 'paradise', while another former resident, Elizabeth Barrett Browning, immortalised it in her poem 'The Deserted Garden'. The village also has the dubious accolade of being the birthplace of serial killer Frederick West, or Freddie, as he was known to his family.

From being a weak child, Freddie grew up to be a short and slight man, with a crop of curly hair and a gap in his teeth. He also had an easy manner and, as Rosie would later say, he could 'charm the birds off the trees'. This was in spite of his country burr which rendered his speech almost inaudible at times, and the smell of pigs' muck that accompanied him when he was younger. Freddie left school at 14, barely able to read and write, and began working on the land with his father where the two of them would bring in the crops at harvest time, go 'ratting', tend the sheep and set off poaching by moonlight. Walter West taught his oldest son everything he knew about the country way of life, and the little boy came to love it himself. At least initially.

Walter, like his son, was also barely educated. He had left school aged 11 to help his grandfather with his horses and carts. Freddie's mother was also called Daisy. Like characters in a Thomas Hardy novel, Walter – a tall, muscular and weathered man – had met his young bride-to-be at the village fair just months before the outbreak of the Second World War. He was 23, and already a widower. His first wife, Gertrude Maddocks, had died just two months earlier. Walter had married Gertrude when he was 21 and she was 45. Two years after their marriage, Walter had come home from work to find his beloved Gerty dead in their cottage garden; she had been killed by a bee sting. Unfortunately Walter found he wasn't able to look after the little boy he and Gerty had been in the process of adopting, and so he returned the child they'd named Bruce to the local orphanage. And now Walter was off to the fair.

At the fair Walter met Daisy Hill, whose father was a local cowman. Daisy and her family lived out of the village and were said by the locals to be a little strange and on the 'slow' side. For this reason, and because their last name was Hill, they were known locally as 'The Hillbillies'. Walter proposed to Daisy, who had only just turned 16 and was almost thirty years younger than his first wife, Gerty. Selecting a naïve young girl for his bride this time was possibly a deliberate move on Walter's part, as he then began to groom her to satisfy his often perverse sexual desires. At this time, rumour began to circulate that something 'wasn't quite right' about poor Gerty's death. After all, as local people remarked, there'd been no witnesses to the first Mrs West's bizarre death, and hadn't her young husband been quick to send the child back? Whatever the truth of the matter, Walter kept Gerty's picture with him, inside the West family Bible, until he died.

Soon after Walter and Daisy married at the local parish church of St Bartholomew's, Daisy became pregnant, and eight months later gave birth to a little girl they named Violet. Violet died the following day and 17-year-old Daisy was devastated. But there was something odd about this turn of events too. Walter would explain to people how his wife had been affected by a policeman calling at the cottage to enquire about a road accident in the village. According to Walter, with his wife being so young and inexperienced in the ways of the world, her being confronted by a policeman had given her a shock that had sent her into premature labour. As Geoffrey Wansell points out, this story is even more implausible than the bee sting, as everyone in the village knew each other, including the local bobbies, whom Daisy would have grown up with.

It was more likely that Walter beat Daisy, resulting in her going into premature labour. Like the sadistic Bill Letts, Walter had also been brutalised as a child by his violent father, a sergeant major in the First World War. Violence, it seems, was a legacy passed down throughout the generations in both the West and the Letts families. And there was to be another shared legacy, that of incest.

A year after baby Violet died, Daisy gave birth to a boy and christened him Frederick Walter Stephen West, or Freddie, as they affectionately referred to the boy. Daisy and Walter then moved into a cottage on the edge of the village, where they would go on to have another six children. This was Moorcroft Cottage, close to the cornfields of Letterbox and Fingerpost Hills, where half a century later the dissected remains of Freddie's first wife, Rena, and his mistress Anna McFall and her unborn child, would be found in three separate graves.

As with the Letts children, all seven of the West siblings would share just two bedrooms. Although the cottage was detached, and bigger than their previous home, the accommodation for such a large family was cramped and basic at best. It did, however, have a tin bath and outside toilet, whereas the family only had a bucket between them before. The bucket had to be emptied into an open sewer that was full of rats. Like something out of the Wild West, Daisy would come out with a shotgun and blast them away.

As soon as Walter's daughters became a little older, he saw them as fair game and would openly proclaim it was his right to 'break them in', a notion which he would pass down to his oldest son. Alongside this, he would beat 'the living daylights' out of Daisy if she did not give in to his desires for sex at various times of the day. Walter was said to have sex on his brain from the moment he got up, until he went to bed late at night. As well as abusing his daughters, he assaulted any other little girls who should cross his path, pushing them down in a field while making his young son watch. Walter also instructed young Freddie on the delights of having sex with animals. By the time the little boy was 8, he'd learnt how to grab a sheep from behind, tuck its hind legs down the front of his Wellington boots and penetrate the poor beast. Freddie was also believed to have been sexually abused by his father and, given Walter's voracious and varied sexual appetite, this seems likely. Fred would later say of his father, 'Dad was obsessed by sex', but he could equally have been talking about himself. As Geoffrey Wansell says, 'his father's example, in the sexual abuse of children, and his own son in particular, led Frederick West to the conviction that everybody does it.' Because of this, 'Sex . . . became his only hobby and consuming passion.' Yet, for all this, Walter and Daisy West would not allow Freddie and his brother John, just a year younger than him, to have girlfriends until they turned 21.

As their mother Daisy grew older, she began to pile on weight and became plain-looking and dumpy. She also started to wear a thick leather belt around her waist to discipline her boys with. If Freddie and John so much as talked about going out with a girl, Daisy immediately whipped off the belt and beat them with it.

In Freddie's case, however, it was not always about discipline, but jealousy. Daisy doted on her blond, blue-eyed, eldest child from the moment he was born; by the time he turned 12, she took the already highly sexualised boy to her bed, where she taught him to have sex with her. This took place on a regular basis, possibly with Walter sometimes present.

Having been initiated in matters of incest before his teens, on Freddie's fifteenth birthday his parents took him into Gloucester to have him fitted for his first suit. This was in the West family tradition, for while they may have been simple farming folk, it was a matter of pride amongst the men in the family that they always wore suits, even to undertake the most mundane of tasks, just as Bill Letts did. The suit was brown and double-breasted, and his next new suit would not go unnoticed when young Rosie eventually met Freddie.

Freddie, like Rosie, was not bright at school; he was also bullied and isolated. This was not helped by the smell of animal dung that lingered on the little boy, or by his mother packing him off with a raw turnip each day for his lunch. And, just as the Letts children were assigned chores after school, so too were the Wests, although everything about them was more extreme. For Fred not only had to carry out tasks such as chopping up firewood and trapping hares for the pot for the family dinner, but he also learnt at his mother's knee how to cut a pig's throat and drain the blood, watched cows being slaughtered and skinned rabbits and squirrels at a young age. And then, of course, he would have to stop to have sex with his mother.

Freddie Leaves Home

In 1957, when Freddie was 16, he started going to dances in Ledbury, where he proved to be popular with the ladies in his new suit, which he wore with his farm boots. His success with the opposite sex ruffled Daisy's feathers who, being only 33 herself, saw the girls as rivals for her lover-cum-son's affections. Fred was in fact becoming so successful that he soon learnt not to use a girl's name when he had sex with them in case he called them by the wrong name. He also carried a number of cheap or stolen engagement rings in his pocket, proposing to the particular girl he was with at the time so that they would have sex with him; otherwise, as he said, it would be, 'no ring, no sex': such were the social mores of the time.

In the summer of that year, Fred got up in the night and left home without telling his parents. He was particularly concerned about how his mother might react. 'Cause we were that close', as he was to say; he knew she would be broken-hearted at his going and that she would try to prevent it. Having earned little money on the land at Much Marcle, and after paying a large proportion of it to Daisy for his keep, Freddie put away what he could into a Post Office savings account. His plan was to buy a motorbike and move to Gloucester, the city he had felt at home in when he had first visited on his fifteenth birthday. Finding himself a job as a builder's labourer in Hereford, Fred slept in one of the half-built houses on site to save money, returning home covered in cement dust – but bearing gifts for the family – some months later.

He then got himself a job at a local cider works and by the autumn had saved up enough to buy his much-desired Bantam motorbike – using it to impress the girls and to proudly show off to his family, being photographed on it with four of his younger siblings. However, while out on his motorbike in a country lane, he ran over a pushbike, left in the road by one of the village girls, and crashed. Freddie was unconscious for over a week, and kept in the local hospital on the John Masefield Ward. Sex was always uppermost in young Freddie's mind. As he began to recover, he told his brother he hadn't been concentrating on the road when the accident happened, but had been consumed by the idea that the girl who owned the bike was behind the hedge, 'dropping her knickers'.

Fred's skull was heavily stitched up and he had to wear metal callipers and a special shoe to support his broken leg, and from then on he walked with a limp. But, aside from this and his broken nose, some of his family believed that the knock on the head changed his personality. While Fred himself always denied it, one of his sisters felt he became a loner, while others thought that he became bitter in the years after the accident, even blaming the murders he subsequently committed on his injury. However, given his hideously abusive childhood, his template, like Rosie's, had also been cast in stone at a very young age, and he would have been sex-obsessed, with or without the injury.

Fred was now 18 and having written off his motorbike, decided to leave home again. Over the next two or three years he worked at Gloucester docks, and became a deckhand on ships going out of Bristol. Although he spent a lot of time shifting manure around and working on the dredges, he later sailed off around the Pacific, going to such places as Australia and Hong Kong and working on the Jamaican banana boats. In between working on the boats, Freddie took a job as a bread delivery man in Bishop's Cleeve, where he got a house-wife pregnant and set off to get another ship. Soon Freddie had enough money to rent a flat in Newent and to purchase a more powerful motorbike: a Triumph 1000, joining a bikers' group in the area and picking up girls. After two years away from home, Freddie returned home at Christmas, 1960. Daisy was 35 by now, and had become a strong and obese woman. As soon as she saw Freddie approaching the cottage, she untied her leather belt with its knotted leather laces attached, rushed out of the cottage and rained blows on her prodigal son. Then, putting the belt back on, she told him, 'Welcome home, son, now we're even.'

Freddie went back to working on the farm with his father and brother John, and it is likely he also began sleeping with his mother again. During his time away, his little sisters had grown, which Freddie of course immediately noticed. Kitty, Little Daisy and Gwen were now aged between 10 and 16, and by November the following year, Freddie was to stand trial at Hereford Assizes for 'illegal carnal knowledge' of a 13-year-old girl, having got one of his sisters pregnant. Daisy senior turned up at the court to give evidence in her son's defence. Freddie's doctor also told the court how the head injury his patient had received three years earlier still caused him to black out. Fred hadn't actually denied the offence when he was accused of having sex regularly with his young sister. He was simply incredulous that he'd been charged with something he'd been brought up to consider as perfectly normal. As Gordon Burn said, he probably thought to himself, 'Well of course he'd had sex with his sister! Wasn't that what her was there for?'

And when a person grows up accepting incest as an ordinary part of family life, they are more likely to continue to do this with their own children. Just like the young Rosie.

Unfortunately, Fred West's sexual offences were never set on record, which could have helped when he and Rose were accused of raping their first victim, Caroline Owens, and later when they raped some of their own children. However, Freddie's sister, probably out of family loyalty, refused to name her baby's father in court, and the case was dismissed. The effect of this on Freddie was to give him increased confidence; he became cocky, there was nothing he couldn't do. And the only thing he had a record for was petty theft of some materials from his works, and a pocketful of ladies' watches he'd stolen in Ledbury earlier that year and given as presents to the women in his family.

After the court case, Fred went out and celebrated by forcing himself on a 15-year-old girl in a field. The young girl was
left so traumatised by the rape that she was unable to report it
for another three decades, until murder charges were brought
against the Wests in the 1990s. In the end, Freddie's sister
was believed to have had a termination, after which Freddie
developed a morbid fascination with abortions that continued
throughout his life.

While the incest charges meant little to the Wests, he'd
brought disgrace on the family by being caught out. He'd
been sent to stay at his auntie's cottage in the village during
the trial, but now had to leave Much Marcle for good. At the
time, he and his brother John had bought a car between them.
This was a Ford Popular – the same make and model of car
that, just a few years later, he would drive around with teenager Rosie Letts beside him, as they went hunting their prey.

Freddie's upbringing had been both brutal and perverse and,
having been highly sexualised by both parents, he lost any inhi-
bitions early on. Brian Masters also suggests that his mother,
by mollycoddling Freddie, did not give him the chance to
grow up and he was to remain grossly immature all his life.
The same could be said of Rosie, who on the one hand was
childlike and intellectually 'slow', but on the other, having
been abused and corrupted by her father, was easily sexually aroused. As Consultant Forensic Psychiatrist Dr Rajan
Darjee – an eminent specialist in sexual offenders at the Royal
Edinburgh Hospital – has found, where a child is neglected or
isolated – and Rosie had certainly been isolated – the closeness of the sexual contact with their abuser can be confusing,
as it is both frightening and pleasurable at the same time. The
victim can then become preoccupied by sex as a means of self-
comfort and coping with negative mood. Rosie had certainly
become fixated with sex at an early age, before she'd even
met Freddie. As one of her lovers, Kathryn Halliday, was to say,

'Rose was absolutely insatiable. She used to say no woman or man could ever satisfy her.'*

And when this disturbed young Daddy's girl met her older, amoral Mummy's boy, it was to be a highly toxic combination of two sex-crazed adolescents.

---

* She also added: 'I don't think she got much sexual pleasure from Fred, he wasn't very well endowed.'

12

Rosie Meets Freddie

Late Summer and Early Autumn, 1969

SOMETIME DURING THE SUMMER, Bill treated himself to a
Lambretta scooter, put some two-stroke fuel in the tank
and set off to visit his family at last. He did not, however, ask
Daisy back at this point, but then he didn't need to for, as Colin
Wilson points out in *The Corpse Garden*, Rosie had 'lost no
time stepping into her mother's shoes.' Rosie and her father
were believed to have been involved in an incestuous relationship while they lived together at Tobyfield Road. Rosie's
former brother-in-law, Jim Tyler, also believed that Rosie was
involved in an incestuous relationship with her grandfather, old
William Letts, who had moved from Northam to be closer to
his family. He said there was something about the grandfather
that 'just wasn't right'. If he was abusing Rosie, Bill is likely
to have known about it and perhaps even encouraged it as a
way of seeking his father's approval which he'd always craved.
Jim also thought Bill showed an unhealthy interest in Jim's own
little girls, aged three and four, as he cuddled and teased them.
'I didn't like the way he did it. There was . . . something I didn't
trust', he was to say.

Only Rosie and her father knew what went on during those
weeks of their being alone together at the house but, despite the
bond they shared, they soon fell out. Rosie was a teenager and
wanted to go out. Bill forbade her, but she carried on staying

out late, disobeying his orders. He knew she was going out and meeting older men, which would have put his nose out of joint. Fed up with him trying to stop her, Rosie then, surprisingly, took the upper hand in the relationship, contacting social services and telling them that her father was being 'restrictive'. A 15-year-old reporting her father to the authorities, at a time when children did not often have a voice, was a rare occurrence, and shows a certain kind of intelligence, if not manipulation. The fact that Rosie did not report Bill's abuse of her means she possibly didn't regard it as such at the time, but saw it as something merely to keep 'Dad' happy. After social services visited the house, life carried on as before.

Daisy's break for freedom with the boys was short lived. The job at Teddington paid very little, and she could not afford to buy furniture for the cottage or to provide new clothes and shoes for her growing children. The cottage was also damp and cold and, with winter just round the corner, Daisy realised it would be difficult to keep warm. Caught in an impossible situation, she then made the tough decision to move back in with Bill.

Settling into married life again, old habits died hard as Bill continued to beat Daisy, but this time even harder to teach her a lesson for leaving him. Daisy did, however, make a stand. Refusing to sleep with Bill again, she spent her nights on the settee downstairs, dreaming perhaps that one day he might just pack up and disappear. But, as luck would have it, the family hadn't been back together long when Daisy's younger sister, Eileen, turned up on the doorstep that autumn with her small son, Ricky, having left her husband. This meant another change of sleeping arrangements at Tobyfield Road, forcing Daisy to share a bed with Bill once more and Rosie to share with Graham and Gordon to accommodate the new arrivals.

Rosie at this time was still working at a baker's-cum-teashop, some six miles down the road in Cheltenham. Neither Bill nor Daisy had expected much of their youngest daughter, who lacked the academic abilities of her sister Glenys, who'd gone to college and worked at GCHQ before having a family, and Joyce, who had by now trained as a nurse and would go on to become a well-respected matron. Despite Rose's limitations, Bill in particular had always encouraged her to try to do well for herself, and he and Daisy were pleased when she found the job at the baker's, even bringing home cream cakes and bread left over from the day for the family.

One evening, as Rosie waited at a bus stop after work in the dark, she claimed to have been frightened by a man also waiting there who'd told her he'd been in the Army. The bus stop was opposite Cheltenham's famous pump rooms and park and, taking fright, she'd run away from the man, across the road towards the park, whereupon he'd chased after her. The park gates were locked, but the soldier, she said, 'just smashed the padlock off with his fists', before dragging her under some trees and raping her. This claim did not come to light until she mentioned it at her trial some twenty-five years later, along with another rape she said had taken place earlier, by a golf course near Cleeve, after she had accepted a lift home from a stranger at a party.

After the second attack, Rosie said she began to catch the bus home in the evening from the main bus station in Cheltenham. And it was here, amidst the gloomy surroundings of the bus depot, the stench of burning oil and the rev of engines, that Rosie was to meet her Prince Charming. She had only been catching the bus home from there that week, when a man in his late twenties, whom she initially took to be a tramp, shuffled over. With his mop of curly hair, shabby suit and a limp, he might have asked the young girl in his usual forthright manner, 'You coming out with me tonight, darling?'

Rosie was frightened and looked away, but not before she'd noticed his twinkling blue eyes and the cocky grin plastered across his face, albeit that she was to say his teeth were 'all ganky and green'. For all of this, the older man with the lucky gap in his teeth and thick country brogue was soon capturing Rosie's attention with his line in banter. An impressionable young girl of tender years, with a short skirt, high heels and sleek dark hair down to her waist, was just Fred's kind. And of course 'her was gagging for it', if Fred knew his women. Yet when he asked her out a second time, she still turned him down; Prince Charming was going to have to work a little harder to get his princess.

By chance, Freddie found out the young girl lived not far from him in the next village, and they travelled back the six miles on the bus together – he taking the empty seat beside her. (Serial killers Peter Sutcliffe, the Yorkshire Ripper, and Dr Harold Shipman were to meet their much younger future wives at bus stops too.) Though probably flattered by the older man's attentions, Rosie studiously avoided his eye during the journey home as he piled on the charm. He soon found out she worked at a bakery in the town, and probably told her about the Sunblest bread round he used to do in Bishop's Cleeve, but possibly not about the child he'd had there with a married woman several years earlier. As he chattered on, the couple seemed to have a lot in common – more even than either realised at this point, including incest. They laughed instead about both having mothers called Daisy, while Fred then regaled Rosie with tales of having sailed around the world, to places like Australia where her father had also sailed – another coincidence. Fred, however, always embellished his experiences, or indeed made them up – he was, after all, a habitual liar. He told the young girl of ice-cream parlours and hotels that he owned in Scotland, omitting to mention that this was where he'd met his wife, and that while working on an ice-cream van in Glasgow he'd run over a small child he'd befriended, killing him. Rosie might have wondered why the man beside her was dressed so poorly and travelling on a bus, but she hadn't been paid this much attention since she 'served' the lorry drivers at Seven Springs and the experience would have been heady for her.

By the end of the ride, Freddie had not only impressed Rosie with his stories, but had made it look as if fate had somehow played a hand in their meeting. More importantly, he also evoked her sympathies, telling her that his wife had gone off, leaving him to bring up their two little girls alone. Fred often used his toddlers as bait to entice underage girls to come to his home, and with Rosie the ploy worked a treat. Rosie had loved looking after babies since her little brothers were born, and the fact that this smooth talker had two small motherless children attracted her like a moth to a flame. Asking her out for the third time, Rosie agreed. Thus, a simple bus ride had quite by chance become the ride to Hell, culminating in multiple murders and a case that would become infamous around the world. Or was it by chance?

Freddie, who owned both a car and a van, must have smiled to himself as Rosie agreed to a date: taking the bus home had really paid off. For, although the couple's meeting appeared accidental, Freddie had almost certainly planned to 'bump into' Rosie. Living in the same close-knit community as Rosie meant that he would have heard all the local gossip about her (where he too had a reputation, as both a flirt and a ladies' man). It is also likely that he had passed the sexually precocious teenager in the village as he drove around in his van looking for young girls. He may also have believed he wasn't going to need to produce one of his rings to get this one into bed.

Freddie was now 28 years old, and had become a charming and seasoned manipulator since leaving Much Marcle to make his way in the world. Finding out which teashop Rosie worked at, he sent his mate round with a present for her, gift-wrapped in brown parcel paper and string. Although Rosie lived just yards from The Swallow pub in Tobyfield Road, she met Fred some miles away at the Odessa pub in Tewkesbury so that Bill wouldn't see her. Freddie bowled up outside the pub in his rusty old ice-cream van. This wasn't a black mark against him for, just as Rosie's mother had at first been impressed by Bill wearing a suit and not drinking more than a half, like her own father Fred Fuller had, Rose was impressed by this Fred wearing a suit and eschewing drink, just as her father did. As the older man and the teenager sat starry-eyed across the beer-stained table, Freddie spotted the gifts he'd bought the girl. 'What's the matter? Don't ya like them?' he asked her in his country burr, though puzzled, as most girls he took out would have had the fur coat on their backs by now. 'No, they're great,' she might have replied, casting her eyes sadly over the fine lace dress, which was probably of nylon mix, and the fur coat which, if not rabbit, was almost certainly stolen, or both. She couldn't accept them, Rosie told him, because if her father saw them, he'd kill her.

In a flash, Freddie turned the situation to his advantage. It was a shame a pretty young girl such as herself couldn't wear the glamorous clothes she deserved. But he had, he told her, the perfect solution. He would keep the outfits at his home, where she could come round and wear them when-ever she wanted. She could also meet his two little girls while she was at it: Charmaine, 6, and little Anna-Marie, not yet 5. Thus, by the time the couple drained their glasses, the man with sparkling blue eyes and something of the romantic gypsy about him had persuaded the young girl to come back to his lair.

As far as Fred was concerned at the time, Rosie was prob-ably no more than a potential notch on his bedpost. But what Fred could provide Rosie with was an exciting escape from life at home with her restrictive parents who insisted she stay in at night. But, as Andy Letts was to say of his little sister, 'Going out with older men made her feel grown-up.' What Andy actu-ally didn't realise at the time was an attachment to an older man was something Rosie was both accustomed to and possibly even seeking as a means of leaving Tobyfield Road forever. As a letter to her pen pal Victor, written in 2005, reveals, 'I started to believe this [Fred] was my way out of the oppression my parents had kept me under for so long.'*

* Published in the *News of the World*, 28 September 2008

13

'Cracklin' Rosie'

Bishop's Cleeve and Surrounding Areas

BISHOP'S CLEEVE AND THE nearby hamlet of Stoke Orchard possess a number of static caravan parks. During the 1960s, as now, some of these were used by holidaymakers, while others were permanent mobile home sites. The Lakehouse Caravan Park, though now a landscaped, luxury holiday park, was said in the 1960s to have a reputation locally as a place that decent folk avoided. Those who lived there were a mixed bag of itinerant workers, recluses and others who got by in the black economy and on the fringes of crime.

Stepping cautiously along the dirt track between the faded Bluebirds and Sprites, the young girl passed clapped-out cars supported on bricks on her way down to number 17: her prince's castle. In some parts of the site, chicken and goats roamed freely, while geese hissed as they guarded the piles of scrap metal accumulated on the site, and barking dogs strained on leashes to sound the alarm. To one side of the park was a dark lake in which the only forms of life were said to be the rats and the algae.

If there was something lawless, uncertain and machismo about this insular little world, it exhilarated Rosie, who had spent most of her life on housing estates in the suburbs. The interior of Freddie's caravan was also very different to Rosie's clinically clean home. The surfaces were caked in grease and grime, while rusty jemmies, spanners, angle-grinders and other workmen's tools were scattered on the sides and the floor amidst dog ends, wood shavings and the children's toys. It was here that Rosie had first been introduced to Fred's little girls as they played amongst the mess. Charmaine was 6, and a bright little girl, whose father was a bus driver from an Asian-Scottish family (though Fred told people the child's father was a wealthy businessman). Fred had married Rena (Catherine) Costello when she was pregnant with Charmaine, and the couple had given the child the West surname. Anna-Marie was now 5, and Fred's biological daughter, who had a mass of blonde curls at this age, just as her father had as a baby.

The little girls had a history of being in and out of care, depending on when Fred hit Rena and Rena upped and left him to go off on another of her travels, working as a prostitute in Bristol and her home town of Glasgow. Rena was a spirited young woman of about Fred's age, who had also had a chaotic and troubled childhood, culminating in her finding her way into a girl's borstal in Scotland. During her absences from her little girls, Fred would either put the children in care, or entice underage girls from the local Cleeve School to babysit so that he could go to work. Invariably, this resulted in him getting the naïve young girls into bed.

The children had two little pack-away beds and a play area at the back of the caravan that was fenced off with chicken wire. Inside this, Fred had made the toddlers a Wendy house, cobbled together with old bits of wood and nails; beside this was a fish pond, drained of water and filled with rubbish. An old van he was in the process of breaking up also stood in the fenced-off area, along with oxyacetylene cylinders and tools he used to break up vehicles with. But Fred had other, more sinister, purposes for the welding equipment and bits of metal scattered around the caravan.

Fred liked to fashion crude metal devices to perform 'home-made' abortions with. He had used one of his rudimentary prototypes on his first wife, Rena. They had gone to a remote spot on the Gloucestershire hills to try to abort the baby that would be Charmaine, while Rena's friend Margaret played lookout. He also carried the bizarrely shaped tools in his van, and boasted to acquaintances that he would help them out should they get a girl 'into trouble'. West's obsession with abortions was such that he kept Polaroid photos in his pocket featuring close-ups of a bloody termination. As well as looking at the pictures for his own perverse enjoyment, he liked to show them off to people, including Terry Crick, his young lodger. Terry left soon after and reported the abortion equipment and photos to the police. But, unbeknown to him, Fred was a police snout, and the very officer he reported it to was West's handler, who took no further action. Later, Fred would fashion implements in metal for other, hideous purposes. Rosie however, knew nothing of such gruesome hobbies at the time, but was just a young teenager who had met a man she believed to be her Knight in shining armour. There was certainly nothing to suggest that she would become the type of person to use some of Fred's terrible inventions for torturing their victims.

On Rosie's first visit to Freddie's caravan, she ate the same meal as his little girls: two eggs, sausage and beans, making a face with them and topping it off with 'hair' fashioned out of the chips. As Gordon Burn remarked, it is interesting that he treated Rosie like one of the children – but then, despite being sexually precocious, she was still childish. With her high, babyish voice, miniskirts, stilettos and her white, knee-high schoolgirl socks – which were her trademark until she went to prison – there was something of the Lolita about her. This appealed to Fred, who liked his women young – the younger the better.

Fred farmed the girls out to a neighbour for the rest of the evening and then courted Rosie with a cup of tea rather than alcohol. It was the late 1960s, but Freddie's taste was more 1950s – just like her father's. Fred played her 'I Hear the Sound of

Distant Drums', and other Jim Reeves ballads, and Country and Western music including 'Lay the Blanket on the Ground' and 'The Crystal Chandelier'. Given her age, Rosie might have preferred one of her own favourites, Neil Diamond's 'Cracklin' Rosie', but if she did, she didn't say so.

Rose began taking time off from work, sneaking down to the caravan park a mile away from her home rather than catching the bus into Cheltenham. Here she would look after the girls while Fred was at work, and have sex with him when he got home in the evening. Her excitement soon stalled, however, when she was met at the caravan door by some girls her own age babysitting for Fred. She recognised them from Cleeve School and soon realised Freddie's caravan was a magnet for truants and runaways. Rosie, with her foul language and the reputation for being hard, saw off her rivals that day but considered her position as she knew she couldn't be there all the time . . .

Fred's daughter, Anna-Marie, or Anne Marie, as she later called herself, remembers her first meeting with the girl who would become her stepmother a little differently. In her 1995 book, *Out of the Shadows*, Anne Marie recalled that she and her big sister Charmaine were in local authority care when her father brought his 15-year-old mistress to meet them. On the second visit, Rose brought her a present: an old-fashioned doll with long blonde locks that moved by battery power. Rosie had played with her dolls until she was older than is usually the case, so the toy was probably one of her cast-offs. It was also the only present Rose would buy her that wasn't a bribe or a threat.

Sometime after this Fred, somewhat amazingly, was allowed to take the girls out of care and bring them home to his caravan, where Rosie became more than just another notch on his bedpost. The couple began to spend time together, playing in the fields around Stoke Orchard with the children, collecting wild flowers and planning a future together where they would have more children. They also talked about his earlier life in

Much Marcle, though probably not the worst excesses of it, as even Freddie knew this wasn't appropriate at the start of a relationship. Rosie was, however, one of the few people who would have understood where Fred was coming from, and she began going into work less and less as their relationship developed.

Fred no doubt found his new young girlfriend uninhibited and open to new experiences. Having been highly sexualised as a girl, she, like Freddie, had abused her younger siblings. Whether each was aware of this at the time is unlikely, but they would very possibly have had the same outlook and, subconsciously, felt comfortable with one another. It might also have marked Rosie out as different to Fred's other conquests – as it had his wife, Rena. Rena had also been a victim of incest, and although she did not go on to abuse, was completely sexually uninhibited.

Despite Rosie's sexual experiences, she'd never had a normal teenage friendship or a friend at school. Now that she had a proper boyfriend whom she could confide in and who didn't laugh at her, she wanted to show him off – to let the bullies know who'd tormented her that 'Dozy Rosie' had someone of her own. She also decided to introduce him to her parents. And, to her surprise, he agreed to meet them. How sad then that Fred, like her father, was a paedophile.

Fred was working as a labourer for Costain's at the time, laying the new M5 which was just a mile from the Letts' family home. Some of Fred's workmates would have known Rosie already from when she'd served them at her sister's snack bar earlier in the year, as the men went there for their lunch breaks. For some reason best known only to Fred himself, he didn't go home to change before the meeting with Rosie's parents, but turned up at her house in his oil-stained work clothes and on his digger, parking it on the grass verge outside. Her parents refrained from asking him through the front door, but invited him to step into the kitchen, where he proceeded to rattle off a succession of fantastical stories about his life in his West Country brogue. He told them how he'd owned a chain of hotels like the Fortes, and was a businessman with caravan parks and ice-cream parlours in Scotland; babbling on and on with his ridiculous lies, interspersed by maniacal laughing, he didn't even stop as he rolled up a cigarette. If Bill had been less than impressed with his son-in-law Jim, who was a small businessman, he got the shock of his life with the 'grubby, lying little tramp' he called Fred. Daisy and Bill looked at each other aghast as Fred set off up the road towards the M5 on his digger. Bill had every square inch of the house scrubbed that night where Fred had been, and, when it was clean, no doubt had it scrubbed again just to make sure.

But the die was cast and Rosie was told never to see that 'filthy gypsy' again. Possibly the young girl agreed for a quiet life for as her mother was to say, she wouldn't argue but would 'just hold herself tight'. But, of course, Rosie had no intention of sticking to it, and as soon as she was out of the house, headed off to her lover's. And, just for good measure, she gave up her job at the baker's too and spent each day at the caravan park – looking after Fred's daughters while he was at work. Fred gave Rosie the £3 a week that the baker normally paid her so that she could still give her mother her keep, and prevent her parents becoming suspicious when she no longer returned home with the leftover cakes. Every morning Rose would head off to catch the bus for Cheltenham and, as soon as the coast was clear, slope off across the fields towards the caravan park.

Fred gave up his job at Costain's and took one at the gravel pits in Stoke Road, nearer his home, so that he could spend more time with Rosie. Rosie, for her part, took over number 17 the Lakehouse as if it was her own home, tidying and scrubbing the caravan like never before. She also collected up the trophy underwear that Fred had stolen from his conquests, probably to use for masturbation purposes. It is likely that in setting out her territory, Rosie also threw out Rena's clothes, which were hanging in the closet, and replaced them with her fur coat and lacy dress. When Fred came home that evening, she thrust the box full of her rivals' belongings at him telling him to, 'Get rid.' And with a grin on his face, he duly did.

Rosie, by day, had now become the little housewife and playmate of her lover's daughters: three children together. In the evening, Fred came home and made love to her before she rushed off to her parents' house, pretending to have been serving bread and cakes all day. And, masturbating one or both of her brothers at night, she fell asleep and dreamed of Freddie: Rosie was in love.

14

The New Order

November 1969 to February 1970

FRED WASN'T GOOD AT SEX. He had a small penis and always preferred the role of voyeur with his wife, Rena, as she had sex with other men. Soon Fred would want to observe his young girlfriend with other men and to introduce Rosie to his other penchant: sadomasochism.

Fred wanted to be tied up and beaten, and purposefully left S&M pornography lying around the caravan for his young mistress to see. He also kept naked pictures of Rena in the caravan and made sure Rosie heard all about his wife's wild antics, from sexual sadism through to voyeurism and orgies. Rena was, he said, a woman willing to do anything for pleasure. He manipulated the highly sexed and curious young girl into joining in with his perverse games, selling them to her as an exciting and 'grown-up' thing to do. And, being young and naïve, Rosie took the bait, indulging her lover in his fantasies in a bid to outdo his wife.

But Fred's fantasies didn't stop there. It was while she was cleaning out the caravan when Freddie was at work that she discovered a pile of letters tucked away, addressed to a Miss Mandy James. Rosie didn't hesitate in opening them, and discovered they were from Rena's clients; that her predecessor was working as a prostitute. Rosie even knew some of the men who'd written the letters – married men whose children she'd gone to school with. Fred's plan had worked and before long there was a new Mandy on the scene: Mandy Mouse. Fred began advertising her services by word of mouth, and soon a steady stream of customers began to call at his caravan to have sex with the 15-year-old . . . But, as usual with Fred, this wasn't about money, but recreating the arousal he'd experienced in his early childhood as he watched his father having sex with young girls in the field.

Bill Letts had heard all about Rena West's services from his workmates at Smith's Aerospace who lodged up at the Lakehouse caravan park. Now rumour had it that his own daughter was doing the same thing. Bill visited the bakery in Cheltenham where his worst fears were confirmed – Rosie hadn't been in to work for some while – and he was incandescent with rage. Rosie tried to explain to her parents how she was now the paid nanny to Fred's children, but Bill knew this wasn't the whole truth. He rang children's services to say that his 15-year-old daughter was having sex with an older man – failing to mention his own abusive relationship with his daughter. Rosie was taken into a home for troubled teenagers in Cheltenham.

Winter began to approach while Rosie was in care. At the care home, she was banned from seeing her lover and had to abide by a strict set of rules dictating where she could go, who she could see and the time she had to be back by. Rosie hated every minute of it and called it a prison – an irony, given where she now sees out her days. Rosie was also said to have felt abandoned by her parents again when they did not make the short trip to visit her in the children's home even once. This claim appears to have substance but, because Bill and Daisy kept secrets from their children, very few of Rosie's siblings even knew she was in care. 'It's news to me, I really had no idea,' Andy was to say of it many years later, even though he and Rosie had been living under the same roof when she'd been taken away. The truth at Tobyfield Road continued, as always, to be fragmented and compartmentalised between different family members.*

Without any visitors, the love-struck young teenager took to meeting Fred illicitly when she left the home to go to work each day. She also began writing to him. As one letter read: 'Dear Fred, I am glad you came to see me . . . You told my Aunt about Rena, but what about telling me the whole story even if it takes all day. I love you Fred, but if anything goes wrong it will be the end of both of us for good. We will have to go somewhere far away where nobody knows us . . .'

Rosie had learnt from her auntie Eileen that Rena had gone back to Fred in her absence. Although Rena would leave almost as soon as she'd returned, this was to have a marked effect on the young girl, who realised she could be usurped again at any time by Rena, who was, after all, the mother of his children. And so it was that she set out to secure her lover for herself.

When Bill found out that Fred was still seeing his daughter, despite her being in care, he was fuming. He knew Fred often went in The Swallow pub in Tobyfield Road after work and, donning a crash helmet and leather gloves, waited outside the pub for Fred to emerge. As soon as Fred surfaced from The Swallow, Bill lunged at him with both fists flying. But Freddie was a lover not a fighter, and took the punches and simply walked away. Soon after, Bill turned up at his caravan, shouting outside it – much to the amusement of other park dwellers. Fred came to the door, where Bill threatened to burn down his mobile home and chop him into little pieces if he didn't leave Rosie alone. Once again Fred just grinned, while Rose took comfort in the knowledge that soon she would turn 16

---

* It was not until Rose's case broke in 1994 that several members of the Letts family discovered their sister Patsy had died sometime earlier.

and be able to do as she pleased. And she was planning to move in with her lover: 'Rosie and Freddie 4ever'. But as she looked forward to that day, on 28 November – just a day before her birthday – Fred was sent down for thirty days for non-payment of fines and a stolen tax disc. It was the first time, but not the last, that Fred would do 'porridge' in Gloucester prison. His two little girls were once again taken into care, while Rosie herself had nowhere to go.

Her father, however, said she could come back home if she found a decent job, worked hard at it and paid her board. Oh, and there was another proviso: she could never see Fred again. Rose was desperate to leave care and agreed to her father's terms, but of course had not the slightest intention of sticking to them and never seeing Fred again. An almighty row broke out between herself and Bill, to which the police were called. A social worker who subsequently visited them said in his report that the family 'presented as quite reasonable'. Bill had managed to pull the wool over their eyes once again.

Christmas came and went with Rosie shut up in her bedroom, where she was not allowed to see anyone or to give or to receive presents. Instead, she spent the whole of the festive period sitting on the bed that she shared with Graham and Gordon, making rag dolls for Fred's two girls. And, at night, she continued to comfort and abuse her little brothers.

But Christmas had given her time to think, and Rosie began to look forward to the New Year with renewed vigour. Fred would be coming out of prison and she wanted to secure their future together, so that Rena would have no further claim on him. Getting up early one morning in January 1970, Rosie set off for his works at the gravel pit near the Stoke Road, where she waited in the foreman's hut for him to arrive. It was freezing cold and dawn had yet to break; the foreman made her a cup of tea as she waited.

Rosie told Freddie why she was there: she was 16 now and

wanted his baby. It had been all they'd talked about as they played in the fields around Stoke Orchard with the children during the warm days of autumn – and now it was time to put that plan into action. Fred threw in his job on the spot and took her off to his caravan, apologising to the foreman. 'The missus. You understand, mate,' he might have said. And soon Rosie found she was pregnant. Keeping it a secret at Tobyfield Road, she rushed off excitedly to tell Fred the good news. As the couple celebrated that night, it is impossible to imagine the fate that awaited their first child together . . .

With Rose now pregnant, Fred began to take Bill's threats seriously and rented a bedsit in Cheltenham to keep out of his way. The bedsit at 9 Clarence Road had a toilet, bathroom and kitchen, which was shared between a whole house full of bikers, hippies and drifters passing through. Although Fred didn't drink or take drugs himself, he didn't mind the parties every night and subsequent police busts. It was an anarchic existence, in which his pregnant teenage girlfriend, who hung out there with him, did not look out of place. Indeed, life at Clarence Road was to make such an impression on Fred that he would later use this as a model for Cromwell Street when he and Rose moved there.

By the time Rosie had slipped away from home to move in with Fred at the bedsit, he had obtained bar work in a pub nearby, and was also working as a tyre fitter at Cotswolds Tyre Company in Cheltenham. Fred wanted to take the girls out of care so that they could be a family. Whether he should actually have been allowed to have them was another matter. He had been sexually abusing 6-year-old Charmaine for most of her short life, rubbing the naked child against his groin with a smirk on his face. 'She'll come if I carry on,' he was to tell Rena's friend Margaret, who saw him do this.

Despite Clarence Road being a cramped bedsit surrounded by 'drop-outs' whom Rosie disapproved of, the children's home allowed Fred to take his daughters home, as he now had Rosie there to help with their care. They knew Rosie was only just 16 and told the couple that checks would be made on them. But, as even Rose herself was to say, the bedsit 'was a real pit, we were all in this little room together . . .'

Rosie was blissfully playing house, cooking dinners on the tiny Baby Belling in the corner and using the dressmaking skills she'd learnt from Daisy to make clothes for the girls on an old sewing machine. With money in short supply, Rosie would simply use one of the girl's old dresses for a pattern, cutting around it with some inches to spare, to make a larger size. The children always looked neat and tidy when they went to school, which probably kept the 'welfare' happy.

Rosie and Fred's happy family scenario was short-lived, however, when Bill began trying to track his daughter down and contacted the police. When the police finally caught up with the couple at Clarence Road, they were taken back to the police station, where a police surgeon examined Rosie. To Bill's chagrin, the surgeon found his daughter was only in the early stages of pregnancy, which meant that charges of underage sex could not be brought against Fred and the police had to let him go. When Daisy first heard news of the baby, she was so angry that she refused to speak to her daughter. Bill, however, responded by giving Rosie 'the hiding of my life', as she was later to say.

Once more social services intervened, sending Rosie to a mother and baby unit for teenage girls, to try to bring her to her senses. Rosie stayed there for a week or two, during which time Bill arranged an abortion for her. Rosie promised her parents that if they let her go home on the Friday evening, she would go into the clinic on Sunday night in preparation for the abortion first thing on Monday morning. Rosie only agreed to this because she yearned to see Fred, and the more 'grief' she got at home, the more she looked on him as her passport to freedom. How sad then that a man as disturbed as Fred had something to offer this young girl, and she him – for by now Fred too had fallen in love. And thus it was that the couple decided they would keep their precious baby, planning like Romeo and Juliet, or Freddie and Rosie, to run away together the night before Rose was due to go into the clinic – only to kill their firstborn sixteen years later.

They had intended that Freddie should park his Vauxhall around the corner at the time Bill was going to take her. She would run over to Fred and he'd whisk her away, heading for Scotland. But, over the weekend, her parents had a change of heart. 'My father told me I could stay at home as long as I . . . had an abortion and no boyfriends. Or I was told I could go off with this Fred West and never see my family again.' Bill Letts also went on to say that, if he ever bumped into the pair together, 'he would knife' them.

Rose knew all about 'Dad' and knives, but was still not deterred. Jumping out of bed that Sunday morning, Rosie yanked open the curtains to let in the day. Such was her excitement that she barely noticed the smoke rising from the neighbour's bonfire as it began to form a giant curl up to the sky. Taking the rag dolls she'd made for Anna-Marie and Charmaine from the window ledge, she stuffed them into her bag, along with the few items of clothing she had, and a pair of shoes. Then, taking one last look around the room and the bed she shared with her younger brothers, she closed the door on her childhood forever.

'You're not going, Rose, are you?' Auntie Eileen asked as Rosie set off that crisp winter morning.

Rosie just laughed, and tossed her long dark hair. 'Yeah, I am!' she said.

'She looked so lovely on the day she left,' her mother recalled at the time of the trial.

'Come back and see us, Rosie!' The boys waved to her from the front gate.

Rosie turned and smiled at them. 'Promise!' she called, not

sure her father would let her, then carried on her way, swinging her bag as she went, not a care in the world.

As the young girl left home, her mother watched after her and worried how she'd cope. Her daughter was pregnant and younger in her ways than her 16 years would suggest – right down to the schoolgirl socks she wore with her high heels. But as Fred was to say many years later, 'Why her father wanted her to get rid of the baby and get her back home was 'cause he'd lost her, sort of thing, when she was with me.'

Bill's incestuous relationship with his daughter was at an end; or so it seemed. While this 'ordinary' young girl who would go on to commit serial murder of many other young girls was anything but ordinary.

Rosie knocked on Fred's caravan at the Lakehouse site in Stoke Orchard which he had only recently moved back to. As he opened the door to his beloved, he might have said, 'Welcome home darlin',' with a grin on his face. That night, as the lovers lay on their foldout bed, sharing a post-coital ciga- rette, Rosie told Fred of the plans she had for them. First they would get the girls out of care – but a poky caravan was no place to bring up two children and a baby. She told Fred she wanted him to find them a roomy flat or a house, a decent place away from the village where they could make a fresh start. Fred, ever the bragger, probably promised to find her a 'palace fit for a princess' as he began house-hunting in Gloucester. Fred had come to love the city since his parents had first taken him there to buy him a suit on his birthday. He liked the privacy and anonymity it offered, in contrast to the claustrophobia he felt in communities such as Cleeve and Much Marcle – particularly now that he and his young mistress were calling themselves Mr and Mrs West.

While Fred was looking for a place for them, the couple went back to the Parklands children's home in Tewkesbury and took Charmaine and Anna-Marie out of care again. The children's services had already warned Fred that the girls would be placed in care on a formal footing if he didn't make permanent arrangements for them, and with Rosie once more at his side, 'I could get the girls back,' as he was to say.

Rosie gave the caravan another scrub-up in preparation for the children's arrival and possibly sat the rag dolls on the end of their beds. The young girl was delighted: all she'd ever wanted was to be a housewife and mother, and now her dream had come true. But the psychological foundations that had been laid in Rosie's childhood would begin to wreak havoc when, by the following year, the teenager would commit her first murder . . .

PART III

House of Bodies: The Later Teen Years

15

New Beginnings and Ends

Gloucester, June 1970

IT HAD TAKEN FRED until the early summer of 1970 to find a flat for his young family to live in. First he moved Rosie and the two little girls into another caravan at the Sandhurst Lane site near Gloucester, then into a tiny flat at Midland Road in the city before finally moving them into a larger flat at number 25, in the same street.

Midland Road was a rundown area of the city at the time housing mostly immigrant Jamaican and Polish families. The large house with steps up to it had once boasted a splendid Victorian elegance, but was by now faded with a gloomy grey exterior. The house overlooked a park at the front with a bowling green and tennis courts, while a main railway line ran at the back, causing the windows to rattle when a train flew by. The Wests' flat was on the ground floor and had a coal cellar below in the basement. The flat was compact and dark and furnished with dilapidated curtains and carpets left by the owner, an elderly Polish man, Frank Zygmunt.

Mr Zygmunt was buying up other rundown properties in the street as they became vacant, and asked Fred to help him do the houses up after he finished work for the day at the Cotswolds Tyre Company. The flat was to be the little family's fresh start and permanent home for the next three years, and Fred revelled in the fact that no one knew them or their business here, unless they told them. Even so, the new Mr and Mrs West must have looked a little odd to their neighbours – the older, scruffy man with a strange way of speaking, his young, pregnant girlfriend, no more than a child herself, and their rainbow tots. Rosie was actually only five months pregnant here, which means that either there had been some confusion with the dates, or that Rosie had lost the first baby and was pregnant again.

The start of the new decade had ushered in the era of glam rock and bands like Gary Glitter and Sweet, along with platform shoes, Lurex tops and kaftans. Edward Heath's Tory government had won a surprise election in the UK, while in the States, Charlie Manson and his 'family' were on trial for the most gruesome and cruel of 'stranger' murders. This included the frenetic stabbing of eight-months pregnant Sharon Tate, wife of director Roman Polanski. As Rosie followed this on the news at night, there was still little to indicate that, very soon, she too would go on to callously murder strangers with Fred.

At Midland Road, as the young lovers continued to enjoy their colourful sex life, Rosie carried on in her role as homemaker and mother: cooking and cleaning and taking a pride in turning the girls out well. Like Daisy, appearances were important to Rosie, and when the Polish lady next door complimented her on her domestic skills, the little housewife was cock-a-hoop. But Fred's girls were not little dolls to play with: at 6 and 7 they were at an age to know their own minds, which became increasingly difficult for Rose to contend with.

While Anna-Marie was described as 'timid' and tried her best to please, Charmaine was bright and spirited and soon realised she could get the better of her young stepmother. This wasn't helped by Fred telling the little girls to call Rosie 'Mum', particularly as Rena was still in the picture. As Anna-Marie recalled in her book, *Out of the Shadows*, while she was unhappy about it but reluctantly complied with her father's wishes, Charmaine flatly refused, reminding the older girl at every opportunity, 'You're not my mum! You can't tell me what to do!'

Rose told the neighbour Mrs Giles, in the flat upstairs, and a mother of two young girls herself, that while she found Charmaine difficult to cope with, she could manage Anna-Marie. Yet there were problems here too. The 6-year-old not unnaturally doted on her father, who had been one of the few people in her short life to show her any affection, and she would delight in telling Fred how she would marry him one day. Fred probably encouraged this, as he was grooming his youngest daughter for the abusive relationship that was yet to come, while enjoying playing off Rosie against Anna-Marie. This would lead Rosie to become jealous of the little girl, in the same way she was of the child's mother. Added to this, Rosie was only 16, and left with all the responsibility for the children. As Graham was to say, 'Fred saw it as Rosie's job "to look after the kids"' while he went out to work. The 'fresh start' the young girl had been planning wasn't quite what she imagined.

With the children's chaotic lifestyle and Fred's abuse of Charmaine, the girls were exhibiting symptoms of disturbed behaviour: from wetting the bed to being defiant and overly eager to please. This would have made it even more difficult for their stepmother (disturbed herself) to care for them. And if Daisy worried that her childlike daughter had taken on more than she could cope with, she would soon be proved right.

On Sunday 17 October 1970, 16-year-old Rosie felt the baby coming and was rushed into Gloucestershire Royal hospital where she gave birth to a little girl. The baby's doting parents named her Heather, and took her home to their spartan flat, where Fred had got a cot ready for his new daughter, and a second-hand pram. It was a requirement of the children's at-risk register at the time that 'very young parents' were monitored. Rosie should, therefore, have been brought under the watchful eye of Gloucester social services, but this does not appear to have happened, even though Rose, and Fred's two little girls, had only recently come out of care.

Charmaine and Anna-Marie were overjoyed as they peered into the pram to see their new sister for the first time. Baby Heather had dark hair and looked the spit of Rose and the Letts side of the family. Yet, incredibly, of the three little girls now in Rosie's care, only one would survive murder at her hands.

At this point, however, Rosie was a proud new mum who, having no mod cons to assist her, boiled the nappies in a pan over the stove to get them as white as possible. But from the moment Heather came home, she was a restless baby who constantly cried. Rosie had to get up several times during the night to see to her and, as tied as she was, could not ask her parents for help as she was still not on speaking terms with them. Fred was there even less of late as he had taken on a third job, as a milkman. As soon as he came in from his day job, he'd go out to do a job on the side for Mr Zygmunt, sleep for a few hours and then be up for his milk round at Model Dairies in the middle of the night – and not home again until the evening, when the whole cycle started over again. While Fred was as addicted to work as he was sex, Rose was leading a solitary and stressful existence that was about to get a whole lot worse.

Fred could never resist 'thieving' anything that he could get his grubby little hands on; it was a legitimate perk of the job, as he saw it. He fraudulently ordered a set of tyres and a spare for his van from the tyre company where he worked, got caught and was sacked. But every cloud had a silver lining with Fred, who was immediately offered a full-time job by his landlord, Mr Zygmunt, who had increased his portfolio of properties and had more houses in need of repair. Fred had just started his new job when, two weeks after Heather's birth, he was hauled in front of the magistrate's bench for the tyres and stealing a tax disc, fined £50 and sentenced to three months' imprisonment. Fred already had a six-month suspended sentence for theft of fencing panels from a building site he'd worked at in August 1969. The new sentence brought this one into effect and Fred was sent down for a total of nine months.

What should have been the little family's first Christmas together had come and gone with Fred warm and fed in the 'local nick', while Rose sat alone in her schoolgirl socks in a cold, damp flat with the baby and two bewildered and resentful little girls to care for. It was not any better than the Christmas before, when Rose had been locked in her room, and now she was a prisoner in a flat with no adult company and no money to buy any food or presents with. On top of that, Fred was brought back in front of Cheltenham Magistrates Court on New Year's Eve and given an extra month for other pilfering offences. As Rosie left the hearing that day in the freezing cold, revellers were beginning to fill the pubs and streets in preparation for the New Year. But Rosie had little to celebrate. Putting the girls to bed that night and trying to settle the baby, she sat alone with just the radio on for company as 1971 came in with an icy blast. And by the time the spring came, the 17-year-old would kill.

At first Rosie had been able to visit Freddie regularly, as he was just a stone's throw away in Gloucester jail. But on 27 January 1971, he was transferred to Leyhill open prison, some twenty miles away in the Gloucestershire countryside, where he served out the rest of his sentence. Although Rose visited him there, it was more difficult with the children and using public transport to get them all there. During these long, lonely months, as Rosie and Anna-Marie silently yearned for Fred, Charmaine continued to refuse to do as her stepmother asked. Rose had no idea how to cope, while her model for parenting was both warped and dangerous. Nonetheless, it was the only one she had, and she began using it: 'erupting' – as Anna-Marie called it – as Rosie began unleashing terrible outbursts of anger on the children, as Bill had done. She also began to implement her father's regime by insisting the girls did all the housework before and after they came home from school. And if the polishing or vacuum cleaning wasn't up to scratch, woe betide them, for Rosie, unchecked and unsupported, would lash out with anything that came to hand: from buckled belts through to kitchen implements.

The problem was Rose was still emotionally a child, and like a child she was egocentric and lacking in any impulse control. But once she'd begun lashing out at the children, it gave her a feeling of power, and this was dangerously heady. In a short space of time, Rosie had turned from a naïve young girl who loved to play with smaller children into a tyrant who, with just one look, could put the fear of God into the girls. This was the same ferocious look that Andy Letts had seen on his father's face. 'I was terrified of him,' Andy was to say of his childhood with Bill, 'too scared to breathe.' And just as Andy and his siblings had not been allowed to have friends or to go out to play, so Rosie did not allow Fred's girls to do so. There was one exception, however: the little girl who lived in the flat upstairs, Tracy Giles. Rosie was on speaking terms with Tracy's mother, Shirley Giles, and allowed Charmaine to play with Tracy when she called for her. Tracy was the only friend Charmaine would ever have, and the little girls became 'best mates'.

One morning, when Tracy popped downstairs with a jug to borrow some milk for her mother, she was shocked to discover her little friend 'Char' standing on a kitchen chair with her hands bound behind her back with a belt and 'the lady with the long dark hair' about to beat her with a wooden spoon. Tracy rushed back upstairs in tears to tell her mother what had happened, and would later give evidence at Rose's trial. Despite the beatings, little Charmaine remained defiant and refused to cry, which disconcerted Rose, as it meant she could not break the child and have full control over her. Anna-Marie, on the other hand, was more like Rosie as a child, and did whatever she could to avoid annoying her stepmother. Even so, the little girl would not be immune from Rose's outbursts. While Charmaine was washing her breakfast bowl deliberately slowly at the sink to antagonise her stepmother, Rosie took her frustration out on Anna-Marie as she waited behind her sister to wash her own bowl. Grabbing the dish from the 6-year-old, Rose brought it crashing down over her head. With blood pouring from the wound, Rose took Anna-Marie to the Casualty department at Gloucestershire Royal, where she had stitches put in her head. Despite the nature of the injury and Rose being a child in charge of two small children and a baby, no enquiries followed and Rosie was able to continue her reign of terror.

Rosie would sleep in the large front room overlooking the park, with Heather in her cot beside her, while the two little girls slept in a small room at the back of the house. Charmaine's child-size bed was directly beneath the window and had a plastic sheet on it as she would wet it, while Anna-Marie's bed was pushed against the wall opposite.

It was here that Rose would strip the girls and tie them to their beds, where they were not allowed to speak or make a sound. As Charmaine was the most trouble to Rose, she would sometimes lock her in the bedroom all day, with her hands tied behind her back and her legs spread-eagled and strapped to the bed. But still the 8-year-old refused to cry or be beaten into submission by the older girl, as it became a battle of wills between them.

If Rose caught the girls talking in bed at night she would beat them across the legs with the leather strap. She also began to gag them with ripped-up sheets or strips of sticky tape over their mouths, so that they wouldn't be heard by the neighbours should they cry out. These were no longer the actions of a girl unable to cope, but something more sinister. This behaviour had its roots in Fred and Rose's earlier sex games involving bondage and sadomasochism at the caravan park, and which would be the modus operandi they would use with their victims. As

Caroline Owens, the Wests' first victim, said, 'They were very efficient with the duct tape, as if they'd done it before.' Clearly Rosie had come a long way quickly, from 'comforting' her brothers just the year before.

After abusing Charmaine and Anna-Marie in this horrible way, Rose would then carry on with her normal domestic routines as if nothing had happened – just as she would later, after the murders. And just as a psychopath has no feelings for others, so the teenager lacked any empathy for her little step-daughters left in her care. Charmaine would whisper to her little sister as they lay shivering in bed at night, 'Mum'll come and save us soon.' And Rena did come, many times, for the children, right up to her death. Rena had long since lost interest in Fred and their marriage, but had fought tooth and nail to get the children back from him. But Fred was increasingly sadistic, and just smirked at Rena as he used the children to torment her. There were times when she would stand outside the caravan door, screaming to see them, but he would not let her have them. Sometimes Rena would come and just take Charmaine away; as the child was not related by blood to Fred, she feared for her, although she had no idea he was sexually abusing her. When Rena was between lodgings, she some-times took Charmaine off school and returned her before the end of the day so that Rosie wouldn't find out. With Rena's own chaotic lifestyle, she is likely to have felt relieved that her husband had Rose living permanently with him to care for the girls. This arrangement also suited Rosie as, despite how diffi-cult the children might be, it gave her a hold over Fred.

The bedroom that the two little sisters shared at Midland Road had large, dilapidated window frames, and the panes would rattle when the wind blew outside. The two little girls would then hide beneath the covers, Charmaine whispering, 'Anna-Marie, Anna-Marie, the witches are trying to get in. They're going to get us.' But as Anna-Marie recalled later in her

Rose aged 6, at infant school in Northam, Devon, 1959.

Rose's mother, Daisy aged 31. Neighbours remarked on her beauty and exotic looks.

Rose aged 5, in the foreground, with her older sister Glenys aged 9, and brothers Andy aged 7 and Graham aged 2, on the sand dunes at Northam Country Park, 1959. Big sister Joyce aged 15, has taken the picture.

Fred aged 12, with his mother Daisy and father Walter. Daisy is 29 and by now Fred is having to have sex with her. It is 1953, the year of Rose's birth.

Fred's younger brother John West aged 18, his father Walter and mother Daisy, standing by the second-hand Ford Popular that Fred and John had recently purchased between them. It is 1960 and the picture was probably taken by 19-year old Fred.

Fred aged 17, on his motorbike with his youngest brother Doug and sisters Daisy, Kitty and Gwen in the garden at Moorcroft cottage.

25 Midland Road. This was home to young teenager Rose and her own little family, and where she was already working as a prostitute.

Picture taken in the summer of 1971, just after Fred's release from prison. Rose is 17 and has already murdered her first victim, 8-year old Charmaine.

Sisters Charmaine aged 7, and Anna-Marie West aged 6 – Fred's children from his marriage to Rena Costello – and Rose and Fred's first child together, baby Heather. Of the three children, only Anna-Marie would survive.

CERTIFIED COPY of an ENTRY OF MARRIAGE
Pursuant to the Marriage Act 1949

Registration District	Gloucester City

| 1972. Marriage solemnized at | The Register Office | in the | County Borough of Gloucester | in the |

| 181 | Twenty Ninth January 1972 | Frederick Walter Stephen WEST | 30 years | Bachelor | Skilled Fibre glass Worker | 25 midland Road Gloucester | Walter Stephen WEST | Farm Worker |
| | | Rosemary Pauline WEST formerly known as Rosemary Pauline LETTS | 18 years | Spinster | — | 25 midland Road Gloucester | William Andrew LETTS | Electrical Engineer |

Married in the Register Office by certificate before

This marriage was solemnized between us, P W S West, R. P. West

in the presence of us, M. Horman, Joe West

A. V. Urban Superintendent Registrar E. H. .... Registrar

Certified to be a true copy of an entry in a register in my custody.

J.M. Winston

31st July 1995.

Rose and Fred married in January 1972. Although Fred put 'bachelor' on the certificate, he had not divorced Rena.

Catherine (Rena) Costello, Fred's first wife, murdered sometime after Charmaine disappeared.

Rose aged 19, with her first son, Stephen West, who was born in August 1973. She had killed twice by this time and in a matter of weeks after this picture was taken, would become a serial killer.

25 Cromwell Street, which Rose and Fred become the proud owners of.

A young Rose photographed by Fred at the couple's new home, for purposes of finding her further 'clients' for her work as a prostitute.

The Black Magic Bar, Cromwell Street, where Rose and husband Fred would entertain their friends and hold sex parties.

Eight of the nine West children, probably taken in 1982. From back, clockwise: Stephen aged 9, Mae aged 10, Heather aged 11, Barry aged 3, Louise aged 4, Anna-Marie holding Rosemary aged 1, and Tara aged 5. The children slept in the basement at different times, where many of the victims' remains laid concealed just inches beneath them.

A section of the basement with the children's paintings, and a bricked up wall.

The ten victims Rose was convicted of killing. From top left, clockwise: Thérèse Siegenthaler aged 21, Charmaine West aged 2 in the picture (aged 8 when murdered), Heather West aged 16, Shirley Robinson aged 18, Shirley Hubbard aged 15, Alison Chambers aged 16, Carol Ann (Caz) Cooper aged 15, Lucy Partington aged 21, Juanita (Nita) Mott aged 18 and Lynda Gough aged 19.

The police digging up the patio at the back of 25 Cromwell Street where the remains of further victims were discovered, including 16-year old Heather West.

Human remains being removed from the cellar at 25 Cromwell Street.

Rose is sent to prison in 1995. She will never be released.

Heather West aged 6, at primary school. She looked very like her mother at the same age. Heather was Rose and Fred's last victim.

DEAREST HEATHER
BIRTHDAY WISHES SWEETHEART, THOUGH
THE YEARS HAVE PASSED, YOU ARE
ALWAYS IN MY HEART, YOU WILL NEVER
BE FORGOTTEN – NOBODY CAN EVER
TAKE AWAY MY THOUGHTS AND MEMORIES
OF YOU – MY LOVE
YOUR EVER LOVING BIG SIS
ANNA-MARIE – X –

Anna-Marie's tribute to her sister Heather.

book, the wicked witch was already inside the flat. And, worse still, she was honing her skills. The girls couldn't even appeal to Fred for help as he had put Rose in charge of 'disciplining' them, before he went into prison. Fred later admitted, 'Rose never liked Charmaine really. I turned a blind eye to it because I couldn't do nothing about it. I wouldn't separate them [the girls]. It was either getting rid of Rose or putting them in a home . . .' Nonetheless, he used the children as a means of testing Rose's boundaries, instructing her that 'Charmaine was old enough for the strap now' – his only stipulation being that she 'didn't hit the children where it showed'. These words must have seemed familiar to Rosie, whose own mother had said the same thing to Bill when he beat her siblings.

Having been mentored by Bill, Rosie was now being 'coached' by Fred and wanted to impress him, even when he was in prison. And when he wasn't, he would tell the children, 'Your mum does it because she loves you.' The lovers were then said to have exchanged a look as if they shared a secret – which they soon would . . .

16

Rosie's First Murder

Gloucester, Late Spring and Early Summer, 1971

ROSE MADE THE FORTY-MILE round trip with the girls and the baby to see prisoner 401317 in Leyhill open prison whenever she could, including on family sports day where Anna-Marie took part in the egg and spoon race. Somewhere around this time, Charmaine 'disappeared'. What actually happened that fateful day, or even which day it was, we will never know for certain unless Rose chooses to talk about it. But what we do know is that Rosie took Charmaine to the local hospital, where she was treated for an injury to her ankle, on the evening of 28 March 1971, just six days after the child's eighth birthday. Anna-Marie was certain her stepmother would have been responsible for the wound, and that she must have realised the seriousness of it for her to have taken Charmaine, whom she despised, for medical treatment. Charmaine was now attending the same Casualty department that Anna-Marie had been treated at, but again this did not lead to any enquiries being made. The strange-looking puncture still remains a mystery, but was possibly caused by a knife.

Meanwhile Daisy, having had no news of their youngest daughter for over a year, pestered her husband to forgive and forget and go to visit her. Taking Glenys and Graham with them, the warring couple set off to see Rosie together – united for once. Or so it seemed, for a more cynical motive would later emerge for Bill's 'forgiveness' of his daughter. When the Letts arrived at the flat, they were confronted by squalor. The wooden floorboards were stained and grubby, dirty terry nappies littered the front room, while unwashed crockery was piled high in the sink.

'The place was a shambles, you wouldn't want your dog to live in it,' Graham was to say. Daisy was shocked while Bill, with his obsessive cleanliness, couldn't even bring himself to sit down. Daisy wasn't impressed by Rose's foul language either, and put this down to Fred's influence. She also noticed her daughter's eyes were red from crying, and that she'd lost weight and was looking gaunt. As her brother Graham was to say to author Howard Sounes, 'Rosemary couldn't cope; it hit her all of a sudden and she got run down.' After the visit, Daisy was so worried about her daughter that she called round to Midland Road twice more, unannounced. On one of these visits, she found Rosie had gone out with Anna-Marie and the baby, leaving Charmaine alone in the flat. Soon after, the plucky little girl would be dead.

The Prison Letters

During Fred's period of imprisonment, the star-crossed lovers sent each other letters with hearts and kisses on them. In Rose's letter of 4 May 1971, she talks about her problems with Charmaine.

To My Darling,
  . . . Hey love, that's great, just three more visits, it'll take up half the time I've got to wait for you . . .
  Darling, about Char, I think she likes to be handled rough. But darling, why do I have to be the one to do it? I would keep her for her own sake, if it wasn't for the rest of the children. You can see her coming out in Anna now. And I hate it.

... Oh love, about our son. I'll see the doctor about the pill. And then we'll be safe to decide about it when you come home ...

Well love, keep happy. Longing for the 18th.

Your ever worshipping wife,

Rose.

The letter is as interesting as it is ambiguous. It could mean she is discussing letting the child go to live with her mother (who should also be the one to discipline her rather than 'why do I have to be the one to do it?'). Or it could be saying something far more sinister, as the prosecution implied at Rose's trial: her intent to murder the child. And if she did intend murder, then the letter shows her utter callousness towards the little girl.

Although Rose's suggestion that the child likes to be ill-treated may sound ludicrous, she had grown up with violence and been coached in sadomasochism by Fred, so she may have believed this to be true. It is also interesting that now she was with Fred, she no longer referred to herself by her childhood name of Rosie, but by the more grown-up Rose. Fred replied a short while after. 'So you say yes to Char, that good. I will see to it when I get out, but don't tell her for you know what she is like and you can have our son as soon as I come out.'

This backs up the notion that the discussion was about letting the child go to her mother's, although Fred warns her not to tell Charmaine beforehand so that she doesn't become overexcited. In fact, Fred would not make it home before the little girl was murdered.

Three days after Fred received the letter, on 7 May, Rose visited him with all the children. During the visit, Fred gave her a painting of herself on her knees, naked, at sunset – presumably painted in the prison workshop from imagination. The couple were then said to have ignored the children as, across the table in the visits room, Rose regaled Fred with her recent exploits involving bus drivers he'd sent her to pick up at the depot. But, even though she was hard up, no money exchanged hands as by the time Fred got out of prison the gas and electricity had been cut off.

A week later, on 14 May, Fred wrote to Rose to tell her about a model gypsy caravan he'd made her out of matchsticks. The caravan turned into a jewellery box on which he had carved a heart and inscribed, 'To Rose love Fred'. On the letter, he wrote at the top 'Our family of Love'. How ironic this would turn out to be.

Although Fred was the dominant partner of the two, at least at this point, he was far less able than Rosie when it came to literacy. In the same letter he wrote the following, which is an extract:

Darling be at home Tuesday for your Table will be cuming so be at home all day until thy cum it will be in the morning if they do cum then cum see me but don't cum to thy cum Darling . . .

Will it won't be long be for the 24 [June] now Darling so get the pill if you want it or will be a mum to or son to son Darling. I love you darling for ever my love. Yous has your say from now until for ever. Darling. Will Darling, untill I see you. All my love I sind to you . . . Fred.'

By contrast, 17-year-old Rose writes well for someone who had been considered 'Dozy'. On 22 May she wrote to Fred, 'Darling, I am sorry I upset you in my previous letters. I didn't mean it . . . We've got a lot to do darling in the next couple of years. And we'll do it just loving each other . . .'

This is a chilling portent, given what their body count would be within the next two years. But in fact what the young girl was asking for here was something quite ordinary. She wanted to get married ('That ring means so much') and to have a future with Fred ('FROM NOW AND UNTILL FOREVER'). The couple already referred to each other as if they were married, signing themselves, 'Your Ever Worshiping Husband' and 'your worshipping wife'. Fred was still married, but there was no mention of a divorce here – although Rena too, like her little girl, would soon cease to be a problem for Rose and Fred.

Things had been building to a head at home for a while. A few weeks after the injury to 8-year-old Charmaine's ankle, Anna-Marie opened the door to their bedroom to find her big sister naked and tied to the bed by her wrists and ankles, with the plastic sheet beneath her. The little girl looked terrified and her hair was wet, as if she had been sweating or crying – although Charmaine *never* cried. It was shortly after this that Anna-Marie came home from school to find her sister had gone.

The prosecution maintained that Rose killed Charmaine somewhere between the first visit on 7 May and Fred's release from prison on 24 June. Rose usually sent Anna-Marie and Charmaine off to St James's Primary School together each morning, and they returned home together each afternoon. On this particular morning, Rose sent 7-year-old Anna-Marie off on her own, keeping Charmaine at home. Although Fred had said he would 'see to it when he got home', it is likely that Rose had arranged to hand the child back to Rena herself – but, if this was the case, it never happened.

Rose was friendly with a neighbour at Midland Road, a Polish lady called Mrs Jagura, whom she would chat to over the garden fence and exchange recipes with. During the course of one of their chats, Rosie had told her she could not 'wait to get rid of Charmaine', and was waiting for the child's mother to come and take her away. She had also mentioned this to Mrs Giles upstairs, who had advised her that Fred's girls should not be separated.

There are various theories about what happened next, but the one which the jury accepted is that Rose lost her temper with the child and murdered her in one of her uncontrollable rages. This is plausible for, if Rena was expected that day, the little girl may well have antagonised Rose before her mother arrived and Rose would then have lashed out at her. As Rose's son Stephen, born in 1973, was to say of his mother later on, 'She had no self control . . . [she] would hit out with anything she could lay her hands on. If she had a sledgehammer in her hand she'd have belted you with it.'* Stephen also described how his mother would grab him and his siblings around the throat with both hands. She had lifted Stephen off the ground this way as a young boy, throttling him until he passed in and out of consciousness. Stephen only survived because Rose had been distracted by Fred coming home, whereupon she loosened her grip, letting the boy crash to the floor without her even noticing. As Anna-Marie was to say of Rose, 'It was as if she had mental blackouts . . . as if she didn't know what she was doing.' Like a creature from a horror movie, Stephen's eyes were entirely bloodshot and his neck was one large purple bruise. Charmaine, however, would not even be this 'lucky'.

Another view amongst those who have studied the case is that Rose stabbed Charmaine with a kitchen knife, just as she'd probably stabbed her in the ankle a few weeks earlier when she'd taken the little girl to hospital. Some years later, Rose would also cruelly cut and stab two of the West children. As coal dust was found on the little girl's remains, it is likely that Rose hid Charmaine's body in the cellar until Fred came home to bury her. Rose would then have had to fob Rena off when she called for the child later that day, as she was to fob Daisy off when she too asked where the little girl she had taken a shine to had gone. However, this logical murder scenario begs the question: why wasn't Rose worried about how Fred would react when he eventually came home? Although Fred wasn't Charmaine's biological father, he still included her in his 'family

---

* *Inside 25 Cromwell Street* by Stephen and Mae West (1995)

of love' and sent kisses for Charmaine in his letters to Rose from prison. We now have the benefit of hindsight and know that Fred was a killer, but at this point Rose didn't know he was. Or did she? Having killed the little girl, why didn't she run away? The most plausible reason for her staying and waiting for Fred to come home and deal with the situation was because she already knew that he too had killed.

Somewhere during the months they'd been together, he'd either confided in Rose his most grisly of secrets, or she herself had found out that four years earlier Fred had killed his mistress, 18-year-old Anna McFall. Anna was a gentle Scottish girl who had been Rena's best friend before she began an affair with Fred. Unlike Rose and Rena, Anna had refused to join in with Fred's sex games but, once she'd become pregnant by him, pressed him to get a divorce in order to put things on a more formal footing between them. But Fred did not want Rena to find out and killed Anna as soon as she became a nuisance to him, cutting their almost full-term baby from her. After dissecting the bodies and keeping bones from both mother and unborn child as trophies, he'd buried their remains separately in a field at Much Marcle, just in sight of his childhood home of Moorcroft Cottage. He then told his father about it, and his mother Daisy a few days later, who cried when she learned what her favourite boy had done.

At the same time as telling Rosie about Anna McFall, Fred may have confessed that he'd killed missing waitress Mary Bastholm before this. And there may have been other murders, including a young boy found hanged whom Fred had been friendly with at his works in Gloucester. Fred could never resist bragging at the best of times, and had been cultivating in his young lover a morbid fascination with sadistic sex as they watched S&M films together, which at some point would include bestiality, paedophilia and snuff videos. Fred probably crowed about the murders to Rose enough times in jest for her to eventually realise he was telling the truth, by which time it would be less of a shock to her. She might even have become accustomed to the idea. (Fred did much the same in the 1980s and 1990s, making jokes to his children that they'd end up under the patio like their sister if they misbehaved. Only when his 'jokes' were taken seriously did it lead to his and Rose's arrests.) It is also possible that John West, the quieter but more cunning and 'manly' of the two brothers, might have told Rose, as he too was sleeping with her at his brother's behest.

There are other plausible theories as to how Charmaine died. Writer Howard Sounes believes that when Fred came home and Rose showed him what she'd done, he shared his own grisly secrets with her and together they forged 'a pact made in blood'. This bloody pact would then keep them together for the next twenty or so years. This still begs the question that if Rose didn't already know Fred had murdered, what made her think he wouldn't go to the police? It's fair to say, however, that Rose knew her beau had no time for the law, constantly being on the wrong side of it himself, and that despite 'his family of love' he actually had little love for the child who wasn't his.

Whatever happened that day, Rose carried on as normal, as if nothing out of the ordinary had happened. One of Rose's relatives believes that she and another of her siblings learnt to block things out as children as a way of coping with their abusive home life. In Rose's case, this appears to have led to a complete state of denial. A photo of her sitting smiling on Fred's lap soon after Charmaine's murder is particularly disturbing, as it shows she lacks even a shred of guilt or remorse – which she wouldn't of course, if she was in denial of what she'd done. Her state of mind regarding the murder is also evident by her reaction when Charmaine's little friend called round to see her soon after the murder. The Giles family had moved out of the upstairs flat to a place in the Forest of Dean some months earlier, but made a trip back to Midland Road especially so that Tracy could see her little pal again. When Rose answered the door, Tracy excitedly asked her if she could see her 'best friend', only for Rose to snap back at her, no she couldn't! 'She's gone to live with her mother, and bloody good riddance!'

Rose's cold and inappropriate response to the 8-year-old gives us an insight into her lack of maturity at best, and at worst reveals her contempt for the child she had just murdered. Tracy burst into tears at this and sank down onto the hall stairs where Anna-Marie comforted her. Anna-Marie was also missing her big sister, but was too frightened to ask Rose where she'd gone. Instead, she waited until her father came out of prison some weeks later who, knocking the ash from his cigarette, confirmed Rose's story.

After returning from prison, Fred had taken the child's lifeless little body back upstairs, where, using all the skills he'd learnt from working in an abattoir some years earlier, he began dissecting it. Rigor mortis would have already set in, but Fred managed to remove numerous small bones from the feet, toes and kneecaps which he kept as mementos. Whether Rose saw his trophy bones is unclear, but what we do know is that Fred then dug a deep, narrow hole outside the kitchen door that night and, possibly with Rose's help, stuffed the child's body into it, pushing her severed legs down beside her. This was to be the little girl's resting place for the next three years, until Mr Zygmunt asked Fred to build a kitchen extension onto the property. Fred then moved the body parts to beneath the new kitchen area, where the poor little mite would remain for another twenty years.

Rose then had the presence of mind to keep the school Charmaine attended off her back by informing the teacher that the little girl had gone to live with her mother. 'Moved to London' was recorded on the child's file, and that was the end of the matter for the next twenty-three years, until police bulldozers moved into 25 Cromwell Street. But Rose either did not have the wherewithal to get her story straight or arrogantly believed she would not get caught. Having told the school Charmaine had moved to London, she then told Mrs Giles that the little girl had gone to live with her mother in Bristol. These were the kinds of contradictory and obvious lies that Rose was to tell the police some twenty or so years later when they questioned her about her daughter's disappearance.

17

Rosie Goes Home

Tobyfield Road, Bishop's Cleeve, 1971

AROUND THIS TIME, CHARMAINE'S murder and Fred's own secrets appear to have become too much for the 17-year-old to bear. Perhaps Rose had a heart after all; or perhaps she was simply terrified at what she'd got herself into. Whatever the case, Rose got up one Sunday morning, put baby Heather in the pram and fled to her parents' house. But Daisy was not the only one who had been visiting Rose at Midland Road in secret. Despite the state of the place, Bill had also been making secret trips there, where he'd repeatedly asked his daughter to come home. Rosie had turned down his requests, but now that she'd finally sought refuge at her parents' house, Bill told her, 'You've made your bed, now lie in it.'

These were, of course, the words of a cuckolded man whose 'mistress' had dumped him for another. Rosie had chosen Fred over Bill, and now Bill was making her pay for it. His refusal to protect his daughter and allow her to come back home was critical, as it could have diverted Rose from the course of becoming one of the world's most infamous serial killers. Instead it propelled her back into Fred's arms, and later to the house at Cromwell Street that would eventually become their killing fields.

Fred had turned up at the Letts' home later that day and called to his young mistress at the back door in his coaxing, hypnotic voice, 'Rosie ... Come on Rosie ... You know what we've got between us ...'

What they had between them was, of course, like no other young couple who'd been living together for less than a year. Rose's father had come to the door, and Fred had said, 'What's the crack then? What's wrong?'

'You treat her like a child,' Bill replied.

Fred then went back to the van telling Bill, 'Right, tell Rose that I'm going to sit in the van out the front there for ten minutes, and if she ain't there, there'll be somebody else in her bed tonight.'

When Rose heard this, she picked up the baby and turned on her parents, 'You don't know him! There's nothing he wouldn't do!'

Bill must have changed his mind, for when Rosie went out to Fred, he ran after her telling her, 'He's only kidding.'

But the damage was done, and Fred was now driving her away, on the road to murdering together as they descended into Hell.

Life Without Rosie

Although Rose had sexually abused her younger brothers for a number of years, when she'd left home at 16, Gordon and Graham no longer had anyone to protect them from their psychotic father. The boys were the only children left in the house, and so when Bill wasn't hitting Daisy, he focused his rages on them. They then began sleeping rough as Andy had done – in public toilets, under hedgerows and in coal holes – anywhere, in fact, rather than go home and get beaten. On one occasion, a neighbour had stumbled across Graham covered in ice where he'd had to sleep out in the winter. Daisy would go out and look for the boys, and the police would sometimes pick them up and bring them home to face more violence. Yet still they received no help, just as the older children hadn't.

Daisy changed her job at this point and began working in the kitchens at the Delancey Hospital during the evenings, which meant she saw even less of Bill. However, relations had begun to thaw a little between Bill and Daisy's sister when he helped Eileen to obtain a job at Smith's. Eileen was much younger than Daisy and still a very attractive woman, which the grey-haired Daisy had once been. This was unlikely to have escaped Bill's attention as he offered her a lift into work each morning. His assisting Eileen, however, was not about any attraction or fondness he may have felt towards his sister-in-law, but simply a means of ensuring that she brought money into the house since Bill was, as ever, money-obsessed.

While the adults were out of the house, the boys, now aged 14 and 11, stole anything they could get their hands on. They used the money to buy drink and drugs as they attempted to block out their miserable lives. This had been going on for some while and, by 12 years of age, Graham had become an alcoholic. When Bill caught the boys stealing, he reported it to the police, whereupon they were hauled before a juvenile court, but again were punished rather than helped. Daisy had even written to Joyce, begging her to come home and help her out with the younger children as they ran wild, including Rosie before she left home. Joyce reminded her mother that she had been the one who'd asked her to leave in the first place, and that the last time she'd tried to visit her little brothers and sisters with a Christmas hamper for them, Daisy had shut the door in her face.

The boys were so disturbed by the time Rosie left home that 11-year-old Gordon had begun stealing women's lacy and satin underwear from the neighbours' washing lines and cross-dressing. He also flashed at people in the street from his bedroom window. This was obviously a scream for help from the child, which could not have been made plainer when, a year later, aged 12, Gordon took himself off to Cheltenham and asked to go into care. He was only in the children's home a matter of weeks when he ran away and went to stay with Rosie, but Fred made him leave when he stole from the couple. He also stole from Daisy's purse, but didn't worry about getting caught as he knew he was 'going to get beaten anyway'.

As an act of rebellion against his cruel and sadistic father, Graham stole Bill's new Toyota from Smith's car park and burned rubber as he hit the motorway. Andy Letts was completely in awe of his younger brother's courage in taunting their father, but terrified about what would happen to the boy when Bill finally caught up with him. As it was, the police got him first and Graham was packed off to borstal, which must have felt like a holiday camp compared to living at home with his father.

The three older girls had fled the nest into early marriages, and Andy had a girlfriend whose family he could stay with. Although when Andy was at home he had no idea about the sexual abuse going on there, he was fortunate in being older than Rosie as he too might have suffered the same fate at her hands as his two little brothers did. As far as Bill's violent mood swings were concerned, Andy believes these mellowed over time. This is a frightening thought as, later on, Bill would lift Gordon up by the ear and swing him round as the mood took him. On one occasion he had accused his son of stealing a radio and picked him up by the ear in front of Jackie Letts, who was so upset by it, she'd had to leave the house. Bill would also send the younger boys up to bed, strip them and flog them with a leather belt as they lay there. This bears all the hall-marks of Rosie's later 'disciplining' of Fred's little girls. Perhaps Fred hadn't had to 'train up' Rosie in sadosexual practices from scratch after all, as he told the police, for she'd already got a head start.

Daisy would later say of her youngest three, it was 'as if they couldn't cope with life'; that they had a 'weakness of character'.

Clearly Daisy was in denial and, as Carol Anne Davis rightly suggests in *Women Who Kill*, how could they be expected to cope when they'd had 'no praise, no fun and been regularly brutalised by their hate-filled father?'

And thus while young Gordon and Graham were out stealing cars and flashing at the neighbours, so their big sister was helping her lover dispose of the body of the child she had murdered.

18

Cruising for Fun

Gloucester, Summer 1971

WITH CHARMAINE 'GONE' AND Fred out of prison, Rose soon found she was pregnant again. The couple were excited by the news and hoped it would be the son they'd been planning on having. And as they celebrated the news, Fred wasted no time drilling holes in the bedroom door and lining up men for Rose to 'perform' with. These men were mostly Jamaicans with whom he'd made friends while doing up Mr Zygmunt's properties in the area. According to Fred, black men were better endowed than white, and he was obsessed with seeing Rose have sex with his black friends throughout their entire marriage. Rosie did not baulk at the idea, and was already calling herself Fred's cow or 'moo'. Had Rose been like most other 17-year-old girls, she might have been out with her friends or the boy next door, but she'd never had the chance to be 'ordinary' and wouldn't have known what it was. And now she was pregnant and putting on a porn show for her lover's entertainment, while he masturbated as he watched her through the spyholes in the door.

As soon as Rose and her 'client' finished, Fred then had sex with her – although he had ejaculation problems and wasn't able to satisfy her. He also had insane ideas about sex and told her that by coating himself in the superior sperm from another man (invariably black) it would help him delay ejaculation.

Rose might even have believed him at the time, although later she would brusquely remind him, 'You didn't last long.'

There were times later on when Rose wasn't keen to do what Fred wanted, but he would go on at her: 'Do it for us. Do it for the marriage,' nagging at her until she gave in. They weren't actually married at this point, but Rose had been dropping hints to Fred to make 'an honest woman of her', particularly now she was pregnant again. It was after they'd had sex one night, had eaten boiled eggs and gone back to bed, that Fred proposed to his young mistress. Rose was delighted and they set the date for January of the following year, by which time Rose would be 18 and not need her parents' consent (which they were unlikely to have given). Dozy Rosie and Weird Freddie were going to get hitched. But the fact that Fred was still married to Rena and this would make him a bigamist seemed neither to concern Rose nor her intended. But perhaps there was a reason for this . . .

During the latter part of August 1971, just two months after Fred had buried Charmaine, Rena came calling at Midland Road. Not finding the child there, she went over to Moorcroft Cottage in Much Marcle, where she helped her father-in-law, Walter West, to bring in the harvest while trying to find out the whereabouts of her eldest child. Walter had not been able to help but, some time after this, although we cannot be sure of the date, Fred agreed to meet Rena at a pub, where he plied her with drink. In trying to track Charmaine down, Rena had become a nuisance to Fred and, like Anna McFall before her, she too would now have to be got rid of. After murdering Rena, Fred butchered her and interred her remains in a field close to where he'd buried her former friend, Anna, four years earlier. It is possible that John helped him in this. Fred then placed a child's small red boomerang beside his wife's remains – the type given away free in cereal packets at the time – which had probably belonged to Charmaine. He and Rose were now free to wed.

Gloucester, Autumn 1971

Although Rena was now out of the way, the path to the altar did not run smoothly for Rose who, before the banns had even been read, discovered Fred had fallen for another woman. This was unusual for Fred, who rarely saw women as anything other than objects for his own sexual gratification. The woman in question was 19-year-old Elizabeth Agius, who had recently moved in next door. Fred had seen her having difficulty lifting her pram up the steps to her front door. He'd rushed over to help and, with his roguish charm, soon discovered her husband worked abroad. Fred introduced Liz to Rose, but continued to pursue her in front of his young 'fiancée', who Liz thought looked no more than 14. At first Fred's friendship with Liz didn't cause problems with Rose as their relationship was far from conventional, but this was to change.

With no relatives in the area and her husband away, Liz Agius was doubtless grateful for the couple's neighbourliness, and when Rose invited her in for a cup of tea, the two young women became friends. Events took a strange turn, however, when the couple asked her to babysit for them. Liz had babysat for Rose and Fred once before without incident. However, on the second occasion, Rose and Fred did not return home until the early hours. When Liz asked them if they'd had a nice time, Fred replied that they'd been 'driving round for hours, looking for young girls . . . virgins and runaways, to put on the game.' He carried on saying that the best place to find these 'lemons', as he called such vulnerable young girls, was at bus stations – and that he and Rose had parked up by the main bus depot at Bristol to continue their search. A bus station was, of course, where he'd picked up Rose and possibly Mary Bastholm.

Chillingly, Fred went on to say that it was easier to pick up girls with Rose in the car, as they would think it was safe to get in. He then bragged that he would bring the girls home to live with him and Rose, and he'd put them on the game if they were willing.

Liz thought Fred was making some kind of weird joke and didn't take him seriously. As she was later to say, 'They seemed such a nice couple.' But these trips were actually dummy runs leading up to the couple's first kidnap; Fred was quite possibly also testing Rose out to see if she would help him to 'abduct a girl', as he would later tell the police. Fred's crowing was a way of testing Liz, too, to see if he could involve her in the couple's sex games. He had also deliberately encouraged Rose to befriend Liz to try to talk her round. At one of their tea-drinking sessions, Rose told Liz that Fred was in love with her as she set about entrapping her. She also told the older, lonely teenager that she had had sex with numerous men while Fred watched her through a hole in the wall, and that he wanted a threesome with them. Rose then showed Liz a bag of sugar-cube-type pills that were probably spiked with tranquillisers, or the 'liquid cosh', but which she, strangely, told Liz were to stop her catching an STD from her clients. It is unlikely Rose actually believed this, as she also kept a pile of condoms in the drawer. But even the condoms had a perverse reason for being there.

With Rose getting nowhere with Liz, Fred became desperate to bed her, and told her she could do whatever she liked to him, with bondage, defecation and sadism top of the list. Still they got nowhere and, as the couple carried on trying to groom Liz, her husband returned home briefly from abroad. Liz brought him round to meet the new neighbours, whereupon the unsuspecting spouse put his arm around his wife, making Fred jealous, who stormed out of the room. He wanted Liz, and if he couldn't have her, he didn't see why her husband should. Threatening to put Mr Agius 'six feet under . . . !', he pointed at the floor where little Charmaine's body parts lay. As Colin Wilson said, 'Emotionally, Fred West was still a spoilt child,' who could not accept Liz Agius's husband had a prior claim. Rose too was like a spoilt child, and what these two narcissistic children wanted, they would make sure they got . . .

Some time after Mr Agius went back to work abroad, Rose invited Liz in for her morning cup of tea as usual. Only this particular morning, as Liz drank her tea, her head began spinning and she passed out. And when she woke up, she found herself naked in bed beside Fred. She remembered him having said to her some time before, 'Oh, what I could do to you . . .' and now he apparently had, with Rose smiling naked on the other side of her. This may have been Rose's first lesbian experience, and soon she would come to prefer having sex with women to men.

Soon after raping Mrs Agius, Fred and Rose tied the knot. In the event, Rose did not invite her family, and told a former neighbour that she met on her honeymoon, 'I don't have anything to do with them now.' Her parents had been against her marrying Fred, and not knowing Rena was dead might have wondered if he was even divorced. Daisy had recently pressed Rose again on the whereabouts of Charmaine and, perhaps as the questions got too close for comfort, it had been in Rose's interest to fall out with her family.

The Nuptials, Gloucester, Early 1972

The marriage between Fred and Rose took place at Gloucester Register Office on 29 January, exactly two months after Rose's eighteenth birthday. Fred was 31 years of age, and Rose by now was five months pregnant. Being highly adept at sewing, Rose probably made her own dress, placing matching small white rosebuds in her shiny, long dark hair. Fred had been working all morning on a car and turned up back at home covered in oil, with only a few minutes to get ready and get to the ceremony. Rose pleaded with Fred to change out of his dirty work overalls, and finally the party of four, Rose, Fred, Fred's brother John and a criminal associate of Fred's called Mick, walked to the register office together. The couple then exchanged vows at eleven, with Fred describing himself as 'bachelor' on the marriage certificate and his witness, who had a number of aliases, having to cross out the first name he'd signed with and put down another. The other witness, John West, had brought with him 'a bottle of Bristol Cream sherry,' as Fred recalled. 'We had a quick drink and went straight back to work.'

Rose did not ask why Fred had put 'bachelor' on the certificate, which means she probably knew her rival was dead. Her memory of the wedding also differed from Fred's. She had asked for a lager and lime in the pub afterwards, but her new husband had snapped at her, 'You have a bloody Coke and like it!' Obviously he was already trying to control her. On the way back from the ceremony, Fred found some money in the park which was enough to cover the cost of their marriage certificate, and he was said by Rose to be 'over the moon' about it. But this short burst of happiness didn't last long. When Fred found Liz in the kitchen one day, he slapped a pair of handcuffs on her and said in front of his new wife, 'Now I've fucking got you!' Rose and Fred began to row so loudly over his infatuation with Liz that the neighbours went round to complain but were promptly told, with a string of expletives, where to get off.

Rose went into labour in June 1972 with her second child; she and Fred called the baby May June because she had been expected in May but was overdue.* Rose had been depressed for much of this pregnancy, which wasn't helped by Fred barely visiting her during her stay in hospital. The birth had again been straightforward, and Rose had been due to leave within a few days, but she refused to go until Fred came to pick her up in the

---

* May later called herself Mae, by which name she is referred to hereafter.

van. But Fred didn't come and only in fact turned up once in ten days. In the end Rose was forced to discharge herself and get the bus home with the baby.

When Rose arrived home she was in for another shock. Anna-Marie and baby Heather were alone in the flat, while Fred was nowhere in sight. Thumping on the door of the neighbour's flat, Fred emerged red-faced and dishevelled. The newlyweds were supposed to be open with each other about 'everything'; sleeping with someone else behind the other's back was not part of the deal, and Rose erupted at her husband. Whether to placate his bride, or for some other reason, Fred agreed to take Rose on a belated honeymoon – albeit that they would have the children and a mystery young blonde-haired woman in tow. Rose had wanted to show Fred her childhood home of Northam in north Devon. Despite all that had happened there, it was a trip down Memory Lane as she hadn't been home since she'd left almost a decade ago. Even though Fred wasn't a drinker, Rose stopped off to take him into The Golden Lion, where she chatted to some of her former neighbours from Morwenna Park Road. As Rita New, a chalet cleaner at Westward Ho! holiday camp, explained:

I used to meet my husband up The Golden Lion at lunchtime, I had my daughter Tracy with me. It was in the 70s. I sat with Margaret Wilcox – Barry Seathe and his wife were sat by the bar. The door opened and in walked a slim man in a tank top which had a fawn background. He had two young women with him – one with a blonde bob and one with long dark hair, who was about eighteen. Barry chatted to them then brought the dark one over to me and said, 'Do you know who this is?' I didn't recognise her, it'd been some years since she'd left [Northam] but she said 'It's Rose.' She was smiling and looked lovely – she was a beautiful girl. We chatted and I asked how she was and her parents. She said 'I don't have nothing to do with them now. This is my husband [pointing to the man at the bar].' I saw him [Fred] at the bar with the blonde. He was all fidgety and on edge. She said they'd got married and couldn't have a honeymoon at the time for some reason, so they were taking a belated one. After a while Rose said, 'We've got to go now – I've taken them to Exeter, now I'm going to show them Ilfracombe.' When they went Barry came over to us. He said that blonde with him at the bar, that's his ex-missus. 'I find it awful funny,' Barry said, 'he takes his ex-missus on a belated honeymoon . . . I find it most weird that's his ex-missus.

Fred was known to be a liar and braggart; but there is often a kernel of truth in people's boasts and lies, and there may have been here. For it is possible that Rena, who was blonde, might still have been alive at this point, as it is by no means certain when Fred actually killed her (and a few writers believe it wasn't until August 1972 that she died). Rena was unconventional and would not have turned a hair that Fred had married someone else while still married to her, or at going on honeymoon with the couple if she thought it might help her find out what had happened to Charmaine. But if it was Rena, she was no longer with them by the time they'd made their way down to Rose's old home in Plymouth. It was here, at Benbow Street, that Rose caught up with her little friend again: Joan Scobling. Joan invited them in, but Fred wouldn't get out of the car. He sat with the children as Joan passed orange squash through the car window to them while she and Rose chatted.

Had Rose then been involved in Rena's murder? Or was the unknown girl Liz Agius, who was also blonde and whom Fred might well refer to as 'the ex-missus'? Or was it someone else? Whoever it was, it is almost certain that all three were sharing the honeymoon bed.

During the stop-off at The Golden Lion in Northam, a

Transit van – the kind of vehicle that Fred owned – had been parked outside a nearby house. The lady who lived at the house came out when she heard loud noises coming from the van, as if there were children inside it, kicking and banging to get out. She looked in the window, where a sheet of boarding separated the long driver and passenger seat from the back so that it was impossible to see inside. She then went into the pub and asked if anyone knew whose van it was, but no one laid claim to it. Moments later, however, Fred, who had been listless and edgy at the bar, suddenly said, 'Come on, we're going now' – and the honeymoon party upped and left. So had this been their van, or did the Plymouth trip take place another time? One chilling thought is, as Rita recalled, 'She [Rose] looked beautiful and spoke so nice, I'd have let her take my little daughter to the shops. It makes you think.'

When the newlyweds finally arrived back in Gloucester, they were about to embark on another adventure together. Old Mr Zygmunt liked Fred: he'd proved to be a fast and reliable worker doing up his properties, and he had availed himself of Fred's young wife on a regular basis. Now Mr Zygmunt wanted to return the favour and suggested, as Rose was pregnant again and their family growing, that they move to one of his more spacious properties around the corner; a three-storey semi at 25 Cromwell Street. The couple jumped at the chance, and walked the few hundred yards with the children and their belongings to their new home.

Rather like Midland Road, Cromwell Street was bedsit-land, with a mixture of students and immigrant workers; the house itself had once been elegant, but was now rundown and gloomy. At the end of the road, close to number 25, was a car park with a cut-through to the main shops in town, which Rose would often use when she went shopping. The house itself had an attic, a garage at the back and a single-storey corrugated hut stood at the side of the house, used as a church by Seventh Day

Adventists. Number 25 also boasted a large cellar with a separate set of stairs down to it at the front of the house; pictures of it which would be beamed around the world some twenty-three years later.

Despite the condition of the house, Fred knew he could soon get it round. At first they rented the house and then later accepted Mr Zygmunt's offer of a loan as a deposit to obtain a mortgage on the house. Rose was now on the property ladder: not bad for a young girl from her impoverished background, or for her husband, who had spent his young life in dark and unsanitary tied cottages. The newlyweds were proud of their achievements, and the very first person they invited round to show off their home to was their friend Liz. Taking Liz on a tour of the house, Fred took her down the stone steps to the large cellar beneath. The cellar was also dark and damp, with a low ceiling that made it difficult to stand up in. 'I could sound-proof it and use it as my torture chamber,' he joked to Liz. And very shortly, this is exactly what he and Rose would do, carrying out a test run on Fred's own little daughter.

Taking on Cromwell Street meant the couple had over-stretched themselves – at least this is what Fred told his young bride as he began turning the upstairs of the house into bedsits to get rental from them. Rose was said to have been against the idea, and he'd hit her, letting her know he was in charge. They'd also drawn up a master and slave contract between them, in which Rose agreed to give in to his every whim, although this was more of a private joke or sex aid in their perverted marital toolbox.

As soon as Fred got home from work each evening, he started knocking down walls, banging nails into plasterboard and drilling and wiring. The children had their rooms on the ground floor and, at the other side of the house, Fred had made a special bedroom for his young wife where she could continue to entertain her Jamaican clients to boost the household coffers. 'You gotta do your bit for the marriage,' he told Rose. But in reality,

Fred was earning enough from all his different jobs to keep the family without Rose having to obtain money for sex, when she paid for it at all, or from letting out the top of the house. What Fred was actually doing was turning their new home into a cross between Clarence Road, which had so impressed him with its numerous lodgers, drifters and others passing through, and his fantasy house, where sex would be on tap and he could indulge his voyeuristic desires whenever it took his fancy – which was most of the time.

The first lodgers moved in two or three weeks later. They were two boys, Benjamin Stanniland and Alan Davis, who were both 18, the same age as Rose, and which was likely to have been a deliberate move on Fred's part. On the day they moved in, Rose and Fred insisted on taking the boys out for a drink, where they were said to have talked nonstop about sex. Ben and Alan were taken aback by this, but the couple were obviously 'testing' them out, as they had done with Liz the previous year.

That evening, when they all got back to the house, the boys were in for another shock when Rose changed into a see-through top and got into bed with Ben and, later that night, with Alan. Fred had either put her up to this or the young girl was learning fast from her Svengali. A night of enthusiastic sex with her lodgers probably also gave Rose a sense of power over the boys, who in the morning dreaded bumping into the landlord. But Fred, of course, had been observing his wife's performances from behind the freshly drilled holes in the wall. And, as the lodgers were soon to find out, while drink and drugs were barely tolerated at Cromwell Street, sleeping with the landlord's wife was a fundamental rule of the house. Thus, between cooking dinner, taking the children to school and keeping house, Rose would happily oblige. As another new lodger, David Evans, was to remark: 'She was the landlady but came upstairs now and then because she liked sex.'

Practising

Fred's jest to his former neighbour, Mrs Agius, would soon prove true when he started work on the cellar at Cromwell Street. The cellar would undergo many changes over the years as Fred dug out vast quantities of earth. At first he divided it into a playroom, a place for his tools and another, larger area, which he soundproofed and equipped with vibrators, some implements he'd fashioned in metal, duct tape and ties made from ripped-up old sheets.

Just a year after Charmaine's murder, and within a few weeks of arriving at Cromwell Street, the couple turned their attentions to little Anna-Marie, whom they led down into the cellar. Anna-Marie's account of what happened next is the first evidence of Rose and Fred abusing together, and of the sheer cruelty and callousness of which 18-year-old Rose was capable.

As the child asked what was going on, Rose grinned weirdly at her, a look that meant 'she was really going to enjoy herself'. Fred ordered the little girl to strip off, but she wasn't quick enough for Rose, who ripped her dress from her. 'You heard your father! Get that off!' she told the terrified child. Having been forced, naked, onto a mattress on the floor, Anna-Marie began to cry and begged her parents to stop. But Rose coldly ignored her distress and snapped, 'Just shut up and be quiet!' After Fred spread-eagled her legs and tied her hands above her head, Rose squatted on the child's face to stop her struggling and started 'scratching and pawing' the little girl, until her undeveloped breasts bled (something she would later do with their other victims).

The couple then produced a glass, Pyrex-type bowl with liquid in it, which later turned red like rosehip syrup. This could have been blood, but Fred's ideas were so insane – he'd even become obsessed with trying to breed Rose with a bull – that the substance could equally have been animal sperm mixed with blood. It could also have been sperm from Rose's black clients, whose used condoms Fred insisted she saved, so that he could mix the contents together and use them for his weird experiments. Whatever the material was in that bowl, he inserted it into the child's vagina using some kind of implement or vibrator, as she screamed in agony. Rose and Fred then left her lying there and returned an hour later, to torture the little girl all over again. And as she tried to resist, Rose repeatedly told her 'not to be so silly' and encouraged Fred to 'get on with it'.

Fred then raped the child as Rose stood by. Perhaps Rose was trying to understand her own experiences as a child, as can happen in cases where women who are abused in childhood go on to abuse with a male partner. At the very least, it demonstrates that Rose was not just Fred's willing assistant in the abuse, but that she'd joined in with it and lacked all compassion for the child. Strangely, however, Rose did apologise to Anna-Marie afterwards. At first, when the little girl couldn't walk because of her injuries, Rose had laughed at her; but then, following her into the bathroom, she had given her a sanitary towel to mop up the blood. 'I'm sorry,' she said. 'Everybody does it to every girl; it's a father's job.' This remark possibly speaks volumes about Rose's own childhood experiences with Bill and her subsequent attitude. She then went on to say, 'Don't worry about it, and don't say anything to anybody. It's something everyone does but they don't talk about it.'

This attack marked the point when Fred had taken Rose onto the next stage in their sadosexual games, and where they would begin to look further afield for their enjoyment.

19

The Dummy Run

Gloucestershire, Autumn 1972

IT WAS ONE SATURDAY evening in September that Rose slipped into the passenger seat beside Fred and they went out for a spin in his grey Ford Popular, leaving the lodger's girlfriend to keep an eye on the children. One of the places the couple liked to drive around was the Tewkesbury area of Gloucestershire. Fred and his brother John had gone to dances there in their teens, and it was not far from where Rosie used to live in Bishop's Cleeve.

The newlyweds had not had much success earlier that evening, and it was getting towards half past ten when they finally spotted their prey: a teenage girl hitchhiking on the other side of the road. Fred turned the car around and they drove back down the road, pulling up alongside the young girl. Sixteen-year-old Caroline Owens looked worried until Rose wound down her window and, smiling sweetly at her, asked, 'Where are you going?'

Caroline 'relaxed' at seeing a teenage girl not much older than herself in the car and went over to talk to her. She told Rose she was hitching back to her home in Cinderford, in the Forest of Dean. Hitchhiking was common practice amongst young people at the time and Caroline knew to be careful. Rose was immediately attracted to the very pretty young girl with an urchin haircut and offered her a lift home. As Caroline had chatted through the window to Rose, she'd noticed the driver of the car was a grubby little man who was much older than his passenger, but felt safe getting in because Rose was there.

Although Caroline was very much a teenager of the time in her check flares and tank top, Rose wore a full-skirted red dress with a Peter Pan collar and white bobby socks – looking more fifties rock and roll (her husband and her father's era) than seventies glam rock of the time. Caroline soon found this was Rose's own unique style of dress – the frock was the same one that Rose's former neighbour, Rita, had seen her wearing on her honeymoon, and both women were struck by how very attractive Rose was at this age.

The couple asked Caroline about herself: who she'd been visiting and where she went; information they would later use to hunt her down. Rose, in particular, made her feel comfortable, so Caroline poured out her heart to her, telling her how she'd been to see her boyfriend Tony in Tewkesbury and about the difficulties she had getting on with her stepfather at home. As she spoke she could see Fred possessed a roguish charm, but still wondered why someone as young and pretty as Rose would be married to him. In the course of the conversation, Caroline went on to tell them she was looking for a job. Rose and Fred glanced at the girl and back at each other, replying in unison, 'We need a nanny to look after our daughters.'

Dropping Caroline off at her house in the Forest of Dean, the couple returned the following day. Only this time they had their two small children in tow, and Rose was clutching the baby. Caroline's parents were apprehensive of Fred, but as he and Rose gave every impression of being an ordinary family, they welcomed them over their threshold. Caroline cooed over the baby and 'fell in love with the children' straight away. Fred knew only too well the power of using his toddlers to entice teenage girls back to his caravan, and now he and Rose were brazenly using the same ploy to entice the young girl to move in with them right under her parents' noses.

The couple told Caroline she would get her own room – and as she was one of fifteen children, this appealed to her. They also promised to pay her a weekly wage of £8 and to take her over to see her parents one evening each week. The tactic of using their children had also worked with her parents, who gave Caroline the go-ahead to move in with them. The following day, as Caroline was packing her belongings, the 'nice' Mr and Mrs West even turned up to give her a hand, reassuring her parents they'd keep an eye on their daughter; that she'd be safe with them. Only little Anna-Marie, as she silently watched the new nanny's belongings being carried out to the car, had any inkling of what Rose and Fred were actually smirking about.

Turning up at Caroline's house to win her parents round and collect their prey was an audacious move on the couple's part, and indicates even at this early stage the lengths they were prepared to go to to get exactly what they wanted. And as soon as Caroline arrived at the Wests' home, she discovered they had lied to her, as she was not given her own room but had to share with Anna-Marie. This turned out to be a godsend, however, as Anna-Marie relished the new nanny being there and clung to her. Even though Caroline was only 16 herself, she realised the little girl was starved of affection and was frightened when-ever Rose and Fred were around. By sharing a room with her, Caroline at least felt able to protect and care for her some of the time.

While Caroline took Anna-Marie to school and cared for baby Mae and toddler Heather, she soon realised their teen-age mother would be entertaining clients in another room. But, despite this side of Rose's life, she always kept the children clean and well turned out, and cooked decent meals for all the family, as Caroline was to say. And there were some fun times to be had at the house in the early days, where 'Alright Now' by Free would often be heard as the boys in the bedsits played it at full blast and joked around. Caroline also made friends with Rose whom she later described as 'simple-minded'. Her 'whiny and drippy' voice irritated Caroline, but the two teenage girls would often spend their evenings together, chatting about boys and television.

After a while, however, things took a different turn, when Rose began playing with the younger girl's hair, stroking it and telling her she had beautiful eyes as they sat on the sofa together. The bathroom door at Cromwell Street did not have a lock on it, and there were times when Rose would just barge in on the young nanny, talking to her and looking at her as she bathed. At night, Rose would then put on transparent tops and, at Fred's behest, try to draw Caroline into their sex games and the parties they held upstairs with their guests – often Rose's clients. After whispering in the kitchen together one day, Fred and Rose came out smiling at Caroline as she nursed the baby. Rose then sat beside her while Fred told her, 'We'd like you to join our sex circle . . . You know – you, me, Rose – you like Rose, don't you? . . . And a few men friends of ours, you'd enjoy it. You haven't tried a black man yet, have you? You wouldn't want a white man after being spoilt by a black man . . . They'd fuck the arse off you. How about it then? Are you game for it?'

Caroline was shocked and frightened, and in her book, *The Lost Girl*, says she could not believe that Rose was sitting beside her, letting Fred talk in that way to her. Caroline laughed nervously and said, 'Tell him to behave Rose!'

But, to her astonishment, Rose just carried on grinning at her and said, 'Oh go on, Car, you'll enjoy it, give it a go!'

When Caroline realised the couple were deadly serious, she protested she wasn't that sort of person. Fred turned nasty at this, threatening to tell her mother and her boyfriend what she'd been up to at their house – 'they won't want anything to do with you any more, will they?' he barked at Caroline, leaving

Rose to comfort the crying girl. As Rose hugged Caroline, she tried to get her to reconsider Fred's proposition, while Fred muttered as he left the room, 'Fucking lesbians!', and told Rose to 'have it sorted' before he returned.

While working as a nanny at the house, Caroline had become increasingly upset by Rose's treatment of Anna-Marie, who she would whack around the head at will and treat like her personal slave. John West was a frequent visitor to the house, and would quietly watch Caroline from the corner of his eye. Fred, on the other hand, talked incessantly and crudely about sex, and constantly bragged about his abilities as an abortionist. He also told Caroline that 8-year-old Anna-Marie was not a virgin, watching the young teenager's reaction to this as he did so. It was another ploy to test her out to see if he could draw her in to the couple's games. When Caroline showed her distress at his admission, he immediately tried to laugh it off, saying the saddle had come off Anna-Marie's Chopper bike and that she'd 'damaged herself' because of it.

In fact, shortly after raping the child that summer, Rose had made Anna-Marie wear large, heavy sex gadgets made out of metal as she walked around the house doing the housework. The contraption had a vibrator inside, which the little girl had to keep in place all day and which buzzed as she worked. Fred had made these hideous contraptions at Permali's factory where he had recently started work; they included a metal surround on a vibrator and a U-shaped gadget with handles on it.

Just after the rape, Rose had asked the terrified child to go down to the cellar again to 'tidy up the toys'. When Anna-Marie had tried to pass Rose on the stairs to go back up, the 18-year-old blocked her way and forced her to strip off. Strapping the U-shaped sex gadget to the little girl, Rose had then gagged the child and begun whipping her, when Fred came home on his lunch break. Rose had obviously put on the 'show' for her husband, who laughed uproariously at his daughter's distress. On this particular occasion, Fred had then quickly raped his daughter and gone back to work. But rather than just acting as her husband's assistant, for his pleasure, Rose decided to continue the little girl's ordeal to fulfil her own sadistic desires. After screaming at Anna-Marie and beating the child, Rose lifted her skirts to reveal a vibrator attached to a belt with which she raped her. The internal cuts inflicted on the little girl were painful enough, but Rose then took great pleasure in making her take a bath with salt in it.

Caroline, of course, knew nothing of this, but had heard enough to cause her to be frightened. After being both comforted and propositioned by Rose, Rose was called away to see to her sleeping children. The moment she left the room, Caroline grabbed her belongings and slipped out of the house, rushing home to her parents in the Forest of Dean. Rose and Fred hadn't been married a year by this time, but like two sex-crazed adolescents they once more decided that what they wanted, they *would* have – whatever it took. Where Liz had been for Fred, this time Caroline would be for Rose. According to Fred in his police interview in 1994, it had been Rose's idea 'to get her', as she wanted to 'satisfy her urges with her'. As Caroline said, 'He kept me in order with violence for her to do what she did . . .'

Fred told the police he'd come up with the plan as he'd wanted to see if Rose would actually go through with helping him abduct a girl. Of course he was a known fantasist and liar (even blaming Rena in court for the tyres he'd stolen from his works). But he was probably telling the truth here as the couple had not attempted to kidnap or rape Caroline when she'd got into their car the first time, although they could easily have done so had they thought about it. Instead, they'd tried to groom and seduce Caroline, but since that had failed, they were now changing their modus operandi. And, as they did so, they were becoming increasingly locked in a *folie à deux*, or shared madness, together – but one which would be far more extreme and insidious than anything Bill and Daisy had shared.

Fred had begun transmitting his delusional beliefs to Rose since she'd first moved in with him at 15. He'd exploited her youth and her nymphomania by encouraging her to outdo Rena in sexual exploration, and to use his children as guinea pigs as he tutored her in his own sadosexual fantasies. Rose was susceptible because she was young and had already been corrupted by her father. And, very soon, under Fred's tutelage, she'd developed an appetite for the power such practices gave her. It was a heady feeling and something she'd never experienced before. Fred had then introduced her to cruising for girls and, as they egged each other on to act out one of their fantasies, they decided to abduct a girl together: in this case, their former nanny. The danger was, while sexual sadism is very rare amongst sex offenders, it is common amongst sexual murderers and serial killers – and Rose and Fred were both sexual sadists.

The Abduction

On 6 December 1972, exactly one week after Rose turned 19, the couple decided to put their plan into action; it was Rose's birthday present to herself. As Rose and Caroline had been friends for a while, Rose knew things about the younger girl, such as where she went and at what times of the day. She was pretty sure Caroline would be visiting her boyfriend Tony in Tewkesbury on a Saturday night and, as Tony did not have a car, Rose knew Caroline would be hitchhiking home to the Forest of Dean afterwards.

Earlier that day, Rose and Fred had begun discreetly trailing Caroline in the car when she was out with Tony. It was just a few weeks since Caroline had left Cromwell Street but, glancing over her shoulder, she noticed the couple driving around in their Ford Popular. Later that evening, as she waited for a lift home opposite Gupshill Manor pub as usual, the Wests pulled up alongside her. Caroline was worried about their response to her leaving them high and dry, without a nanny. Rose, however, had got that one covered, and jumped out of the car, beaming at her.

'Hello Caroline! How are you? I'm sorry you left. We've missed you, haven't we Fred?'

'Yeah, and the kids have too,' he nodded at her from inside the car. 'Look, I'm sorry for what I said, I was only messing around. Can we give you a lift home?'

Perhaps pleased to see some friendly faces as she stuck her thumb out that cold December night, but against her better judgement, Caroline accepted their offer. Yes, the couple were odd, she told herself, but she'd worked for them and they hadn't actually hurt her or anything. She'd be all right.

The car only had two doors, and Rose got out to let Caroline climb into the back. The moment Fred pulled away, Rose said she wanted a 'chat' with her, and clambered over the passenger seat to sit beside her in the back.

At first the two young women talked about the children, but as Fred drove through the dark countryside towards her home, Caroline saw him leering at her in the rear-view mirror. He then demanded to know if she'd had sex with her boyfriend that night. Caroline was frightened and begged Rose for help, 'Tell him to leave it, Rose.' But Rose didn't answer; instead she grinned weirdly at Caroline, just as she had at little Anna-Marie, before she and Fred had pounced on the child. 'Have a feel, Rose!' Fred chimed in, smirking. 'See if she's wet!' Rose didn't hesitate and grabbed the girl's crotch. Caroline pushed her hand away in shock, whereupon Rose chortled and began fondling her breasts. Caroline burst into tears and said she wanted to go home, which only made the couple laugh all the more. As Caroline recalled, 'My fear just seemed to turn them on even more.'

The terrified girl then realised that Fred had taken a turning towards Chepstow, which was in the opposite direction to her home. When she asked where they were going, Fred pulled up at a grass verge just past the Highnam roundabout in an isolated part of the countryside, where Rose tried to maul and kiss her all the more. As Caroline fought her off, Fred yelled 'bitch!' at her and turned to help Rose. Licking his lips, he then lined up his punches, smacking the young girl on the temple several times until she lost consciousness.

When Caroline came round she found her hands were tied behind her back, and Rose was gripping her securely in a bear hug while Fred wrapped layers of duct tape around her head and mouth, making her gag. Caroline remembers the whole operation as being 'very efficient', and taking only seconds. Rose then pushed the girl into the foot-well of the car, and sat on her (just as she had Anna-Marie), while Fred turned the car round and drove them back to Cromwell Street.

They arrived back at the house a little before midnight, where Fred got out of the car to check no one was around, and gave the signal to Rose to bring the trussed-up girl inside. They then took her to a first-floor bedsit facing onto the street, where Fred told her to be good and they'd tidy her up and let her go; but of course they had no intention of doing any such thing and were just playing a cruel game of cat and mouse with her.

To keep their game going, Fred sat Caroline on the settee while Rose, bizarrely, went off to make them all a cup of tea. Fred took out a knife and began cutting off the duct tape around Caroline's head, all the while talking gently to her. In the process he nicked her skin, making her bleed, for which he apologised – quite forgetting he'd knocked the poor girl unconscious only minutes earlier. Rose brought in three cups of tea and also assumed the role of the caring kidnapper, cooing at Caroline, 'There, there, you'll be all right.' The couple freed the girl's wrists so that she could drink the tea, and then tried to talk her into coming back to work for them. Fred told Caroline that Rose 'had a bun in the oven' again, and needed a nanny even more now. He also told her they were hoping for a boy this time, while Rose smiled at Caroline, 'Go on Car . . . it will be better this time.'

Clearly, the couple had lost touch with reality to believe that the terrorised young girl would ever want to see them again, never mind work for them, after all they had put her through. Rose then put her arms around the young girl, and began kissing her on the lips. Caroline pushed her away, screaming at her to leave her alone, at which point Fred grabbed hold of Caroline's head and forced her face-down into the settee, instructing Rose to 'get the cotton wool'. Rose scurried off and returned with a large wad of the cotton wool which, clearly practised at, she stuffed into Caroline's mouth. The couple got out some strips of old torn-up sheeting (the kind they'd used on Charmaine and Anna-Marie) and tied a strip around her head to keep the cotton wool in place, using another strip to blindfold her with.

As they busily worked together, they swore at the girl, calling her a 'fucking bitch'. Fred waved a fist in her face, threatening her: 'Do you want some more of this, bitch?' He and Rose then stripped Caroline, and bound her hands together with rope. Having rendered the poor girl helpless, they then pushed her onto a stained mattress on the floor. Rose stripped her off and assaulted her digitally, examining her vagina. Fred joined in, both describing the appearance of her vagina aloud for some time, as if the pair were, once more, performing some strange laboratory experiment like two white-coated, insane boffins. Fred instructed Rose to hold the girl's legs apart and then lashed her with the buckle end of a leather belt, telling her he wanted to 'flatten her clitoris' and how she'd 'enjoy sex much more after this.'

Fred and Rose would always tell their victims they were torturing them for their own good; and perhaps they even believed it, as they might have been told this as children, although it was actually about their pleasure as they stood grinning at Caroline's pain.

As soon as Fred finished, Rose left the room and came back with some water; which she proceeded to wipe Caroline with to 'cool her down'. Once more Rose was the kindly caregiver. As Caroline remarked, Rose 'was a sadistic, demonic, sex-crazed beast' one minute, and a softly spoken 'Gloucester housewife' the next. Rose then performed oral sex on Caroline while Fred had sex with Rose from behind. Rose and Fred eventually fell asleep with Caroline still tied up beside them. Early that morning, the doorbell went and Fred answered. The girl could hear a man in the hall and called out for help. Rose began cursing at her and pushed a pillow over her face, pressing all her weight onto it, smothering her. Caroline acted dead in the hope she would release her grip, and when the pillow was finally removed it was Fred's face staring down at her.

He was furious with Caroline, and threatened to keep her in the cellar and let his 'black friends' have her. 'And when we're finished we'll kill you and bury you under the paving stones . . . !' Fred had used this same threat to Liz Agius regarding her husband. He then told Caroline there were hundreds of girls killed and buried in the cellar, and that nobody would find her there. Although this was just a boast at the time, Fred was becoming increasingly preoccupied with the idea – to such an extent that he was now fantasising about it.

It was breakfast time and the children were starting to get up. While Rose went out to see to them, Fred took the opportunity to rape Caroline. As soon as he saw she was upset he, bizarrely, started to cry himself. He begged her not to tell Rose and insisted Caroline was there 'solely for Rose's pleasure', and the young girl had no doubt he was telling the truth. 'When Rose is pregnant, she gets these lesbian urges . . . and she wanted you,' he explained, looking nervously at the door, fearing his volatile wife would 'kill both of us if she finds out!'

His fear of Rose finding out appears to have been genuine as he didn't ejaculate inside Caroline, but withdrew rather than leave traces of what he'd done. And in a bid to buy Caroline's silence, Fred then struck a deal with her. Rose desperately wanted Caroline to stay, he told her, and if she kept quiet about the rape and agreed to move back in with them, he'd let her go. Doing whatever it took to stay alive, Caroline agreed. Fred then tied the naked girl to the chair so that Rose didn't suspect anything, and went out to tell his wife the 'good news'. Rose came rushing back into the room and threw her arms around Caroline, delighted she was staying.

Caroline was untied and they helped her bathe: Rose washing her hair in the bath while Fred gently brushed the gum left from the duct tape from her hair afterwards. They then allowed her to get dressed and have breakfast, after which she helped Rose with the vacuuming as if nothing had happened, as the young girl silently looked for her escape route. Later that morning, Fred ran Rose, Caroline and the children down to the launderette at Eastgate Street, then drove off to his job at Permali's. After helping Rose sort the washing into the machines, Caroline told her she was popping out to get some cigarettes but ran home to her mother's again, who, on seeing the purple cuts and bruising to her daughter's face, called the police. Caroline believes that the rape saved her life. 'I think I was going to be taken to that cellar. It was her hands around my neck,' she said.

When police officers knocked at the door of Cromwell Street later that day, Rose launched into an onslaught of expletives: 'Don't be so fucking daft! What do you think I am?' The police then asked to search the couple's car, at which Rose snapped, 'Please your bloody self!' Once more, Rose was either in denial of what she'd done, or she arrogantly believed she wouldn't get caught. This is typically symptomatic of narcissism. Narcissists see themselves as special and as not having to follow the same rules as others. They are also self-centred, with little regard for anyone else. As well as being to some extent genetic, this behaviour is also partly as a result of early disturbing experiences. It is seen in abused and neglected children and can develop from feelings of worthlessness in childhood. Narcissists also often fantasise about getting their own back on others, and this is important in the development of sexual sadism. Rose appeared to exhibit this personality trait. As did her father, Bill Letts.

As the police looked over the car, they found a button that had been ripped off Caroline's trousers in the struggle. Officers then searched the house, where they found evidence of the parcel tape that had been used to bind her head, and a substantial amount of pornographic films and photographs. The newly-weds were arrested.

At the police station, Rose admitted sexual assault, but said she had stopped when Caroline had asked her to. Fred denied raping Caroline, which, again, was because he feared Rose's reaction if she found out. The case was heard by Gloucester Magistrates' Court on 12 January 1973. Caroline was too traumatised to relive her ordeal by giving evidence in the witness box. Facing the perpetrators of her attack in court was a hideous prospect for any teenager still suffering nightmares from it. Partly because of this, charges of rape against Rose and Fred were reduced to indecent assault and ABH, which the couple agreed to plead guilty to.

The prosecution argued that as Caroline had not screamed when the gag came off, and because she had not tried to escape the following morning, she had offered 'passive cooperation'. They might as well have said, 'She'd been asking for it.' Fred wore a suit and did his best to look remorseful. 'I don't know why I did it, Your Honour sir, it just happened', he told the bench. And because the case had collapsed against him some years earlier when he'd got his young sister pregnant, it meant he had no sexual offences on record. Besides, the Gloucester builder looked a 'docile' kind of chap, the court decided. Rose, who had no record of any kind, must have looked pitiful as she stood in the dock in her schoolgirl socks, a teenage mum with three children at home and another on the way. In trying to get herself off the hook, Rose bizarrely told the court that she was going to receive psychiatric help for her 'lesbian ways'.

After weighing it all up, the bench looked favourably on the psychopathic couple, and fined them just fifty pounds each. It barely rated as a telling off, and a small piece featured in the local paper, the *Gloucester Citizen*, that night: 'City Pair Stripped and Assaulted Girl'. Knowing her family would see the article might have shamed most people into stopping, but Rose lacked all inhibition and never once cared what others thought of her. This kind of grandiosity, and being only able to focus on one's own needs at the expense of the feelings of others, is also found in individuals who are narcissistic and psychopathic.

As Stephen West was to say of his parents' case many years later, the court had effectively told them to 'go for it'. And they did, for just two months later a young girl would be dead, and there would be five more murders in the next two years alone.*

The case was also a slap in the face for 17-year-old Caroline, who had been brave enough to report her terrifying ordeal. 'It made me feel like I wasn't worth anything,' she said years later, and after the case she attempted suicide. Some crime writers believe the verdict also led Rose and Fred to make a pact to avoid finding themselves in this situation again. That is to say, they would not let their future prey go, but would quietly murder and dispose of them instead. As author Colin Wilson suggests, this

---

* Fred was possibly also spurred on by the 'loads of kinky letters' he received after the case, reinforcing the notion he held that this was perfectly acceptable behaviour.

may have encouraged Fred to increase his sadism towards his victims, as he knew they were not going to live to tell the tale. The same could probably be said of Rose. But what seems more likely is that, as the couple became increasingly wrapped up in their joint madness, death was almost certain to have happened sooner or later as their sex games escalated to the next level to get their kicks. Caroline had lived, as they had not yet reached the next stage; the court case had the effect of hastening this.

The couple also appeared to be delusional, as they did not seem to think they would be caught or even that, given half a chance, Caroline would run off from the launderette and call the police. Neither Rose nor Fred believed normal rules applied to them. This was, however, the last chance of diverting Rose from the path she was now on with Fred, as the cruel, perverse couple left the court to carry on with their sex games. And in the New Year, Fred would finish his work in the cellar, turning it into a torture chamber.

20

The First Murder Together

Gloucester, March 1973

ROSE WAS FIVE MONTHS pregnant and, already having three small children to care for, decided she needed another nanny. It was then she remembered Lynda Gough. Or, at least, she remembered Lynda, and the job was the pretext for luring her to the house. Lynda had been the girlfriend of Ben Stanniland, one of the lodgers at Cromwell Street. When her relationship with him had broken down, she'd gone out with another lodger and had become a regular visitor to Cromwell Street. During that time, Rose had taken a fancy to the pretty girl and encouraged her to share her 'men problems' with her; Lynda had also babysat for the couple on occasions.

Lynda worked as a seamstress at the Co-op on Barton Street, and still lived at home with her parents in Gloucester. Fred took Rose round to see Lynda one evening, waiting in the car, out of sight of the house, while she knocked the door. He'd learnt from their last sortie to Caroline's parents that it was less likely to arouse suspicion if Rose turned up alone. Rose smiled sweetly at Lynda and suggested they go for a drink together, where she asked the young woman to move into Cromwell Street to be the couple's nanny. June Gough, Lynda's mother, briefly caught sight of the young woman who called round for her daughter, describing her later as dark, slightly overweight and several months pregnant.

The following month, just two weeks before Lynda's birthday, June Gough came home to find her oldest child had gone, taking her clothes and belongings with her. She had left her parents a note to say:

Dear Mum and Dad,
  Please don't worry about me. I have got a flat and will come and see you sometime.
  Love Lyn.

But, tragically, her parents never saw her again.

Lynda, like Caroline before her, was vulnerable. While Caroline had problems with the fallout of her parents' divorce, Lynda had slight learning difficulties. She had attended Longford Special School and completed her education at a private school in Midland Road, close to where the Wests had lived before. Her mother, June, and father, a fireman in the city, worried about their daughter, but being sensible parents wanted to give her enough rein to achieve her independence and find out what she wanted to do with her life, rather than being overly protective towards her.

Lynda was petite with long fair hair, and wore a maxi-coat and black-rimmed glasses that were fashionable at the time. She was also feisty and headstrong and it wasn't long before Rose wanted to possess her. Rose and Fred had already rehearsed with their children and Caroline Owens, and were now about to give full vent to their brutal sexual fantasies with the new nanny, whose murder would mark the start of a pattern of grooming, kidnap, bondage, sodomy, torture and death of at least another eight victims.

Whether Lynda died from her injuries or by being strangled or by some other means is not known. But when her body was eventually unearthed from beneath the bathroom floor, her decapitated head was still gagged and bound with the same sticky brown parcel tape that the couple had used on Caroline Owens. Lynda's eyes had, however, been deliberately left uncovered so that she could see what was about to happen to her. This meant Rose and Fred could enjoy watching the young girl's terror and pain as they meted out the kind of sadism they'd seen in the hard-core pornographic materials – possibly including snuff videos – they kept in the house. At some stage during Lynda's horrific torture in the cellar, her trussed-up, naked body was suspended upside down from a hook in the ceiling, where further abuse took place over a number of days. (Fred had drilled holes in the cellar ceiling to hang the girls from, as he would later tell his son.) Lynda was believed to have been anally and vaginally raped during the attack, and Fred's hand-made implements used on her before death.

Rose's actions immediately after the murder demonstrate her cold and callous attitude towards the young woman she had deliberately sought out to replace Caroline as her lover, nanny and, finally, victim. Going up to Lynda's room, Rose began sifting through her belongings. The clothes Rose didn't like, she discarded in black bin bags and burnt them; those she took a fancy to, she kept and wore herself without a shred of remorse. Fred even expressed shock at this, for, as he was to say many years later: 'Fuck me, she'd killed her and had her fucking clothes on. She's wearing the girl's shoes . . . and her dressing gown. I said "You wore her fucking clothes after you killed her." To which she replied, "I washed 'em."'

Fred, meanwhile, had the body to dispose of. Using his skills from the abattoir to dissect the body was something he was likely to have derived sexual pleasure from, as there was no practical reason for him to do so: there was plenty of room to bury the girl intact either at Cromwell Street or in the fields around Much Marcle. Yet none of the victims would remain whole. Fred's apparent addiction to death and dismembering corpses also tied into his obsession with abortions. While there is nothing to suggest Rose shared his enthusiasm for dismembering, she didn't appear to care what he did to the bodies as long as she 'got rid' of them.

Fred cut down the tiny girl and laid her out, then began slicing off her legs at the hips and decapitating her. Finally he removed over a hundred bones which, along with the fingers and toes, he kept as macabre trophies. Lynda's remains, such as they were, were then dropped into a concrete hole (the mechanic's pit) in the garage-cum-lean-to at the back of the house. The clothes Lynda had been wearing were also tossed into the pit, along with her partial denture for the front tooth she had lost. The hole was then filled in with rubbish and dirt, as if the poor young woman was garbage herself. After this, Rose probably scrubbed the copious dark blood from the cellar, as she was to do at their last murder scene in the 1980s. The couple then went back to their normal daily lives: Rose cooking the children's meals and Fred at Permali's during the day and building at night – neither sparing a thought for their victim whose young life they'd so cruelly snuffed out.

Ten days after Lynda left home, there was a knock at the door. Rose opened it to find Mrs Gough on the doorstep. June Gough had been to the Co-op where Lynda had worked prior to going to the Wests'. The manageress of the needlework room had pointed her in the direction of Cromwell Street. Lynda's concerned mother asked to see her daughter, but Rose denied any knowledge of her. 'No, never heard of her,' she told the poor woman, as did Fred when he came to the door behind her. But Mrs Gough recognised the pregnant woman as having called round to her house to see Lynda just a few weeks earlier. However, still getting nowhere with the couple, she was about to go when she spotted something familiar about the slippers and cardigan Rose was wearing: they were Lynda's. Looking around the side of the house, she also saw her daughter's clothes flapping on the washing line in the breeze.

Rose had to think quickly, and came up with the story of yes, now she thought about it, Lynda had been there for a short while. But they'd had to sack her because she had been hitting Anna-Marie (this was clearly a case of Rose projecting what she'd done to the child onto the nanny). Lynda had simply left the things she didn't want any more at the house, she told Mrs Gough.* June Gough then asked the couple if they knew where her daughter had gone. 'Ah yes.' They suddenly remembered she'd mentioned something about going to Weston-super-Mare, the nearest seaside to Gloucester, and shut the door on her.

To put an end to any questions that might be raised in the house, Rose then went upstairs, sat on one of the lodger's bed and told him, 'She hit the children while she was babysitting. She won't be round the house any more.'

There were by now eight young male lodgers at Cromwell Street. And, with all the comings and goings of the house – Rose's clients, the lodgers' music blaring out, the parties and Fred banging away in the cellar doing his building work – no one suspected any different. Not least Mr and Mrs Gough, who went to Somerset to look for Lynda, and tried the Salvation Army and other missing persons' agencies, but who would have no word of their daughter for over twenty years. While back at Cromwell Street, Rose and Fred breathed a sigh of relief some weeks later as they realised they'd quite simply got away with murder.

By this time Fred had committed at least three murders, which under UK classification made him a serial killer; for Rose, it was the second. Lynda was, however, Rose and Fred's first murder together, and sharing this evil act would have increased

---

* Although twenty years later, Rose was to stand in the dock and deny all knowledge of the clothes. 'I'm not the kind of person who would wear anyone else's things; I'm rather proud that way,' she was to say.

the sexual excitement and sense of power they derived from it. Rose, in particular, would have felt empowered by murdering a young woman her own age, and may have wrought her revenge on Lynda as an act of contempt for her peers who had spurned and bullied her since her childhood. It would also have made her realise she could kill anyone, not just a small child, and this would have felt as heady as it was compelling when, six months later, she and Fred went out hunting again.

21

The Killing Fields

The Summer of 1973

DURING THE HOT SUMMER that year, the Seventh Day Adventist church in Cromwell Street was having work done, which meant there was scaffolding all over the neighbouring garden at number 25. This gave Fred an idea and, just a few weeks after murdering Lynda, he decided to extend the house to make a second bathroom with toilet and shower on the ground floor – all 'knock-off', of course, as were most things in the house.* The new bathroom would be for the use of Rose and the family, rather than their having to share the upstairs facilities with the lodgers. After knocking down the garage-cum-lean-to attached to the kitchen, Fred built a brick extension and put in a concrete floor over Lynda's remains. Rose helped him with this work. 'She could mix plaster all right. Dig holes, everything,' Fred was to say of his wife who, although small and heavily pregnant at the time, was still as physically strong as ever. One of Fred's former workmates who called round remembered seeing a pregnant Rose standing on the extension roof at night in a pair of boots, applying tar from a bucket by lamplight. The only time Rose stopped was to see to the children or to have

---

* Fred was a kleptomaniac and rarely purchased anything unless he had to – including the materials he used for the cellar and new extension.

sex with Fred's workmates. 'When I was at Permali's,' Fred bragged, 'the blokes were taking an hour off and going up and fucking Rose.'

By August the work was almost finished when Rose went into labour. Bringing the new baby home and admiring the extension, effectively a mausoleum to Lynda, the couple then set off on holiday with all the children and Bill (Grampy) Letts in tow. Rose's parents had made their peace with their daughter some time before, and her father had become a regular visitor to Cromwell Street. Perhaps because Fred was not literate and Rose had always been the organiser of the two, she booked the family holiday at Westward Ho! caravan park, just a mile down the road from her childhood home of Northam. Fred and Bill took turns with the driving, while Anna-Marie sat beside her dad making roll-ups for him. Rose had only booked one caravan, which would have to be shared between Fred, the newborn baby, three small children, Bill and herself. Daisy, possibly not wanting to spend any time in such close proximity with either man, declined to go.

Rose, who by now had broken every taboo, including murder, was sleeping with her father again. As Rose's loud groans came from the family trailer at all hours of the night and day, her appetite for sex continued to be insatiable, even though she'd only given birth two or three weeks earlier. In Gloucester Maternity Hospital, Rose finally received the news – 'it's a boy' – which she and Fred had been longing for since his spell in prison two years earlier. Fred was so delighted to have a son that he'd rushed down the ward bearing a huge bunch of flowers and a box of chocolates for Rose – her only presents from him since the coat and dress he'd given her three years earlier and, like them, probably stolen. The happy couple called the little boy Stephen – but were about to find out that Fred already had a son by the same name when the Department of Health and Social Security (DHSS) and a former girlfriend got in touch after his return from holiday.

Fred had worked with Margaret McAvoy on the Mr Whippy ice-cream van in Glasgow in 1966, eighteen months after Rena had given birth to Anna-Marie. Margaret had been a quiet girl who had fallen for Fred's charms only to be let down by him. Now she was having a breakdown and needed help with the 8-year-old until she recovered. On top of this, the DHSS were after Fred for back-maintenance for the child he'd denied was his – yet with the same curly hair and twinkling blue eyes, Steven was the spit of his father. And, strangely, given Rose's attitude towards her other stepchildren, she agreed to take the little boy in.

Bill offered to take Fred to pick up his son from a car park in Preston, which was halfway between Fred and Margaret's homes. He'd volunteered as it gave him a chance to show off the brand-new Mazda he'd recently bought himself. While spending next to nothing on his family, Bill had taken out an annual replacement deal with a garage in Cleeve. This caused further problems between he and Daisy, who must have wondered what the unlikely friendship that had recently developed between her husband and her son-in-law was all about. What she couldn't have guessed was that it was based on their mutual obsession with sex, and was now as cemented as the concrete floor Fred had just laid in the bathroom.

While Rose might have welcomed the little 8-year-old to her home, she probably changed her mind when she opened his little suitcase, as it was full of nappies. Her own baby Stephen was just six weeks old, and Mae, a year old, was also in nappies. With Heather not yet 3, Anna-Marie coming up to 9 and Steven now living with them, Rose had five little ones to care for, including the baby. On top of this, Fred insisted she still see her clients and made a large sign for the house at work, spelling out '25 Cromwell Street' in metal letters, to make sure no one who might want to call missed it. And the services on offer at the house soon became so well known that the local sex shop directed their trade there. Rose was 19 and washed out, and Fred's suggestion to buy herself a bottle of Sanatogen to keep up her strength did little to help matters. Soon the couple decided they needed a new nanny.

November 1973

Just days before Princess Anne married Captain Mark Phillips, when the country was awash with souvenirs and bunting for the occasion, 15-year-old Carol Ann Cooper fell prey to Rose and Fred. Carol, who called herself Caz, was a willowy girl with pretty blue eyes. She was also vulnerable. Her parents had separated when she was 4, after which she'd lived with her mother. But her mother died suddenly when she was 8, and Caz was sent to live with her father, who had since remarried and was living in Worcester. Colin and his new wife did their best to care for Caz, but she had been through a difficult time, and it didn't work out. By the age of 13, Caz had arrived at the Pines Children's Home in Worcester, just a few miles from the Gloucester border.

Caz wore denims and inked her name on her forearm, making a permanent tattoo. She became a rebel and would sometimes sleep rough and shoplift to get by. She had biker friends in the Scorpion gang who occasionally dossed with the lodgers at Cromwell Street, and may have been part of the trail of people passing through the house at that time, although no one will ever know for certain.* Caz was having her first official stay away from the children's home that weekend, and had been on a night

---

* Fred had modelled Cromwell Street on Clarence Road, and the police would later track down some 150 people who had passed through there by the time of his arrest.

out in Worcester with a group of pals including her boyfriend, Andrew Jones. The group had stopped off to have fish and chips after seeing a film at the Odeon. Caz had then said her good-byes to her friends and Andrew had accompanied her to the bus station, where he waited until she boarded the number 15 for her grandmother's house. As he waved her off at 9.15 p.m., little did he realise that it would be the last time he would ever see his girlfriend again.

Caz had stayed at her grandmother's the night before, and there was no reason to suspect she was going elsewhere that Saturday evening when she got off the bus at her destination. It is likely, however, that Rose and Fred spotted her when they were out cruising as she walked the last part of her jour-ney home. They may even have been hanging around the bus station looking for young girls, as they'd told Liz Agius, and could have followed the bus when they saw her get on it alone. As they pulled up beside the young girl, Rose would have wound down her window and smiled at her. Caz was wearing a bandage on her left hand from a burn she'd received from hold-ing a firework on Bonfire Night; this would have given Rose the opportunity to ask her what she'd done. Caz was a young girl who craved attention and would have enjoyed the Wests showing an interest in her. 'I just want to be loved,' she'd told the other girls in the home.

Pushing back the front seat to allow the girl to climb into the back, it is not too difficult to imagine Rose and Fred exchang-ing a smirk, as they had with Anna-Marie and Caroline: they'd got their next victim. As the two girls chatted away, Fred would have joined in, demanding answers to more personal ques-tions – while both he and Rose relished the prospect of getting their prey home. If they didn't know Caz already from passing through Cromwell Street, they would have discovered she was a frequent absconder from the children's home where she lived. If she just happened to disappear again, it wouldn't even look suspicious. Keeping everything normal and calm at first, Rose probably mentioned baby Stephen to her and asked her if she'd like to come back to their house to see him. 'We need a nanny,' she might have said. 'When you leave school, we have just the job for you.'

The young girl's remains were unearthed in March 1994 from beneath the cellar floor. Her severed limbs and trunk still had their bindings on them, and surgical tape and strips of fabric were wrapped in layers around her head. Before death, she had been terrorised and tortured – much of which is believed to have taken place while she was dangling from a hook in the ceiling. After the couple had tired of indulging their sadistic and merciless pleasure, the 15-year-old was cut down. While on remand in 1994, Fred had intimated that he'd indulged in necrophilia with some of the corpses. He also later admitted that Carol had died as a result of 'kinky sex'. The pathologist, however, found a large dent in Carol's skull. This might have been caused by her being stabbed as Fred dismembered her body, although it is possible that the young girl was still alive when she received this injury and that it happened when Fred decapitated her. As Geoffrey Wansell suggests, Carol's fingers and toes were probably also removed prior to death to increase the pleasure of her tormentors. After dissecting the body and scoring her thigh bone in the process, a vast number of bones – the Wests' signature to the murders – were kept; although, as with all their victims, these were never found. Fred then dropped the bones into the shallow hole, carefully positioning Carol's head the right way up, on the top.

Lynda and Carol's murders had taken place when Fred was making further changes to the house. In particular, he was lowering the cellar floor to make it possible to stand up without having to crouch. This would make it easier for the couple to carry out the torture and murder of their next victims, and indicates a high degree of planning and organisation. Indeed, they were so well prepared that the police and their forensic advisers believed the victims murdered in the cellar had been killed over the holes Fred had dug for them beforehand. The young teenager, who'd only been looking for affection, was Rose's third murder, which now gave her the dubious accolade of being a serial killer.

Mr and Mrs Cooper knew Carol would not just go off and leave her belongings at the home, and reported her missing to the Worcester police. But there was nothing to link their daughter to Rose and Fred or the Gloucester area. And, although the police were regular visitors to Cromwell Street, they were usually there for drug busts at the lodgers' upstairs or to nick Fred for one of his many petty thefts. Neithe they nor the public had any idea there was a serial killer team on the loose. Or that one of them was a teenage mum of four.

22

Welcome to the Torture Chamber

A Ménage à Trois

AROUND THE TIME THE couple murdered their first victim together, Rose began taking driving lessons from her father – despite Bill not holding a driving licence. Fred would refer to the driving lessons with a nod and a grin, realising this amounted to little more than father and daughter going off into the Forest of Dean to have sex. As Fred later told the police, 'He was fucking her [Rose] regular . . . I actually caught them in bed. He was well in.'

Fred, like Rose, had blurred boundaries, and maintained that his wife had never told him she was abused by her father. 'Whenever I seen her with him she was more than willing to get them off, and having a good time at it.' And soon Fred would join them for threesomes, just as he had on holiday that summer, doubtless finding comfort and sexual pleasure in recreating sleeping with his parents as a boy in Much Marcle. Possibly to please Fred, Rose also took to wearing a thick leather, weightlifter-type belt beneath her skirt, just as his mother Daisy had done. Only before lashing Fred or a client with it, Rose would wet it to make it more painful.

The friendship between Rose's father and husband had begun after Fred had invited Bill to join him and Rose on one of their drives out to the countryside, where they'd stop off for a drink. Paedophiles soon find each other out and, after a few of these trips, Fred and Bill would drive round together looking for girls. Bill also picked up and befriended a young prostitute, Shirley Robinson, on his own, who, in a few short years, would become another one of the Wests' victims.

Fred and Bill had slept with their daughters as a matter of course, and Rose had little problem with this. On one occasion when Anna-Marie was 12, the little girl had rushed into her stepmother's bedroom, telling her, 'Grampy's going to sleep with me!' Rose snapped at her, 'Go back to bed. He's not going to eat you; he's only going to fuck you . . . I am sure you will love that.'

And when the little girl told her that her Uncle John (Fred's brother) was also abusing her, Rose had simply laughed it off. 'It was of no consequence . . . it was all perfectly all right,' Anna-Marie was to tell the court many years later.

This gives us an insight into Rose's attitude about her own abuse as a child. On the one hand she has contempt for the little girl and relishes her suffering at the hands of Bill, as she had herself as a child, while on the other she tells the young girl she is sure she will 'love that'. Consultant Forensic Psychiatrist Dr Rajan Darjee found that men who had been sexually abused as children and involved in sexual activity from an early age to the extent that it became a preoccupation, did so as they found it self-soothing and a way to cope with negative moods. The same could be applied to women, as Rose frequently uses the word 'enjoy' when abusing her victims.

Fred's attitude to incest appears to have been pragmatic when he said of Rose's relationship with Bill, 'Making love to your father, you don't have to have a chat-up line, I shouldn't think.' It has been suggested that Fred manipulated Bill into joining their sex circle to give him a hold over his father-in-law. Even so, he was still a powerful figure in Rose's life for, as Fred was to say, 'Rose's father is heavy into her, and she was heavy into him, because what Rose tried to do, I think, was to get me the same as him.'

As the two men came to share Rose, Bill was increasingly to be found at Cromwell Street. After his arrest, Fred hinted to the police that there were others involved in the murders and told his solicitor repeatedly that his brother John and Rose's father were 'both mixed up in it, up to their necks'. Bill certainly had the stomach for it and was – as even his son-in-law hadn't failed to notice – an 'evil bastard'.

27 December 1973

It was the day after Boxing Day, when Christmas lights and tinsel still hung in shop windows and people were still full of seasonal good cheer, that Rose took Fred and the children to visit her parents and her brothers, Graham and Gordon, in Bishop's Cleeve. Some time later that evening, another young woman went missing at a bus stop on the A435, the main road between Cheltenham and Evesham.

Lucy Partington was studying English at Exeter University and had recently celebrated her twenty-first birthday. From a middle-class background, Lucy had attended the private Pate's Grammar School for Girls in Cheltenham and was the niece of author Kingsley Amis and cousin to writer Martin Amis. Lucy's mother and father had separated when she was younger, and now Lucy had come home to spend Christmas with her mother Margaret at Gretton, the small Cotswold village where she'd grown up. Lucy was pretty, with long brown hair and trendy John Lennon-style wire-rimmed glasses. On this particular evening she'd been to visit her old school friend, Helen, in a suburb of Cheltenham. Helen had not been well and she'd been keen to see her. During the evening, as the two girls chatted Lucy compiled an application to do a Masters at the Courtauld Institute. Helen's mother gave Lucy a stamp and she set off to catch the grey Kersey bus home at just gone ten. The Kersey bus was the one that most people used as it was cheaper than the normal service. It also stopped along the A435, the Evesham Road, which Rose and Fred often used on their way to Rose's parents in Bishop's Cleeve; and this particular evening was no exception.

Lucy was last seen as she hurried towards the bus stop, by a man out walking his dog. She was wearing a terracotta-coloured mac, pink jeans and red mitts; clothing which might have caught a person's eye in passing, even though the streets were badly lit – or not at all – that winter because of the fuel crisis. Lucy was not particularly vulnerable, except for those few minutes while she waited alone in the dark for the bus to come, when a pair of serial killers would just happen to pass. Lucy's family and friends were certain that she would not have accepted a lift under any circumstances, even with a woman in the car. She had become extra-cautious after her friend had been scared by a man fitting Fred's description, who'd tried to get her into his car a few years earlier.

It was, however, a filthy night as the sleet came down and the bus was already ten minutes late. Perhaps because the Wests had the children with them – baby Stephen might even have been on Rose's lap – Lucy felt safe enough to accept a lift from them. She may also have recognised 'cheery' Fred, from when he did his bread round in the village she grew up in. A former in-law of the Letts, Ellen White, claimed to know that Fred and Rose had baby Stephen with them in the van that night when they picked up Lucy but, as Gordon Burn says in his 1998 book, *Happy Like Murderers*, Ellen has never spoken about how she knows this. However, if Lucy wasn't enticed into the couple's van that night, then she may have been abducted by force. Fred and Bill Letts had disappeared from the Letts' house and hadn't been seen all that afternoon and most of the evening, while other members of the family had waited for them. After this, Lucy was not seen or heard of again, until her remains were unearthed from the cellar over twenty years later. She was the second victim to be buried there.

Just as before, Lucy was bound, gagged and kept alive for several days while she was tortured, terrorised and sexually abused as she hung from the ceiling. Her head was found buried in a hole in the cellar, still heavily bound with tape, and there were pieces of knotted rope that had been used to bind her limbs, and the gag, beside her. Her clothes were never found. Fred presented himself at the Casualty Department of Gloucestershire Royal Hospital just after midnight on 3 January, exactly one week after Lucy had disappeared. He had a deep knife wound to his hand but, as he was skilled at dismembering bodies, he was highly likely to have sustained this while Lucy was still alive, as the prosecution maintained at Rose's trial.

Rose's bedroom for entertaining was at the front of the house, above the cellar. One of her clients was alarmed by hearing a scream coming from below at night, but Rose had merely shrugged it off, 'It's nothing.' Lucy was buried at the front of the cellar, in the 'nursery alcove', as the police dubbed it, because of the fairy-tale-type wallpaper in that room. Unusually, one of the knives used in the attack was buried with Lucy's remains, and was later identified as a cheap stainless-steel kitchen knife that is normally given away free as part of a mail-order set. It usually sat amongst the other knives on the kitchen shelf, and Rose admitted in court she had probably been the one to sharpen it. Rose may have used the knife to torture Lucy with, as she had cut and stabbed her own children and stepdaughter.

Two young women were now reported missing and despite appeals in the newspapers and on television, including a reconstruction of Lucy's last movements, Rose went about her daily life as if nothing had happened. One of Rose's relatives believes she learnt to completely blank things as a way of coping as a child, and carried this on as she grew up.

23

Rose Gets the Key of the Door

Gloucester, 1974

IT WAS JUST FOUR years since Rose had left home, full of hopes and dreams for the future – but instead she now had the blood of four victims on her hands, including her own little stepdaughter's. The voting age by this time had been lowered to 18, as had the right to marry without parental consent, but Rose had still not reached what was considered adulthood at the time: 21. In fact, it would be another year, two more murders and many more rapes before Rose would have the 'key to the door'.

Steven was still living at the house and although his mother, Margaret, had fully recovered from her breakdown by the autumn of the previous year, neither Rose nor Fred would allow the little boy to go home. This was sheer spite on Rose's part, who didn't want him there but could use him as a means to torture Fred's former lover and exert some control over the woman she probably saw as a rival. Rose was also very cruel to the little boy, spearing him in the face with her stiletto heel when she caught Anna-Marie reading him a letter from his mother that Rose had deliberately kept from him. She also enjoyed humiliating the child, making him stand and watch her naked on the toilet until she'd finished, just inches from where the remains of Lynda lay, and on one occasion insisting that the 8-year-old watched while she had sex with his father.

In the springtime, with numerous calls made to the house from social services, Rose and Fred were forced to let the little boy go. And, in his wake, they went out cruising again.

Filling the Cellar

Thérèse Siegenthaler's murder took place in April. Like Lucy Partington, Thérèse's life was as different to Rose's as it could possibly be. She was a little older than Rose, at 21, and a German-speaking Swiss from Bern. Thérèse had been studying for a degree in sociology at a London college and had a part-time job in Bally's in the Swiss Centre. She lived in Lewisham and had gone to a party the night before setting off to see a friend in Ireland. She was not worried about hitchhiking from London to Holyhead to catch the ferry, as she had taken self-defence lessons in judo, telling her friends, 'I can look after myself.' How she fell into the path of her murderers only Rose to this day knows, but Fred mistook her German accent for Dutch and nicknamed her 'Tulip'.

After taking the poor girl back to the cellar in Cromwell Street, Rose and Fred gagged her with a brown scarf, possibly her own, and tied it behind her head with a bow. It is highly unlikely that Fred tied the bow as a man would be much more likely to knot it and leave the ends dangling. The bow is a damning indictment of Rose's handiwork while Fred kept a grip on Thérèse. The murder then followed the same pattern as before, and a rope used in the killing was pushed into the hole along with the young woman's remains. Chillingly Fred was to say that he'd decapitated the body 'to make sure she was dead'. Numerous bones were kept as trophies, including fingers, toes and wrist bones, along with part of the collarbone. Fred disguised Thérèse's narrow grave by building a false chimney breast over it. He also kept the cellar locked – with just one key for himself and the other for Rose.

Although the young woman was reported missing, there was nothing to link her to ever having been near Gloucester. Four months after the murder, at 11.00 p.m. on 13 August, Rose went into hospital with a knife wound to the fingers of her right hand. It was similar to the laceration Fred had presented with the year before, and it was also late at night. If it was another murder victim, the body has never been discovered, but Rose was to change her story at least twice as to how she sustained the injury – from 'playing about with knives' to 'cutting wood'. The injury was bad enough for Rose to be admitted to a ward and kept in for two nights. Her explosions of anger may have been responsible for the wound, just as when Fred had come in from work one day and had been prodding her to tease her as she cooked his dinner.

'Watch it, boy, just watch it look, or I'll fucking have you,' she told him. Fred carried on, laughing, as he then began to poke her quite hard. Rose swung round, grabbed the carving knife and chased him upstairs with it. Just as she lunged at him with the knife he ran into a bedroom and slammed the door in her face; the knife landed in the middle of the door instead of his back, taking her fingers with it, which were literally hanging off her hand. 'Right, fella,' she told him without shedding a tear, 'you've got to take me to the hospital.' She then wrapped her hand in a tea towel and Fred took her to A&E, where a surgeon managed miraculously to sew her fingers back on, saving her hand. Strangely, she hadn't even flinched at her own pain, later sticking one of her knitting needles down the plaster cast when her fingers began to itch. She had simply learned to 'hold herself in', as Daisy was to say of Rose as a child – so that whatever pain had been inflicted on her at that time, it no longer touched her.

Not long after moving into Cromwell Street, Fred had begun turning the house into a fortress against the world, erecting heavy iron gates that barred the way to the front door which had two bells on: one for Rose's clients, the other for general callers who were not made welcome unless invited. Ironically, although Rose had been desperate to leave home as a young girl, the isolated world she and Fred had created here replicated elements of her own childhood home at Northam and Bishop's Cleeve. 'We don't want to have anything to do with people outside,' Fred told Anna-Marie, while Daisy Letts would shout at any callers for her children to 'go away!' Rose would time Anna-Marie and the older girls on their way back from school to make sure they didn't stop to speak to anyone, and if they weren't at the front door by 4.15 in the afternoon, they would be in trouble. These were the same rules Bill had imposed on his children and his father on him. And then, of course, they all had to do the housework.

However, unlike herself and her siblings, Rose's children grew up imprisoned in an overtly, highly sexualised home. Fred would return from work and put his hand straight up Rose's skirt, sniff his fingers then put them under his children's noses. 'Here, smell your mother!' was his normal greeting to them, and Rose's only complaint was that his hands were dirty. For some while now, Rose had stopped wearing any knickers, and would sit with her legs open in front of the children and anyone else who happened to be there. 'I bet you wish you had something to fill this?' she liked to goad Fred. And, if it was hot, Rose would wear nothing more than an apron.

A few short months after Rose and Fred's first attack on Anna-Marie, the little girl was being forced to have sex with her father on a regular basis. This would happen when he took her out to help him on various jobs, raping her in the back of the van between the cement bags and tools. Afterwards, he would buy her sweets and ask her not to tell Rose. Anna-Marie was only too happy to keep it secret from her wicked stepmother, as it made her feel she had one over Rose. Although, in reality, when Fred took Anna-Marie out in the van, Rose would have known full well what the little girl's fate would be. And Rose was also using the child to perform oral sex on herself wherever and whenever Rose wanted it.

Three months after Rose's trip to the hospital, in November 1974, 15-year-old schoolgirl Shirley Hubbard went missing as she got off a bus. Shirley was another beautiful but vulnerable young girl who had been fostered out at a young age. Shirley had just begun work experience on a make-up counter at Debenham's in Worcester on Saturdays, and on that fateful evening, she'd met up with her boyfriend Daniel in town after work. Despite the cold, the young couple then spent the evening together, eating chips and watching the boats go by on the river. At 9.30 that evening, Daniel saw Shirley off on the bus back to Droitwich, arranging to meet her at the bus stop the following day – but Shirley never returned and was never seen again until her remains were unearthed at Cromwell Street some twenty years later. Shirley had been buried in the 'Marilyn' area of the cellar, so-called by the police as Fred had papered it over with pictures of Marilyn Monroe in different poses, embossed with film titles including, disturbingly, *The Misfits* and *Bus Stop*.

Shirley had no connection with the Wests, but had caught the same bus home that Carol Ann Cooper had exactly a year earlier, from the centre of Worcester. This was obviously one of Rose and Fred's favourite haunts as they went out looking for young girls, and was what police call an 'anniversary trip'. It is likely that they saw the teenager getting on the bus alone and followed it, offering her a lift home when she got off it, just as they had done with Carol. Taking her back to the house, this poor, slight 15-year-old was subjected to the worst bondage of all the victims before death mercifully came. Wrapping layers of brown parcel tape around Shirley's head until she was completely mummified up to her scalp, the terrified young girl could neither see nor cry out for help. Fred then inserted a narrow piece of tubing, like a drinking straw, through the mask into one of Shirley's nostrils to keep her alive for several days as they raped and tortured her for their own sexual gratification. After death, Fred cut off the girl's head from the front and dismembered her, burying her with various bones missing and still in the hideous mask.

West later told the police that Shirley had died as a result of an accident; that he'd 'trussed' her up and tried to hang her upside down for 'kinky sex', but it had failed and she'd died falling on the cellar floor. Fred had been sacked from Permali's by now, but was working at Wagon Works in Cheltenham where he told a co-worker that at first he and Rose had both had sex with the girl, but when she'd refused to go on the game, they'd 'sexually tortured her'. Rose, he said, had used 'instruments to penetrate the girl', which was probably true as she had used them on Anna-Marie and would go on to rape others using excessively large vibrators and dildos both anally and vaginally. He said he'd left the girl in Rose's hands to go to work and, when he'd got back, 'she was in a bad way.' Unsurprisingly, his workmate did not take him seriously, but it is highly likely this is what happened to Shirley. 'I think the cruelty bit in her was for women, she wanted to hurt women,' Fred later claimed of his wife.

After the young girl's death and dismemberment, there would have been a vast amount of blood in the cellar once more. As some of the lodgers sat tuned to *Kojak*, laughing at 'Who loves ya baby', and 'Billy, Don't Be a Hero' blared out on another tenant's record player that evening, Rose unlocked the cellar door and silently made her way down the steps with a stiff brush and a bucket of water. Scrubbing the murder scene clean, she then went back upstairs to celebrate her 'coming of age'.

PART IV

A Portrait of the Young Girl as a Grown-Up: A Misspent Youth

24

Falling Apart

Gloucester, Spring 1975

A s ROSE TURNED 21 in the previous winter of 1974, the public was shocked by the murder of the nanny at the Belgravia home of Lord 'Lucky' Lucan, who then disappeared – while at the young woman's ordinary-looking semi in Gloucester, the remains of five young women lay silently interred.

Just four months had passed since the couple's last murder, when 18-year-old Juanita Mott went missing from the area. Juanita's profile fitted that of most of the girls and young women murdered at Cromwell Street in that she was also vulnerable. Juanita was known as Nita to her friends and had been in care at different times of her life. Her father, Ernie Mott, was a US serviceman who had gone back to Texas when Nita reached her teens, and her mother, Mary, from Coney Hill, Gloucester, had since married again.

Nita had twice been sent to Pucklechurch Remand Centre in Bristol to await sentence for stealing pension books and Giros (benefit cheques). She had also been a regular at the Pop-In Café in Cheltenham, where earlier victim Caz Cooper sometimes met her biker friends. Fred was also known to frequent the café, particularly at the time when 15-year-old Mary Bastholm, the waitress, had disappeared from a bus stop some years earlier. Nita may have met West at the cafe, as the year before she vanished she'd told friends she had met a man called Freddie who she thought looked like a gypsy and who had bought her presents. However, after meeting one of the Wests' lodgers at a bottling plant in Cheltenham where she worked, she had also briefly lived at Cromwell Street, where she obtained her own bedsit. But Nita had only been there a matter of weeks when she lost her job and had to move out – although Rose would not forget her . . .

The young girl had moved on to stay with family friend Jennifer Frazer-Holland in nearby Newent. Some months later, on Saturday 12 April, Nita was expected to turn up to babysit Jennifer's small children while she got married. On the Friday evening before, Nita had hitchhiked from Newent to Gloucester for a night out, but was never seen again. While Nita was a troubled teen she was, nonetheless, reliable, and her not turning up at Jennifer's bungalow to babysit for her was said to be 'totally out of character'.

Fred had travelled the route from Newent to Gloucester numerous times, while Rose would have made a point of befriending the young girl to find out things about her before she left Cromwell Street. Rose is also likely to have been attracted to the pretty dark-haired young girl who looked like herself at that age, as did several of the couple's victims. As Carol Anne Davis writes in *Women Who Kill*, 'it's been said that the female serial killer often tries to kill an early representation of herself, as if trying to snuff out a painful memory.' Rose had a lot to block out, and certainly exhibited a cruel contempt for these girls.

As the car slowed down beside Nita that early evening, she might have been pleased to see her former landlady roll down her window and greet her with a warm smile, before offering her a lift back to her friend's. Soon after, Nita would be bundled into the cellar where she was gagged with a pair of knee-high white nylon socks – the schoolgirl type that were Rose's trademark. The psychopathic couple, who had made Shirley Hubbard's gruesome head mask with just a straw poked through into a nostril a few months earlier, were now set to raise the stakes again. Wrapping two pairs of tights and a bra around Nita's head and under her chin, she was then restrained in one of Fred's home-made metal harnesses and trussed up multiple times, like a mummy, with a long plastic washing line.

At some stage during her capture, Nita's skull had been shattered, 'as if a ball-ended hammer had been hit against the skin', the pathologist was to say. Almost a hundred bones were kept as the couple's signature trophies, including the ribs and kneecaps, as well as the usual fingers and toes. As to the missing kneecaps, Geoffrey Wansell suggests these were removed while the young girl was still alive to ensure she remained the couple's prisoner while they tortured her on a mattress in the cellar. His theory appears to hold water as Rose's own children later spoke of their mother hitting and kicking them on the kneecaps to incapacitate them. And it is likely that Fred's brother, John, and Bill Letts were invited to participate in this grisly attack, as with the others that Fred spoke about near the end of his life. Nita's fingernails had probably also been pulled out while she was still alive and were found buried in a heap alongside her legs, trunk and decapitated head. Fred had taken up the brick flooring to dig the burial chamber in an area where he normally fenced stolen goods for his criminal mates. But with no more room in the cellar, and an offensive smell seeping through the ceiling to the upstairs, he decided to concrete over the cellar floor. Rose's brother Graham, who had no idea what lay beneath, came round to help him seal in the bodies and to turn the area into a bedroom for the growing brood of West children.

The Murders Stop: 1975–8

Following the death of Nita in the spring of 1975, there were to be no more murders for another three years. This is highly unusual for serial – or addictive – killers, who need to get their regular 'fix'. It may simply be the case that the couple carried on abducting and murdering young women away from the house, as Fred had done with Rena and Anna McFall; although, that said, no other bodies have ever been found. It is perhaps more to do with the couple's relationship problems at the time. Fred had been suffering from black moods and depression for a while. He wanted to see plenty of boisterous action when he spied on Rose entertaining her clients, but if she appeared to be enjoying herself too much, he became jealous and punched her. Fred was also finding it hard to sleep and sat up in bed in his clothes until morning, or carried on working around the clock. With the cellar full up, perhaps he was finding it hard to live with the guilt of his and Rose's terrible crimes; he was unable to eat at this time or, if he did, was physically sick. It is more likely, however, that Fred was finding it difficult to cope as Rose began asserting her independence from him.

Fred was used to being in charge. 'When Dad was home, that was it, he took over,' Stephen was to say. 'When Dad wasn't there, Mum was in control.' Fred had been sending Rose out to pubs in the evening for some while to bring back men to sleep with. At other times Rose would ring to say she was staying out with a man, and he would wait for her return in the morning to hear all the details of the sex. But Rose was becoming tired of this way of life, and trying to impress Fred had lost its appeal; besides, with Rena dead, Rose no longer needed to compete. But if she refused to go out, Fred kicked her and kept on at her, 'You're a bad wife!' The more he complained, the more Rose comfort-ate and began piling on the pounds again. Going around town, she looked frumpy and careworn but, as those who knew her remarked, she just didn't care. However, all this was about to change when she befriended a Girl Guide whom we will call Zena, and began to claw back the teenage years she'd lost out on in being a young mum. Like any other 'teenager',

Rose put on her best togs – in her case her bobby socks and stilettos – and set off with Zena for the disco, where they would innocently while away the evening sitting like wallflowers at the side of the hall, or dancing around their handbags together. The next evening the mother of four would put the children to bed and service several callers to the house, or Fred would send her out to pick up men to sleep with.

Rose had realised for some while that she preferred sleeping with women, and although Fred had kidnapped at least two of their victims specifically for her, he'd now become jealous of this too. When Caroline had been their nanny, he'd asked Rose to talk her into having sex with them, then stormed out of the room, swearing 'Bloody lesbians!'. But, during that summer, Rose began to have consensual lesbian relationships and took off with a female lover for a holiday to Devon; 'for a week in a red Mini', as Fred was to say, leaving him in charge of the children. Whether he actually looked after the little ones in her absence is unlikely; the task was probably left to 12-year-old Anna-Marie, who was still also required to sleep with her father.

As Rose continued to pull away from Fred, he continued to be sick and to toil away at all hours, turning up for work exhausted in the mornings when normally he'd had an abundance of energy. He also took on an allotment in Saintbridge in Gloucester at the time, where he put in onion sets, potatoes and carrots. While this was probably a displacement to take his mind off his problems with Rose, he could also have used it to conceal his large collection of human bones. The allotment had a shed on it which, like the disused farm buildings, he could have used for dismembering bodies. For whatever reason he took on the allotment, it soon became clear it wasn't to produce vegetables, as he allowed all his crops to run to seed.

During 1976, as the economy went into recession, so Rose and Fred began to feel the pinch. Under changes to fire-alarm regulations at the time, the couple had to ask the lodgers to leave until Fred had made the necessary changes. Without income from the bedsits, and with little work around, Rose could have started to charge her black clients (who, unlike the white ones, didn't have to pay), but neither she nor Fred considered this as an option. Fred did, however, manage to find work laying pipes for British Gas. The job was in Cumbria and, for the next seven months, Fred moved in at the Belted Will Inn near Carlisle as the couple had a break from each other. Just a few months earlier cuts had been made at Smith's Aerospace, where Rose's father had taken voluntary redundancy. Bill's pay-off was around £3,000 – which was enough to buy a small house with at the time. But this was of no interest to Bill who, to the family's shock, suddenly upped and left his long-suffering wife Daisy – who possibly hoped he wouldn't return.

Vanishing into thin air without even leaving a note, the next sighting of Bill was in Northam, where his former neighbours were surprised to see him standing outside his old house. It was a hot day, but he was wearing his mac and beret as he stood silently staring at the house, as if recalling old memories. After a moment, he walked away without a word. It is believed he then carried on touring round all his old haunts in Devon and Cornwall with his tent – possibly even sleeping under canvas in a wood near to where he'd once worked in Bideford. Bill did not reappear again until 10 July, when he turned up with his daughter Glenys at the wedding of his eldest son Andrew and his girlfriend Jackie at Cheltenham Register Office. The bride and groom were as shocked as Daisy to see him there. Rosie wasn't there as Andy hadn't invited her after discovering she was working as a prostitute.

Somewhere along the line, however, Rosie and her father had been in touch during that long, hot summer of 1976. With Fred still working away, Rose and Bill had taken the children and set off once more for the holiday camp at Westward Ho! But, before the children had even had time to settle into their chalet, Rose had begun working her way through the camp orchestra. She was 'at it like a dose of salts', her stepdaughter Anna-Marie recalled in her memoirs. Rose became a standing joke at the camp but, as ever, she neither cared nor noticed what people thought of her.

Bill did notice, however, and became enraged with the monster he'd created just down the road in Northam some years earlier. The staff who worked at the camp – from the cleaner through to the chef – were Bill's former neighbours and he was embarrassed. But he was also furious with his daughter, as it meant he was now back of the queue for her sexual favours. Fred had told the police after his arrest that Rose and her father had been 'heavily into each other' and that their relationship did not end until Bill's death. The holiday camp incident, however, marked a shift in the balance of power between Rosie and her father: she had outgrown her childhood Svengali and now had the upper hand in their relationship, just as she was developing a dominant role in her relationship with Fred.

Without Fred there to force her to sleep with other men, Rose should have been able to take it easy as she'd told Fred she wanted to. But she couldn't – and of course had been sex-obsessed long before she'd met Fred. And if testimony were ever needed of Rose's insatiable sexual appetite, one only had to open the fridge at Cromwell Street, which was packed to bursting with pork pies from one of Rose's clients who worked in the meat trade.

After Bill had a succession of rows with his daughter at the holiday camp, he packed his bags and the family holiday was cut short. Fred also fled his digs equally unexpectedly, and set off for home, neither paying his hotel bill nor collecting his wages. With his own sex obsession, he too couldn't go anywhere without causing a stir. While in Cumbria he'd obtained a woman's phone number during a radio phone-in for second-hand goods, whereupon he'd plagued her with obscene calls. And there were other unknown problems he'd had to escape from.

When Fred arrived back in Gloucester, Rose does not appear to have welcomed him home with open arms, but he and Bill became closer. 'He was a devious bastard, and he was a bastard too with young kids,' Fred was to say of Rose's father, although he could well have been speaking about himself, such was their common ground. Both men enjoyed hard work and, using what was left of Bill's redundancy money, decided to set up in business together. At first they applied to join the Federation of Master Window Cleaners to start up a window-cleaning round, and Fred even talked about turning the basement into an annexe where Grampy Letts could live. In the event, although Grampy Letts did move in, he declined to live in the basement as he very probably knew what was below it. The 'odd couple' then found themselves a former butcher's premises at 214 Southgate Street, Gloucester, which, with Jim Tyler and Graham's help, they stripped out and set about turning it into a café. Although Fred's building work was of his usual botched standard, the décor was modern, and Bill furnished it with expensive tables and quality elm chairs perforated with stars. The pair then decided on the name, The Green Lantern, and had a sign painted over the front. But Rose knew both men well enough to know the cafe wouldn't work and she took no interest in the project.

At the time, Rose had begun introducing Anna-Marie to her clients, making her take turns while Fred watched through his peepholes. When the little girl had reached 12, Rose had dressed her up, daubed lipstick and blusher on her and taken her down to the pub. The dresses Rose normally made her wear were her own billowing, floral cast-offs, which looked ridiculous on the child but were part of Rose's humiliation of her. On this occasion, Rose gave her a blouse and skirt to wear that was tasteful and made her look grown-up. Fred dropped them off in his Bedford van while Rose plied the young girl with Gold Label barley wine to get her drunk (just as her own father had with Pat and Joyce years earlier.) After a few drinks,

Rose and her stepdaughter began to laugh together and enjoy themselves, and during the course of the evening, some men came over and bought them drinks. Rose had obviously taken Anna-Marie there as bait, but something went wrong – possibly the men realised the girl's age – and Rose and Anna-Marie left in a hurry.

Despite this, Rose and Anna-Marie's happy mood continued until Fred's van appeared round the corner to take them home. But as soon as Rose set eyes on Fred, her mood turned dark and she snapped at the young girl: 'If you think you're going to be friends with me, you've got another fucking think coming! You're fucking joking!' Thrusting Anna-Marie into the back of the van and climbing in after her, Rose then gave her 'a real hiding', as the young girl later said. As Rose beat Anna-Marie, Fred pulled the van over – he didn't stop the attack as his daughter hoped, but joined in beating her as well. After the beating, Rose held Anna-Marie down while Fred raped her and Rose scratched her breasts until they bled.

This attack gives us an interesting insight into Rose and Fred's relationship. It was as if once the couple clapped eyes on each other, they were immediately turned on to the prospect of abusing together. And, despite Rose's dissatisfaction with Fred, these horrific assaults and murders were the glue that held them together in their *folie à deux*.

The Approved School

As well as turning Anna-Marie into a teenage prostitute, Rose had been grooming girls from the Jordan's Brook House Approved School. She and Fred had often cruised by in the van and would hang around outside, chatting to the girls and offering them a shoulder to cry on. Serial killers are said to have a 'normal face', and Rose appears to have learnt how to groom young girls before she'd even left Cleeve secondary school. Fleetingly making friends with a girl in a year or two lower at school, Rose and Joy McConnell walked home together after school.

'I was about thirteen or fourteen, and she was a bit older,' Joy recalled. 'She was a slim girl, taller than me with long dark hair. I didn't really know Rose before, but she was really warm and lovely and spoke to you as if you were her best friend.'

When Rosie invited her new friend round to her house to play, Joy waited by the gate as Rose instructed her, while she went in the house.

'I waited there for quite a few minutes,' Joy said, when 'her mother came out and really shouted at me, telling me to clear off. I was really upset.'

Joy went home and didn't see Rose again, but to this day remembers how charming she was. Only a few short years later, Rose would use this charm to lure young girls into the Wests' car and back to Cromwell Street.

Miss A, as she became known at Rose's trial, had been a victim of incest and was desperate for affection; and, like the younger Rose, the 14-year-old girl was crying out to be rescued. Miss A had been sent to Jordan's Brook House Approved School in Gloucester after being found in a stolen car with her boyfriend at the wheel, who was himself sent to borstal. Soon after arriving at the approved school, Miss A was taken to Cromwell Street by one of the older girls, where she found Rose to be 'nice and pleasant, understanding and caring.'

Quite by coincidence, the young teenager's boyfriend turned out to be none other than Rose's own brother, Graham, who was now 18. Miss A had no idea at the time that Rose was his sister, but was obsessed with Graham and, while at Jordan's Brook House, sent him a picture of a baby that she said was his. Graham had lost interest in the girl by now and knew he couldn't possibly be the father of the baby – but while this young girl was being rejected by him, Rose was being kind and affectionate to her. And when she turned 15 the following year, Rose and Fred sent her a birthday card.

For some time now, the Wests' house had become known as a good place for the young and the lost to hang out. Rose would give them squash, biscuits and sympathy, and during the following summer of 1977, Miss A began to spend more time there. Sometimes she would stop off at Cromwell Street before catching the bus to visit her mother at the weekend. During these visits, Rose sat close to the young girl on the settee and began talking to her about girls' things, gradually throwing in inappropriate questions such as, 'Do you play with yourself?' as if it was perfectly normal to ask. Soon Miss A would run away from the approved school, sometimes sleeping rough or turning up on Rose's doorstep, seeking shelter. Rose let her stay, but on one occasion touched the girl's breasts. Miss A had pushed her away, and Rose had let her sleep on the settee. Leaving the teenager alone had done the trick, for some six weeks later she turned up at Cromwell Street again, where Rose invited her in. Rose was wearing a see-through chiffon blouse and, as usual, no underwear, and was in the early stages of pregnancy again.

During her stay, Miss A went to use the bathroom, whereupon Rose followed her, calling up to Fred. When Miss A came out of the bathroom, Rose took her to her bedroom where, to the young girl's horror, there were two other girls in the room, both of whom were naked. One was sitting on the floor, and the other lying on the bed – they were both about 14 years old. The girl on the floor was Anna-Marie who, in her book, identified herself from the home-made tattoo on her arm that Miss A described to the police, although Anna-Marie has no memory of the attack. Her stepmother had given her a bowl of Weetabix spiked with sedatives at breakfast. When Anna-Marie had tried to spit them out, Rose had given her a back-hander and told her, 'It's only a piece of grain, put it in your mouth and eat it!' Anna-Marie was too scared to go against Rose, who stood over her until she'd swallowed every last bit of the drug. The assaults on the underage girls that Miss A was about to become a victim of that day had obviously been planned.

Rose then came up to Miss A and, putting her arm around her said, 'It's all right to touch, to feel, enjoy and show affection.' She then took off the girl's clothes as Fred watched. Having been abused before, Miss A was frozen with fear and felt help-less to stop her. Rose also used the same type of manipulative language that Miss A had heard before when she'd been abused, and it is the same kind of language Rose would have learnt herself from her abuser or abusers. Rose then turned her atten-tions to the 14-year-old lying naked on the bed. Rolling her onto her front, Fred bound her wrists with duct tape and tied her ankles either side of the bed. 'He almost split her,' as Miss A remembered. Rose then anally raped the girl with a vibrator. The girl was crying with pain, but Rose merely turned to Fred who had an erection and asked him, 'You enjoying this now? That turn you on?' Fred then raped the girl from behind while Rose fondled him. After he finished, Rose, with a look of pure hatred on her face, ripped the duct tape from the girl, deliber-ately hurting her. Once more she exhibited her contempt for other young women.

Rose then buggered Miss A with a white church candle as she screamed in pain. At one point she also felt Rose's hand inside her, scratching her. As Rose did this, she said, 'This is fun! This is great!' and coaxed the young girl with, 'Enjoy!' Fred then raped her, Rose encouraging him to ejaculate over the girl's back, and rubbing it in. After cutting off the girl's bind-ings with a small pair of sewing scissors, she allowed her to go to the bathroom to clean herself up. Miss A was bleeding and in shock and pain but, using all her strength, managed to pull on her dress. However, she had to leave her shoes behind in order to slip out of the house without being noticed – and this probably saved her life.

The rapes of the young girls had taken place in the middle of a Saturday afternoon, yet there was no sign of any other West children in the house. Miss A then caught the bus home to her mother's in Tewkesbury but felt too degraded to tell her or anyone else what had happened. 'Because,' as she said, 'if you were in care you were bad.' And Rose and Fred understood this only too well. Such was the shock and distress caused to Miss A by the attack that, some weeks later, she went back to Cromwell Street armed with a can of petrol and matches, 'to put through the letterbox of the house and set it on fire.' In the end she could not go through with it, and it would be another twenty years and three murders later before she would get her wish, and Cromwell Street would be razed to the ground.

During that same year, Fred had met another young woman: 17-year-old Shirley Robinson. Shirley had been sexualised at an early age; she was also an exhibitionist and openly bisexual: in short, she was a young Rosie Letts who had every intention of becoming the next Mrs West. And, as far as Rose was concerned, that just wouldn't do . . .

25

The Young Pretender

Gloucester, 1977

BY THE SPRING OF that year, Fred had sent Bill Letts packing from Cromwell Street, whereupon he moved into the flat above the Green Lantern. Bill had met Shirley and her friend when he gave them a lift from Bristol, where the teenager sometimes worked as a prostitute. Bill had allowed the girls to stay upstairs at the Green Lantern, and Shirley soon began to work in the café below, where David Soul's 'Don't Give Up On Us' would come on the radio, along with the Elvis hits being played after his death in the summer.

One morning Fred had come into the café; Shirley was looking ill and he'd asked her what was the matter. Shirley, he claimed, had confided in him that Rose's father was making life difficult for her there. Bill had removed the locks from the bathroom and bedroom doors and would constantly walk in on her. 'Touching me up', as Shirley was to say – just as Bill had tried to do with some of his daughters.

Fred had previously called round to 'keep an eye' on his business partner, and on one occasion had found him on the low roof at the back of the café, covered in hessian sacking as he spied on his two female lodgers. He jumped down from the roof when he saw Fred approaching and, as Fred recalled in his memoirs, Bill then told him, 'I picked up two young girls in Bristol. They were coming to Gloucester and they stayed the night. They're having a bath together. If you get on the roof you can see them.'

Fred, ironically, offered the young woman a 'safe haven' at Cromwell Street, even giving her a hand to move the few possessions she had to his home. Just as he had become smitten with Liz, so he had fallen for this young girl, who was so small and thin, he, chillingly, nicknamed her 'Bones'. Despite Shirley's slight frame, like Rose, she was actually very strong, and helped Fred with his latest building endeavours: turning the house into two separate units, and completing the extension which had been started a few years earlier. Shirley slotted into Fred's way of life just as Rose had, and with his 23-year-old wife increasingly dissatisfied with her lot, Fred groomed Shirley to take over from her.

Rose did not appear to have a lesbian lover at the time, but continued to go out to pubs and clubs to have a social life rather than to pick up men for Fred's satisfaction. Liz Parry, one of the lodgers at Cromwell Street, worked at Tracy's nightclub in town, where Rose sometimes went. Rose's diary entry of 24 February 1977 read:

> Went to Tracy's with Anna [Anna-Marie]. Met two fellas. Not much good . . . 12 o'clock got home. Hopeless! Fella not a lot of good. 12.30 o'clock with Fred, that's better. Got a cuddle.

Despite her desire to have her freedom from Fred, Rose is obviously still fond of him, and the diary entry reads almost like a disappointed teenager going back to the comfort of a father-figure.

In the new arrangements at the house, Rose kept her own special room for entertaining her clients, while she and Fred shared a bedroom on the ground floor. The children were moved into new bedrooms in the cellar, which was now more like a basement, where they slept only inches from the remains of their parents' victims. Since the fire regulations problem,

Fred had turned the upstairs of the house into self-contained bedsits with cookers and sinks for their lodgers, who were now all young women. This meant Rose could have her pick of those lodgers interested in having a lesbian relationship with her, and still have her male callers, whom Fred could watch.

Shirley was delighted to have a permanent roof over her head that spring, and Rose was happy to have her helping around the house. This was particularly the case since Rose had discovered she was pregnant again, the baby being due that winter. Rose was also attracted to Shirley. This was mutual and they soon became lovers, as did Fred and Shirley – all three possibly sleeping together at one stage – until problems set in . . .

Tara West was born on 6 December 1977. Rose had been in bed with a client when she went into labour, and had named the little girl after the hotel she sometimes used with a customer. Tara's father was one of her Jamaican clients, nicknamed Rosco,* and the strikingly pretty little girl was Rose's first mixed-race baby. Fred was delighted. He'd been trying to breed a 'master race' for years. His experiments in this field had involved syringes, copper piping and the contents of several used condoms from Rose's black callers, which he would mix together and use to inseminate both Rose and Anna-Marie with, making his daughter sit still for at least an hour afterwards. Rose did not appear to turn a hair at his insanity, but later conceived two other children naturally by her Jamaican clients: Rosemary junior (Ro-Ro) and Lucyanna (Babs); and had two further children, Louise and Barry, by Fred, all in rapid succession.

Things were still not good between the couple though, and Rose continued to go out – even when she was pregnant – to have the social life she'd missed out on as a young girl. During

---

* Rose's Jamaican clients often used nicknames. This is a substituted nickname.

the winter of 1977 when she'd felt Tara coming, she'd asked the man in bed with her at the time to accompany her to hospital. Fred was hurt by this; when he asked her why she hadn't wanted him to take her, she replied, 'I thought you were at work,' to which he said, 'If you stayed at home a night or two you would see me.' Rose was always ready to remind Fred he was not enough for her in bed. 'I need a man to keep me happy,' she responded, to which he replied, 'Thank you Rose.' 'I could not believe how hard Rose could be to me,' he recollected in his prison memoirs.

Spring 1978

By March of the following year, things were a little better between the couple, even though Shirley and Rose had discovered they were both pregnant by Fred. Shirley's baby was due in June and Rose's child in November. Fred and his wife and mistress planned to bring up their children together, but this would never happen.

During late spring, while 18-year-old Shirley was heavily pregnant, she would sit on the wall outside Cromwell Street, eating Mr Men ice lollies and chatting away to the neighbours. She would tell them how well things were going between herself and Fred, which must have raised a few eyebrows, but obviously the young girl was completely love-struck. During these warm spring days leading up to summer, Shirley developed a craving for red ice lollies, which the shopkeeper at the Wellington Stores down the road would reserve specially for her. The teenager's childlike ways were reminiscent of Rose's at the time, who still wore her white schoolgirl socks with her high heels and spoke with a babyish voice. As a former lodger at the Wests' said, 'She dressed as a child. I didn't think she was quite right in the head.'

Rose would sometimes join Shirley outside, sitting on the

front step of Cromwell Street in her maternity dress with no knickers on and her legs wide open. A neighbour remembered passing when Rose pointed happily to Shirley's stomach and said, 'That's Fred's'!' and, gesturing to her own swollen belly, pondered, 'I wonder what colour it will be?'

During the early months of Rose's pregnancy, she was still sleeping with Shirley, as was Fred. But things changed when Fred began flaunting his relationship with the bubbly younger woman to make Rose jealous. Fred loved provoking Rose – usually poking her hard in the ribs until she exploded with rage – but now he could use Shirley to provoke an even stronger reaction. His psychological torture of Rose was made worse by Shirley parading around the house in just her underwear, or naked (as Rose had at Tobyfield Road a few years earlier). Fred also liked to pat Shirley's stomach to taunt Rose and tell her that the young girl would soon become his next wife. While it was all a game to Fred, who was a sadist after all, Rose knew only too well that she could be usurped by the younger woman as this is exactly what she herself had done to Rena, seeing her off once and for all by having Fred's baby.

A little before Shirley's murder, the young pretender had made the mistake of posing for a formal photograph with Fred, the two of them holding hands. She sent this photo to her father, a welder in Germany, enclosing a letter saying, 'This is the man I am going to marry. What do you think of him, Dad? I have never been so happy.' The picture was actually taken for an advert to sell their baby to a childless couple to make money – but, as soon as Rose saw it, she was incandescent with rage and it sealed her rival's fate.

Although Shirley was streetwise, she was still young and naïve in believing that because Rose and Fred had an open marriage of sorts, she could conduct her affair with her lover right under her landlady's nose. She had not bargained on Rose's outbursts, which were so terrifying she would foam at the mouth, with spittle flying off in all directions. Shirley in fact became so frightened of Rose that she tried to stay close to Fred for his protection, but this was impossible as he was almost always at work. Shirley became too afraid even to use her own bedsit, and was forced to seek refuge in another lodger's room during the day, and at night slept on her settee. It is likely that she also became frightened of Fred, who was now tiring of his young mistress, complaining that she was always 'mooning and hanging around' him.

By May of that year, as Rose became even more furious at the situation, Fred knew he had to make a choice – his wife or his lover. And there was no contest, for as Fred was to say, 'I've got Rosie, I don't want nobody else . . . She's got to fucking go.' And little more than a year after Shirley had moved into Cromwell Street, the young girl was dead.

When one of the lodgers returned home one evening, they found Rose in Shirley's room, going through her clothes. Rose quickly shut the door, but kept back the clothes she wanted, putting the others in a black bin bag – just as she had Lynda Gough's belongings. Rose then put the sack out for the dustmen. Fred's brother, John West, happened to drive the council dustbin lorry at this time and collected the rubbish from Cromwell Street. He was also abusing two of Fred's daughters when he visited the house.* As well as disposing of Shirley's clothes, John may have taken away the dozens of trophy bones Fred kept back, disposing of them in black bin bags in the back of his dustcart.

Rose told the lodgers that Shirley had gone to visit relatives in Germany and wouldn't be coming back. Fred felt a weight had been lifted from his shoulders; the girl's death would help to heal

---

* In 1996, John West was being tried on charges of rape against Anna-Marie and another of Fred's daughters, but hanged himself in his garage while on bail.

his and Rose's relationship problems and, for a while, they were happy again. A few weeks later, Rose told the lodgers that Shirley had given birth to a boy and called him Barry. Fred may have removed the baby from Shirley's womb after death to find out the sex of the child. He had wanted another son, but it would be two more years before Rose had their second son, whom they would name Barry. Fred's almost full-term baby with Shirley was buried in the hole in the garden beside her, beneath the jerry-built extension that Shirley had helped Fred to finish.

There was no evidence of the tragic young girl having been trussed up and tortured before death. She had simply been got rid of as a matter of convenience because she was a threat to the Wests' marriage. Fred told the police he had used electrical flex to strangle some of the victims with and, if this is true, he may have done so with Shirley. He then chopped up the corpse into numerous pieces in what appeared to be a frenzied act of contempt. It had taken Fred several blows with an axe or meat cleaver to smash the young girl's thigh bone in two, and as well as chopping off her head, he removed her wrist, ankle and rib bones and kept her amputated fingers and toes as souvenirs. Some of the little baby's bones had also been taken. This whole bloody scene was probably undertaken in the cellar and it would have taken Rose several hours to scrub it clean.

Unusually, no hair was ever found in the young girl's shallow grave, which meant that either Fred or Rose had scalped her and kept it as a grisly souvenir of their crime. The only living memento of the 18-year-old was a strip of photographs taken in the booth in Woolworth's that morning with her lodger-friend Liz. While Liz was sticking her tongue out in the photos, Shirley was making her eyes bulge, as if in a horror movie – which was exactly where she would be that afternoon. And with no one to report her missing, Rose and Fred simply got away with murder. Again.

Changes

As Anna-Marie was to say: 'Initially my mum was young and impressionable, but as she got older she became more dominant.' Shirley's death marked another shift of power in the couple's relationship, whereby Rose began to look after all the money that came into the house. Fred gave Rose his wage packet and the lodgers' rent money still sealed in envelopes. Rose recorded the amounts in her diary, and gave Fred enough back to buy cigarettes for the week and whatever was left, she put into her Co-op Savings Account. Fred, however, was still very much in charge when he wanted to be and would wear Rose down, making her sleep with his West Indian friends when she wanted a night off, or hit her if she refused. Fred also refused to wear condoms when he had sex with Rose, although he knew she could not take the Pill as it made her ill. By making sure Rose was 'potted', as he called it, by himself or someone else each year, he knew that it would be almost impossible for her to leave him. Perhaps Bill had suggested this to Fred as a way of ensnaring his daughter, as he had done the same thing with Daisy.

For now, however, the couple were said by a lodger to be 'very happy' after Shirley's disappearance; even possibly putting in a fraudulent claim for maternity benefits in Shirley's name after her death. A social security officer sent round to interview Shirley found she was no longer living there, and with no midwifery or antenatal checks, that was simply the end of the matter.

The happy couple could relax again, and such was their blissful state of contentment that they carried on with their lives in their own inimitable way. Rose placed an ad in contact magazines: 'Sexy housewife needs it deep and hard from VWE [very well endowed] male while husband watches . . .' and Fred installed baby intercoms from Boots and Mothercare in every room so that he could hear his wife having sex with her clients wherever he was in the house. He also carried on having sex with his daughter, Anna-Marie, in secret, and by the end of the year, when Rose had given birth to another little girl, Louise, their happiness was complete. This was despite the child being white, and therefore not part of Fred's master race.

The couple's new-found joy would soon be tested, however, when news reached Rose about the death of her former Svengali. This culminated in Rose and Fred's next sadosexual murder after a gap of over four years, since they'd tortured and killed Juanita Mott in 1975 for their own pleasure.

26

The Death and Secrets of a Tyrant

Bishop's Cleeve, Gloucestershire, 1979

IN MAY THAT YEAR, while Thatcher and the Tories swept into power and Blondie was in the charts with 'Heart of Glass', Bill Letts died in hospital, aged 58. He was buried a month later, on 5 June, which also happened to be the birthday of Andy Letts' wife, Jackie. As communication between the members of Rosie's family was at best fragmented, neither she nor Andy knew which hospital their father was in – or even why he was there – before his death. The funeral was to be no different.

When Bill had left his job at Smith's a few years earlier, he'd had to give up the house at Tobyfield Road and move into a local authority property, a maisonette, at Crown Drive in the village. Two years later, with his redundancy money gone and the Green Lantern struggling, Bill decided to return home, without consulting his estranged wife, Daisy, who was out at work at the time. Bill's eldest daughter Pat had found her father making himself comfortable in the maisonette when she'd made a surprise visit to see her mother. As soon as Bill saw her there, he bawled at her to 'clear off!' Pat fled in tears; the years had obviously not mellowed Bill as much as the family might have hoped. Pat rang Daisy at work to tell her their father was at the house, and for reasons best known to herself, Daisy let him back into her life. Agreeing to give Bill a hand with the cooking and cleaning at the café, shortly after, she moved in with him there.

Yet, while she was prepared to forgive her errant husband, she had cut off all ties with her youngest daughter, Rosie, since she'd begun producing her brood of mixed-race children.

A few months later and despite Daisy's best efforts, the Green Lantern closed its doors for the last time. Rose's parents then moved into a flat in Regent Street in Lydney, in the Forest of Dean. This was to be their 'fresh start' and Bill soon found himself a job as an electrician at a local sawmill, while Graham and his new young wife Barbara moved into the flat below them. But the Letts' fresh start turned out to be anything but, for when Graham popped upstairs to his parents' flat he found his father had Daisy 'pinned up against the wall'. He had already 'slapped her' and was about to hit her again.

Aside from Bill's psychotic illness he was also not physically well by the spring of 1979, when he was taken into Frenchay Hospital in Bristol, dying a few days later of pleural mesothelioma or asbestosis, the disease he'd been diagnosed with at Devonport dockyard. Having given Daisy a life of hell, he intimated to Graham just before his death that his marriage to his mother had been a mistake, and warned him against marrying 'the wrong person'. For her part, Daisy did not appear to be unduly upset by Bill's death, and the funeral arrangements were finally made and paid for by Andy and Jackie, as no one else seemed willing or perhaps able to do so. This wasn't helped by Bill leaving scores of unpaid bills from his selfish lifestyle, which Daisy had to work her fingers to the bone to pay off after his death. Summing up the feelings of most of the family, one of the older girls said, 'The only reason any of us went [to his funeral] was to make sure he went down that hole.'

The funeral, which was described by one family member as 'a shambles', took place at Cheltenham cemetery. It didn't start off well when some family members refused to follow the coffin into the chapel. The oldest children, Joyce and Pat, had a falling out beforehand and sat away from each other and the main cortège; Graham followed the coffin behind Andy, Daisy and her sisters Eileen and Dolly, while Jackie Letts and Jim Tyler prudently sat it out at the back. Gordon arrived in handcuffs with police officers either side, which Daisy begged them to take off to no avail, while Bill's father, William, who had moved in with another woman and went on to live until he was almost 100, didn't turn up.

As it was Pat and Joyce had never got along, since Pat had been favoured over the younger girl for most of her life. Daisy was still not on speaking terms with Rosie, who clattered along to the cemetery in stilettos, schoolgirl socks and a miniskirt – or, as Gordon Burn referred to it, 'in clothes that the staider members of her family regarded as the uniform of her profession'. At the graveside, Gordon Letts, looking sedated and still in handcuffs, began sobbing that he loved his father; Graham stood opposite, professing his hatred for his old man; while Andy was upset that his cruel father had gone but couldn't understand why he felt this way.

Rosie's oldest sister Pat was prim and proper, and had found visiting Rose just the once since her marriage to Fred was more than enough. As Rose went over to comfort her big sister, it ended up in a scrap, with Pat throwing Rose into the dirt where she might have thought she belonged. And while all this was going on, Bill's former partner-in-crime, Fred, was a no-show.

Rose was angry that Fred hadn't gone with her to see her father buried after they had been so close in recent years. But Fred, who had called Bill evil, was probably the only other man he could look at and see a mirror image of himself. As Gordon was to say many years later, 'Everyone seemed so glad when he died. Gone and out of the way. My mother hated my dad intensely.' Bill's grave still, to this day, is unmarked by a headstone.

A week after the funeral, Graham broke into his widowed mother's flat, took what he could sell to fund his drug habit, and did the gas meter over while he was at it. Daisy had barely had time to deal with this when she was shocked to discover the secret Bill had been keeping from her and the family for years. After reading her husband's medical records, she found Bill had been diagnosed as a paranoid schizophrenic in his youth, a condition that appeared to have gone largely untreated since then. Had Daisy known about this, or if Bill had received treatment for it, how different life might have been for the family and Rosie. Although Bill was still, of course, a sadist.

Fred later told the police that Rose's sexual relationship with her father had continued right up until Bill's death. And now that Rosie's childhood mentor had gone, the murders would peter out; although her cruelty, if anything, intensified.

A Last One For Bill

Three months after Bill's funeral, 16-year-old Alison Chambers, known as Ally, was murdered. She too was from the Jordan's Brook House, and had the same profile as most of Rose and Fred's other victims. Alison lived in a fantasy world to cope with her sad life. She wrote poetry and drew pictures of an idyllic farmhouse where she dreamed of living one day. Ally also had a friend at the approved school who visited the Wests, and she went with her one day to Cromwell Street.

Rose soon began to befriend Ally, exploiting her vulnerability in the most callous of ways. After presenting the young girl with a necklace with her name engraved on it, she told Ally that she and Fred owned a farm and, to back up her story, showed her a photograph of a picturesque farmhouse. What the young girl did not realise was that Rose had obtained the picture from an estate agent's 'For Sale' brochure. Rose told Ally that when she left Jordan's Brook House she could stay at the farm and spend her time writing poetry there. Going back to the approved school later that day, Ally lay on her bed, daydreaming and drawing foliage growing around the farmhouse door.

Perhaps the couple's fear of being caught had also played a part in their abstinence from murder for the three years between Juantia Mott's murder in 1975 and Shirley Robinson's in 1978, as Rose had begun telling the girls who called at the house not to say where they'd been if the police stopped them. Sadly, however, the police didn't stop Ally, who on 5 August that year left Jordan's Brook House and gave up her YTS scheme to become the Wests' live-in nanny. Ally was just four weeks off her seventeenth birthday, and wrote to tell her mother that she was now living with a 'very homely family'. But by the following month, she was dead. Ally's naked remains were found with the gag still in place, which this time was a purple fashion accessory. Rather than moving to an idyllic farmhouse in the countryside, this tragic young girl was stuffed in bits into a hole in the garden beneath the extension. And, as usual, the couple kept their signature body parts.

When Ally's friends from Jordan's Brook House called round to see her soon after, Rose showed no remorse or emotion but fobbed them off by saying she was living on their farm. When they asked to visit her there, Rose became nervous and told them they'd have to wait a while. Later, she changed her story again and told Ally's friends she'd gone to live with her relatives. Ally's murder, coming so soon after Bill's death, seemed as if it was one last one for Bill. It was also the couple's last sadosexual murder; their next would not happen for another five years and, when it did, would be a matter of convenience. Rose was now 25, and perhaps she and Fred had lost their nerve, or their cruel and perverted interests lay elsewhere. But when the couple did kill again, it would be their last known murder together, and was perhaps also their most hideous – for this time Rose and Fred would kill their first child: 16-year-old Heather.

The 1980s and the Final Murder

After having her second son, Barry, by Fred in 1980, Rose went on to have Rosemary West junior in 1982, when the Falklands War was in full swing, and Lucyanna the following year, by one of Fred's West Indian friends. Having given birth to eight children in all, Rose decided enough was enough and was sterilised in 1983. Because of the age differences between Rose's older children with Fred, and the younger ones, what she had in effect was two separate families (just as she'd grown up with herself). Anna-Marie had already left Cromwell Street by this time. Unsurprisingly, the young girl had been in trouble at school for bullying and carrying knives and, at 15, discovered she was pregnant by her father. The baby, however, was found to be growing in the fallopian tubes and Anna-Marie had to have an abortion.

The teenager's pregnancy did not trigger an alert with the authorities, though Anna-Marie was probably glad of this. This was because as the last time social services had visited Cromwell Street, following up a report from a teacher who had noticed bruising on her, Rose had beaten her again when they left. The poor girl, who had only ever known a lifetime of abuse, packed her bags and ran away in the night with nowhere to go. The knock-on effect of Anna-Marie's departure was that Fred turned his attentions to his next daughter, Heather.

Although Heather was Rose's first child, as she grew up Rose treated her only marginally better than Anna-Marie, laughing at her distress and calling her a lesbian when she protested about her father's abuse of her. Rose also beat Heather and, because of the bruises on her body, Heather refused to do PE at school, which meant she was often given detention. Rose would also time Heather coming home from school to ensure that neither she nor her younger siblings stopped off to speak to anyone on their way home. This meant their grim existence at Cromwell Street remained hidden.

Heather left school in the summer of 1987 when she was 16. Despite all the problems at home, the young girl managed to pass a string of GCSEs. But there was a harsh recession in Thatcher's Britain at the time, and the young girl had been unable to find work. This meant she had to spend more time at home which, with Fred's abuse and Rose's lack of protection of her, was the last place she wanted to be. She wrote a secret code, FODIWL, in her books, and began having nightmares and biting her nails until they bled. Then one day she simply disappeared.

Fred shoved her naked remains into a dustbin until he was able to bury them in the back garden at night. With the help of his sons, Barry and Stephen, he then built a pink and cream patio over her and turned it into the barbecue area. And in the summer, Rose dished out hot dogs and burgers to her children by their sister's grave.

Before her death, Heather had discovered that the father of one of her school friends was also the father of two of her little mixed-race sisters. Heather was becoming belligerent as she made it clear she didn't like what was going on in the house, and this had made her even more 'difficult' for Rose to manage. She had already spoken to her school friend, Denise, about the abuse at home. Her friend had seen her terrible bruises and knew she was telling the truth. But when word got back about it to Rose and Fred, they gave the 16-year-old a terrible beating and kept her under guard, making sure she didn't speak to anyone, not even her half-sister. When Anna-Maria had tried to approach Heather in the garden to find out what was wrong, 'My stepmother or my father would be there in an instant,' she recalled in her book.

Anna-Marie hints at other excesses going on at Cromwell Street at the time that made it too dangerous for Rose and Fred to let Heather live. This ties in with her friend Denise's theory that the Wests deliberately waited until Heather finished her last term at school before killing her, so that she wouldn't be missed.

Heather might have lived, however, had she succeeded in finding work away from home. She had been desperate to escape Cromwell Street and had found a job at a holiday camp in Torquay. But when this fell through at the last minute, Heather was devastated; it also meant she had to die. Fred told the police he'd choked Heather to death as she'd lolled against the washing machine, 'coming the big lady', and that he'd then shoved her remains in the wheelie bin behind the Wendy house until he'd buried them. He said Rose had played no part in their daughter's murder, or any other of the young women's murders. But according to one of their younger children, this was a lie . . .

After Heather's murder, Rose told the children that their big sister had gone away to work at the holiday camp. They were shocked that she'd gone without saying goodbye, as the older children had always stuck together and tried to protect each other from their parents. But they were even more shocked to realise their mother had been crying. Rose never cried, but her daughter's murder was perhaps one of the few times she *ever* displayed a shred of remorse. And such was Rose's desire to avoid confronting the truth of what she and Fred had done, they made a rare trip to see her brother Graham and his wife Barbara, telling them, 'She's disappeared. She's a lesbian. That's it, closed . . . I don't want you coming round in future if you do mention Heather.'

Heather's siblings were also told they were not allowed to mention her name again and photographs of her were removed from the house. The 16-year-old had loved to be in the outdoors: alone and free, and barefoot. And when the secret code she'd written in her diary was finally cracked, it turned out to be both her dream and her escape plan: 'Forest of Dean I Will Live'. She had gone on a school camping trip to the forest once and, enjoying the freedom she'd experienced there to such an extent, had decided she'd move there one day to live as a hermit – surviving only by nature. It was reminiscent of the desires of the couple's penultimate victim, Ally Chambers, who'd dreamed of living in an old farmhouse in the countryside where she would spend her days writing poetry.

27

'It's All Over Now'

Gloucester, December 1987–9

A FTER HEATHER'S DEATH, ROSE cut back on her hours of prostitution and was said by some of her children to have become a better mother. As her (now) oldest child, Mae, was to say, 'she never hit me again, you could really see the change.' That Christmas, Rose bought the older children bikes when all they'd ever had before was one gift each costing under ten pounds, which they'd had to choose from the Argos catalogue. The three younger children even got a gift each, wrapped in Christmas paper: one of the girls received crayons, the other slippers and Barry a toy car – whereas before Rose would simply blurt out that Father Christmas didn't exist.

Rose and Fred began taking more interest in the children's schooling: Rose made costumes on her sewing machine for the little ones for a school competition, and Fred picked them up at the school gates, giving a lift to other young mums and their children in the van when it was raining. Fred even became romantic towards Rose again. Taking his teenage son Stephen out to teach him how to steal bikes, he also insisted on showing him the bus stop where he and Rose had first met: number 13. This indicates some degree of remorse on both Rose and Fred's part, as well as romantic fantasy. However, not all the children appear to agree with Mae's view of their mother at this time. In an article in the *Daily Mirror* supplement, 'Britain's Worst Serial

Killers',* Barry remembers Rose tucking him and his siblings up in bed at night and cuddling them, then the next morning 'we'd wake up to her kicking us in our beds. She'd be shouting, "Wake up you little ****s." There'd be no reason for it. We were terrified.'

Long before Heather's death, Fred had been pestering his next oldest daughter, Mae, for sex. Mae and Heather had always looked out for each other and the younger girl had managed to thwart her father. Now that Heather was gone and Mae had a boyfriend, Fred began focusing his attentions on a neighbour who had moved into the street at number 11; this was 31-year-old divorcee Kathryn Halliday. Fred was called in by Mr Zygmunt to repair a leak in the flat above the one Kathryn was renting with her female partner. Possibly in an attempt to take Rose's mind off her daughter, Fred invited the dark-haired young woman back for a drink. Fred had installed a bar in their lounge, complete with a tropical motif and a row of optics – he and Rose called it the Black Magic Bar as both a double entendre and private joke – where the couple invited friends and clients to their sex parties. Rose and Kathryn soon began a sexual affair, with Fred usually watching or occasionally joining in. Kathryn was older than the couple's victims, but she soon became frightened by their increasing acts of sexual sadism. This was particularly the case with Rose, who starved her new lover of oxygen, cut her stomach with a knife and tried to force enormous phalluses into her, including an eighteen-inch flesh-coloured one with nodules on which she called her Exocet.

The couple also took her to their secret room in the house, where they showed her whips, a bed with wrist and ankle restraints on it and meat hooks over the bed-head, rubber bondage suits and leather masks with zips over the eyes and mouth. Kathryn had seen these worn by young women in the porn

* Published in the summer of 2010

films that Rose had showed her, and which Fred had shot in their bedroom. Rose became very excited by the films, especially the part where a young, fair-haired girl was in pain and the camera zoomed in on her fear. During sex with Kathryn, Rose had placed a pillow over her head, keeping it there for some time and taunting her, 'What's it like not to be able to see?' and, 'Can't you breathe?'

As Kathryn was to tell the court at Rose's trial: 'Once she got you to the bedroom she wanted to make you vulnerable.' Rose asked her how she would like to be tied up all day and only returned to occasionally to be tormented. This is a telling indication of what she and Fred did to the girls and young women who they tortured and murdered. 'She would cause as much physical pain as she possibly could,' Kathryn would later say of Rose, who she believed dominated the clowning Fred. 'She had no limit to what she would do,' Kathryn said.

Kathryn was not a young girl, but soon realised she was out of her depth and stopped the relationship. Luckily, as she lived with her partner, Rose and Fred did not pursue her as they had others who'd left them – otherwise the outcome might have been very different. By this time, however, Rose no longer appeared to be enticing young girls back to Cromwell Street. This may have been because she was said to have been in a long-running relationship with a much younger girl from Jordan's Brook House at this time. Or perhaps, since Heather's death, neither she nor Fred had the stomach for it . . .

In a shift of power in the Wests' *folie à deux*, Fred bought into Rose's denial about Heather's murder and, quite soon after, Rose found herself answering phone calls from her eldest daughter. Her children remember her saying as she took the first call, 'Hi Heather, it's your mum.' After mother and daughter chatted away, a row broke out and Rose thrust the phone at Fred in anger, 'She's calling me every name under the bloody sun! You can talk to her!' Fred 'calmed her down' and told Rose she'd call another time. A few days later, Heather called again and Fred asked her if she was okay, then put Rose on to speak to her although, once again, Heather's siblings were not given the chance to speak to her. Rose told Stephen after her arrest, that as far as she was concerned the calls were from Heather.

Later Rose told her son that Fred had set up the calls using someone he knew to impersonate Heather and that as there was always background noise on the line, as if she was in a pub, it was hard to hear properly. Rose, however, knew they couldn't be from her daughter and, to this day, the caller's identity has never been established. Fred had set the calls up as a means to placate Heather's siblings, who missed their big sister and were upset that she hadn't even sent them a postcard, and to deter any unwelcome enquiries from outsiders. But primarily it was his way of helping Rose keep up her pretence to herself that her eldest child was 'working away in a holiday camp', and Rose was happy to do this. It was only some years later, when Fred claimed to have seen Heather in the street, that Rose would tell him to shut up – acknowledging, if only between themselves, the truth of what they'd done.

Rose had never dressed or behaved like other people since she was young and she had always stared a lot, but as time went on, she became increasingly odd. Around the time of Heather's death, Rose had taken to wearing a bobble hat and her white socks while pushing a shopping trolley to the shops. When the children begged her not to go out like that she replied, 'If you don't fucking like it, you shouldn't be looking.'

Neither Rose nor Fred had any idea what normal behaviour was. As Mae and Stephen West were to say of their parents in their book, *Inside 25 Cromwell Street*, Rose would answer the phone and snap, 'What?' and hang up without saying goodbye. Shopping trips with Rose were little better: on one occasion, when she'd taken the children with her to choose a new fridge, to their horror she began walking around the store opening the doors of all the fridges and kicking them shut to see which closed best with a kick. She also never used changing rooms, but stripped in the middle of the shop floor to try on new clothes.

In the summer, the kids' swimming trips consisted of Rose taking them for a dip in the public fountain at the King's Walk Shopping Centre, despite there being a pool in the leisure centre just down the road. Stephen and his siblings would fish out coins thrown into the fountain for luck, while horrified shoppers looked on. But Rose seemed to neither notice nor care. She'd always spoken in a whiny, baby voice, but over the years had taken on Fred's country brogue, using phrases such as 'Watch it boy!' and 'Stop it fella!' These were the types of thing she would say to Stephen when she made him eat a fried egg that she'd plucked from the waste bin or when he looked away from the porn films she made him watch as a boy. The films featured bestiality and adults abusing children, and to stop him turning away, Fred made him a metal head cage at his new job at Wagon Works. The cage had a hook at the back that went over the settee and if Stephen still tried to look away from the screen, Rose would hit him in the face with an ashtray.

The 1990s

Three years after Heather's death, in 1990, Rose began to pull away from Fred again. Fred was approaching 50, but his interests remained the same: work, sex and voyeurism. Rose, on the other hand, was still in her mid-thirties and itching to have the young life she'd missed out on. Reading an advert in the local paper for a singles club, she turned up at the hotel on the Bristol Road, where she met one of the bar staff and started a relationship with him. Rose became a regular at the 'Bristol', and started going to country and western 'dos' there. Fred, for the second time in their relationship, became jealous, and beat his wife when she returned home from a New Year's Eve party at the hotel. Rose hit Fred back, but he could always get the better of her because of his physical strength – and he beat her black and blue. But as Caroline Owens said, Rose wasn't frightened of Fred but 'stood her ground with him' during the six weeks she worked as a nanny for them. She also didn't feel Rose was coerced by Fred during their attack on her, and it was Fred, in fact, who had been frightened of Rose finding out about the rape.

Rose continued going out to the Bristol Hotel, where she would tell her friends that her miserable so-and-so of a brother, Fred, had a cob on. By March of 1991, Rose was so aggrieved with her lot that she took a flat in the Stroud Road to start a new life. Calling herself Mandy West, she told the landlord she worked as a 'nanny', even taking little Lucyanna with her to back up her story (and probably telling the child not to call her 'Mummy' in front of him). Although she kept the flat a secret from Fred, he was devastated by developments and began obsessively cleaning – from the house through to the back garden, sweeping the patio over and over where his daughter's remains lay. When there had been problems between he and Rose in the past, he had lost sleep. But now, although he slept, he began to have terrible nightmares. And, in the day, he would see horrific car smashes with dismembered bodies. His appearance became wilder too, as he let his hair grow until it resembled a bird's nest. Fred was on the edge of a breakdown and appeared not just terrified at the prospect of losing control of his wife, but of actually losing her. Unlike his first wife Rena and his lovers, Anna McFall and Shirley Robinson, he'd never once thought about murdering Rose. And Rose never appeared frightened or concerned that he would, as either she was reckless or she knew that Fred really loved her, as he was to say while on remand for the murders.

Falling In Love Again

Some months later, things came to a head when Rose's landlord turned up at Cromwell Street looking for her. Fred answered the door and was fuming when he found out about the flat, going straight round there and clearing it out. Rose's latest bid for freedom was over, but she was tired of Fred and his sex games and, in a bid to get back at him, stopped sleeping with his friends. Things had not improved much between the couple when, a few weeks later, Fred's role model and father died. Fred hadn't visited Walter while he was in hospital, which was probably because he was phobic about such places, but he was badly affected by the death. While his relationship with his father had always been difficult, Walter had taught Fred all about taking sex where and when he liked, and that it was a father's right to 'break in his daughters'. And Fred needed little reminding.

Fred wouldn't touch his 'daughters' who had been fathered by his friends, so turned his attentions instead to another of his girls, raping her anally and vaginally and videoing it, when Rose was out shopping. The young teenager was screaming for him to stop, and when the other children in the house tried to intervene, Fred locked the door and replied wearily, 'For fuck's sake.' The young teenager had to take a week off school afterwards, and Fred asked her, 'Are you bigger now?' He raped her again the following week in the Black Magic Bar; Rose was in the house this time, but she did not stop it. Instead, she followed her distressed and bleeding daughter into the bathroom after the attack where she brusquely said, well what did she expect? She'd been asking for it. Soon after, the young girl confided in a friend who told another friend and so on, until, like a chain reaction, there was a knock on the door of 25 Cromwell Street.

A team of four policewomen and two detectives stood on the doorstep that warm Thursday morning in August 1992. They were brandishing a search warrant to look for Fred's film of the rape of his daughter. Rose's immediate reaction was as it had always been: she lashed out at the officers, hitting one policewoman and wrestling another back down the stairs. She had to be physically restrained. The police took away almost a hundred pornographic videos, as well as bull whips, rubber suits, rice flails, gimp masks, huge and various vibrators and dildos, and harnesses. Although the police didn't view the bulk of pornographic material they seized, they immediately found photographs of two of the West children naked, and, as officers dragged Rose out to the police car, she screamed at the children, 'Don't you dare say anything!' – only possibly with more expletives.

Rose was charged with inciting Fred to have sex with a 14-year-old girl, and with cruelty to a child. He was charged with three counts of rape and one of buggery and held on remand. The five youngest children were taken into local authority care, and Rose and Fred were banned from making contact with them. As Rose packed up her children's clothes, for perhaps only the second time in her life, she broke down in tears. In the end, however, the child sex abuse case collapsed when the witnesses (three of the West children) felt unable to go through with it. Like many incest victims, they felt a confused loyalty towards the very people who had committed the abuse and wanted the family to be together again – and so they said they had lied. Anna-Marie, a witness herself, was also scared. She'd had two daughters since leaving home and, knowing what her parents were capable of, feared they would come after her little girls if they got off.

While Rose was awaiting trial, she was bailed to Cromwell Street, from where she rang Anna-Marie, threatening her, 'If you think anything of me or your Dad . . . you'll keep your mouth shut.' She also tried to manipulate the situation by swallowing a bottle of Anadin and was taken to Gloucester Royal to have her stomach pumped. Her plan worked, and with all three witnesses no longer willing to testify and the videotape of the attack not found, Rose and Fred were simply told there was 'no case to answer'. The serial killer couple whooped with joy at this, and hugged each other. They were free to go, although the authorities had enough on them to keep their younger children: Tara, Louise, Barry, Rosemary and Lucyanna, in care.

For the ten months between August 1992 and June 1993, when Fred had been held on remand pending the case, Rose had found the house empty without the children. And she'd even missed Fred. Putting their past grievances aside, the couple began romancing each other and fell in love all over again. Rose rang Fred on the 'nonce's wing', calling him 'sweetheart', and sent him love letters with hearts drawn on and arrows through them, just as she had when he'd gone to prison in 1970, at the start of their relationship.

During the long months that Fred was locked up this time, Rose obtained a cleaning job at the local art college to keep herself going. She also 'sprung' two dogs from the local dogs' home for company, Benji and Oscar, but mistreated the poor creatures, just as she had her own children, and soon they would be rehomed by the RSPCA. Once more Rose cut an eccentric and solitary figure as she wheeled an old pushchair across from her house, through the town's main car park to the city centre shops, where she became a familiar face. When she got back home, Rose would simply strip off and stuff her face with cream cakes while watching children's cartoons such as *Snow White* and *Road Runner*, screaming with laughter as Wile E. Coyote got battered. This wasn't the kind of behaviour expected of someone awaiting trial for child cruelty, or whose children had been taken into care.

Rose was not allowed to see Fred while he was on remand in prison, but when he was transferred to Carpenter House bail hostel in Birmingham, she took the train up to see him two or three times a week. As long as Fred got back in time for roll call, he could leave the hostel without being missed. Mae and Stephen sometimes went with Rose to visit their father, but as soon as their parents clapped eyes on each other, they ripped off each other's clothes and had sex in the bushes and on the grass in full view of anyone passing, like a pair of unabashed, sex-mad teenagers. Stephen and Mae, on the other hand, became the parents to their parents, buying Rose and Fred a little igloo tent from the Argos catalogue, so that they could have unofficial 'conjugal visits' out of the public gaze.

On these visits, Fred would produce gifts for Rose: plastic Kinder egg toys, empty crisp packets and a child's dummy – discarded rubbish that he'd lovingly picked off the ground for her. And Rose kept these presents, 'displaying them in her glass cabinet at Cromwell Street as if they were priceless china' as Howard Sounes was to say in *Fred & Rose*. The psychologist who interviewed Rose and Fred just before their child sex abuse case found them to be a 'close and caring couple' who 'discuss everything together' and all their decisions are 'jointly made'. But clearly Rose and her husband were also insane delinquents locked in adult bodies.

After their reprieve, the middle-aged serial-killer sweethearts were reunited back at Cromwell Street that summer, where they decided to start another family together. Since the case had become public knowledge, the couple had lost most of their friends as well as their children. Rose was not on speaking terms with most of her family, and Fred had fallen out with his brother, John, over money. So it was just the two of them again – Rosie and Freddie – as it had been at the start of their relationship, over twenty years earlier. This state of affairs influenced their decision to have more children, and that summer, Rose went into the Gloucester Royal to have her sterilisation reversed. And just before her fortieth birthday, as winter approached, Rose found she was pregnant again. But the couple's happiness would not last when, some weeks later,

Rose suffered a miscarriage. And, after that, things were about to get a whole lot worse.

While in care, one of Rose and Fred's younger children had spoken to a social worker of the patio he'd helped his father build. The other children also mentioned how their father had joked that he'd put them under the patio like their big sister, if they misbehaved, guffawing as he saw the funny side of it. Mae and Stephen had long since worried about these boasts, and had sat their parents down to watch episodes of *Brookside* and *Prime Suspect 2* on television, which had featured storylines about sex abuse and bodies hidden under the patio. They had observed their parents' faces closely as they watched the programmes, but there had never been so much as a flicker of emotion from either of them. However, as the social worker raised the alarm, a detective who had wanted to talk to Heather about the abuse of her siblings before the case collapsed could find no trace of her.

28

Betrayal

Gloucester, 1994

DC HAZEL SAVAGE HAD run a check on Heather's National Insurance number, but found she had neither signed on nor worked in the years since she'd 'left home'. The detective also knew about Fred from his first wife Rena, whom she had escorted back from Scotland to face charges of theft in Gloucester in 1967. As the two women chatted away, Rena had told DC Savage how her former friend Anna McFall was now living with Fred and her children in his caravan near Cheltenham, and that Fred was violent and quite possibly 'mad'. When the detective tried to find Rena in 1994, she found she too was missing – as were Anna McFall and Charmaine – and DC Savage would not let it rest.

Rose was watching *Neighbours* in the living room at Cromwell Street at lunchtime as usual, when, on Thursday 24 February 1994, Hazel Savage arrived with a search warrant and a team of officers. Those in blue boiler suits began lifting the patio slabs, while others searched the house to look for evidence as to Heather's whereabouts. Rose screamed at the police and poured scorn on the warrant, then rang Fred's work, yelling at his employer to send him home. Although Fred was only twelve miles away, it took him over three hours to arrive back at the house, so it is likely he was hiding some evidence of their crimes, possibly at the deserted farm building he sometimes used. By late afternoon, as darkness fell, the back garden was lit up by industrial lamps and the diggers moved in.

When DS Terry Onions questioned Rose in the Black Magic Bar later that day about Heather's whereabouts, he was taken aback by her lack of concern for her missing daughter, 'But come on,' she said, 'there's hundreds and thousands of kids go flipping missing.' She told him there had been a row the night before she'd left home. She also made disparaging remarks about her daughter being a lesbian (based on her refusing Fred's advances), even though Rose herself was bisexual. Rose maintained she'd given Heather £600 to start a new life with when she'd left that morning. When asked for details of the bank account she had taken the money from, Rose was indignant. 'I cannot fucking remember, it's a bloody long time ago.' Pushing her further on this, she replied, 'What do you think I am? A bloody computer?'

DS Terry Onions told Rose he did not believe her story and that he thought Heather was probably just a pile of dust and bones by now, at which she scoffed, 'Oh you're lovely, aren't ya?' The only bone the police found that day was a chicken bone, which caused Stephen West, who was staying at the house at the time, to flap his arms and cluck like a hen. Even though he was all too familiar with the family joke about Heather being buried under the patio, it was just too bizarre and appalling to believe. And Rose probably blocked the image out for the same reasons.

By the time Fred arrived home, the police had finished for the day and he took himself off to the police station. He stuck closely to a familiar story: Heather, he said, had gone off in a red Mini with her girlfriend, when in fact it was Rose who had gone on holiday with a lesbian lover in a red Mini almost twenty years earlier. Having nothing as yet on Fred, the police allowed him to go home where he immediately unrigged the illegal wiring of his electric meter, out of sight of the policeman sitting in the back garden on all-night watch. Rose washed up, while keeping one eye on the policeman outside and whispering to her husband. The couple then took the dogs out for a walk, something they never normally did together – then probably spent that night and the following morning together, as they usually did, having sex. And at some stage during these activities, the couple struck a pact with each other . . .

DC Savage turned up early the next morning at Cromwell Street, asking for Daisy's address as she wanted to interview her. Rose became very upset by this; she'd had no contact with her mother for the past fifteen years, since Daisy had cut her off when she'd had her first mixed-race child. Rose was said to have felt abandoned by her mother again, and probably feared the police getting in touch with Daisy over Heather's disappearance would only make things worse. Fred was sensitive to Rose's feelings and promised her he'd sort it out with the police. Telling Rose to go upstairs, he turned to Stephen. 'Son, I will be going away for a while. Look after your mum . . .' Then, leaving the house with the police, he yelled at the top of his voice, 'I didn't kill her!' creating pandemonium in his wake and bringing out the neighbours to watch the spectacle. Fred then got into the police car where, turning to Detective Constable Savage, he quietly said, 'I killed her.'

Fred was, however, at pains to stress that Rose was not involved and wasn't even in the house at the time. He also said that Heather's death was an accident. He'd grabbed her by the throat to wipe the smile off her face, but 'the next minute she's gone blue', as he'd held her longer than he intended. As well as trying to protect Rose, Fred was also trying to manipulate the police to only dig the area in the back garden where he told them to, so that Heather's remains alone would be found. That way he knew he would be looking at just one life sentence and could be out in twelve years, or perhaps even get a lighter sentence for manslaughter – rather than he and Rose both attracting whole life sentences, which they would if they found all the bodies. Rose is believed to have agreed to this and said she would stick by him – Rosie and Freddie forever – while he served out the sentence.

At first the police couldn't find Heather's remains, but when they did, they almost immediately unearthed a third leg (of Shirley Robinson) and the game was up. Fred still tried to keep Rose out of it, asking detectives such questions as, 'Have you told her what I've done?', so that she would know he had kept to his side of the pact by taking the blame. Despite Fred's attempts to establish her innocence, Rose was arrested and taken to the police station, where she continued to be morose and either said 'no comment' to police questions or protested her innocence. Rose didn't know Fred had admitted to killing Heather at this point. The police didn't tell her until 6 o'clock that evening, but when they did, she immediately distanced herself from him.

Since the day Fred had walked out of the house, the couple had not been allowed to have any contact with each other. While Fred was on remand in prison, however, he managed to pass on messages of love and support to his wife through their two oldest children, Stephen and Mae. But Rose did not respond, and it would be another six months before the couple would see each other again. During this time, and even though Fred often changed his story, he cooperated with the police in trying to help identify the victims and pinpointing where he'd buried the remains of all twelve.* Rose, on the other hand, who was interviewed almost fifty times over the same period of time, gave the police nothing other than to profess her innocence.†

---

* The couple did not know the names of some of their victims and dental records were used to identify the deceased.

† Typically serial killers either can't wait to talk about their crimes, as a way of boasting how clever they've been to get away with them, e.g., Peter Sutcliffe and Dennis Nilsen; or like Rose West and Peter Tobin, for example, they *never* speak about them.

The couple finally saw each other again when they stood side by side in Gloucester Magistrates' Court to face the initial charges against them. Fred had twice gently touched his wife on the arm to get her attention, but each time Rose shrank from him – refusing even to catch his eye. The third time he put his hand out to her, an officer moved between them: 'Rose and Fred forever' was over and the hearts and arrows all gone. The apprentice had betrayed her tutor, husband and co-accused. And Fred, the sexual sadist and serial killer, was hurt deeply by it. Their *folie à deux* of the past twenty-five years had been broken, and Rose was now looking out for herself.

Parenting the Parents

Rose was 39 and Fred was 51 by this time, yet, separately, they still behaved like a couple of disaffected juveniles. When the police asked Rose if she felt she'd been naïve about Fred murdering Heather, she replied, 'I feel a bit of a cunt, to be blunt about it.' And even though Fred was on remand for twelve counts of murder, he continually worried about the police messing up his home improvements back at Cromwell Street. It is particularly telling that once the police began to interview the couple, they immediately appointed each of them an 'appropriate adult' to support them through the process. Appropriate adults are normally called in where the police consider a person is 'vulnerable': that is to say, anyone who is under 17, or who has mental health issues or learning difficulties.

Stephen and Mae, the couple's eldest children, had already taken on the parental role in relation to Rose and Fred since the last court case, and their parents had responded like children.

While Mae worried about her mother's well-being, Rose was 'demanding', as her daughter put it, asking her to send her money for clothes, cigarettes and batteries. At the time of Rose's trial it was costing Mae £300 a month which, as she said, 'puts a great demand on my income.' Rose did not appear particularly concerned about whether Mae could afford this, or even how she was coping, given that the case was attracting worldwide media attention and with all the stigma it inevitably involved. Instead, Rose again comes across as self-centred, like a child who believes they are the centre of the universe. Fred was only a little better in his dealings with Stephen, but did at least tell him to sell his story to make some money from it. But Fred was also completely deluded, for when he wasn't worrying about his new patio being ruined by the police, he was busy telling detectives about the relationships he'd had with some of the victims, including medieval scholar, Lucy Partington.

Fred was devastated that Rose had abandoned him and broken her side of the pact, and later began implicating his wife. Of 16-year-old Ally Chambers' death he said to his solicitor, 'Rose was too bloody vicious. What she did to that little girl was unreal. I was making love to the girl and Rose got a vibrator and shoved it straight up her arse. Fuck me, the girl nearly went right through the fucking wall. I would never allow Rose to tie me up . . .' He also said his brother John was involved in the murders, as was Rose's father, Bill. In fact, there was only one more sadosexual murder after Bill's death − that of Ally Chambers − before the series stopped.* But then came an even bigger shock; for, having admitted to murdering his eldest daughter Heather, Fred went on to say he was *not* her father − that Bill Letts was. If this is the case, and some members of the Letts family believe it is probably true, then Rosie would have become pregnant by her father around the time she left home in early 1970, when she had just turned 16. By killing Heather, Rose could have been snuffing out every last memory of Bill.

---

* Heather was killed eight years later as she was an inconvenience to the Wests, just as Shirley Robinson had been some years earlier.

Rose was first remanded to a safe house and then to prison, where she started to read for the first time in her life: books such as *The Shell Seekers* and *The Prince of Tides*, becoming an avid reader. At the same time, it became obvious to Fred that Rose had not only outgrown him but that she actually despised him; there would be no reconciliation that he had been hoping for. During the autumn, Fred volunteered for shirt-mending duties, cutting off and saving the cotton ties from the laundry bags as they arrived in. Just after midday on New Year's Day 1995, Fred knotted all the ties together and quietly hanged himself in his cell in Winston Green Prison. One of the notes found in his cell afterwards had been intended for Rose's birthday at the end of November. It read:

'The most wonderful thing in my life was when I met you. Keep your promises to me. You know what they are. You will always be Mrs West all over the world. I have no present. All I have is my life. I give it to you. Come to me, I'll be waiting.'

Fred had told Stephen on several occasions that he planned to kill himself so that all charges against Rose would be dropped. However, this letter could be asking Rose to kill herself too – 'Come to me, I'll be waiting'. Even if Rose had received the note before his death, Fred knew he'd lost her; when he killed himself it was in fact his final act of control over his victims, the authorities and, more importantly in Fred's mind, Rose herself.

When Rose was given the news of her husband's death she was busily crocheting baby clothes in her cell for her grandchildren.* She remained unperturbed by Fred's death, not shedding even a single tear for the man she'd been married to for over twenty years. Sister Mary Paul, who had befriended Rose on

---

* Stephen's wife had twins, and Mae and another sibling each had a child by now.

her visits to the prison, suggested they pray together, but as far as Rose was concerned it was Amen to Fred as she focused on getting herself off the hook.

Or could it have been, as she claimed while pouring out her heart to Sister Paul, that she loathed Fred because he'd deceived her? That she had no knowledge of the murders as she claimed all along, and that she was actually innocent of murder?

Was Rose Innocent?

The evening after her arrest, when the police told her that Fred had admitted to Heather's murder, she sounded genuinely shocked. '*What?*' she shrieked in anguish, unable to take it in. She asked again, 'So she's dead? Is that right?' When the police confirmed it a second time, she rallied briefly when told it implicated her, but she began sobbing and had to have a break. After she returned to being questioned she was upset and subdued, and later threatened to kill Fred should she ever get her hands on him.

With Cromwell Street surrounded by the press and TV crews, Rose was bailed to a series of safe houses in Cheltenham for her own protection. One of the houses she stayed in for several weeks was bugged entirely by police listening devices – from the curtains through to the three-piece suite and the cupboards. But despite Mae staying with her mother, and with all the background interference on the tapes from the TV and stereo playing, Rose was never once heard to mention the murders. Instead she watched children's cartoons on television and played Scrabble, where the only words she made were crude sexual references. Clearly old habits died hard for, although the police had excavated twelve sets of human remains by now, sex was still uppermost on Rose's mind.

As regards the case, there was no hard evidence whatsoever against Rose; no one had seen her kill anyone or even witnessed her with the young women near to the time they met their deaths, and there was no forensic evidence to directly link Rose to any of the victims. In the end, however, Mr Justice Mantell allowed similar-fact evidence to be heard, which meant that the jury would hear from the surviving West victims, the attacks on whom formed a pattern of behaviour repeated in the killings.* That is to say, Caroline Owens, Miss A, Kathryn Halliday and Anna-Marie, amongst others, all took to the witness stand. However, as the four main witnesses had all sold their stories to national newspapers, the defence suggested they therefore had a vested interest in making their evidence sound as lurid and sensational as possible. As Rose's QC, Richard Ferguson argued, 'No newspaper is going to pay out large sums if Rosemary West is acquitted.'

Rose was initially charged with nine murders and Fred with twelve, which included Anna McFall, in 1967, and Rena and Charmaine. A few days after Fred's suicide, however, charges were brought against Rose for the murder of her 8-year-old step-daughter, after dental records examined by an expert dubbed the 'Tooth Fairy' established that the little girl had been murdered while Fred was in prison.† There is, however, another view: that with a relaxed regime at the open prison where inmates sometimes stayed out all night, Fred could have hitched a lift the twenty miles to his home, raped and murdered Charmaine, and got back in time for the next roll call.

---

* Citing Bluebeard, who chopped off the heads of his wives, Mr Justice Mantell said that had one of Bluebeard's wives escaped death at his hands to tell her story, this would have been admissible of him committing a series of murders.
† Forensic orthodontist Dr David Whittaker projected a photo of the little girl smiling, exposing her lack of front teeth, taken shortly before her death. He then superimposed a transparent image of her skull over this, showing her burgeoning new front teeth, and from this estimated when the child had died.

It is also possible that Charmaine was murdered after Fred's release from prison, as the dates are not definitive regarding her dental growth, and were refuted by another dental expert whose report was lost. Fred had in any case confessed to the police that he'd murdered Charmaine while taking Rena for a drink. He said he'd left the little girl asleep in the back of the car while he plied Rena with alcohol to get her drunk, took her back to his childhood home of Much Marcle, where he'd strangled her in a field, dismembered her body and buried the remains. He had apparently forgotten about the child until he went back to the car and, not knowing what to do, had strangled Charmaine and taken her back to Midland Road to dispose of her body. The child would have slept through her mother's murder because he had given her alcohol. Fred had recalled the ground was hard as he tried to dig it to bury Rena and so, as Brian Masters points out in *She Must Have Known*, it was likely to have been July or August.

The prosecution also drew on Rose and Fred's letters, written and received while Fred was in Leyhill prison in 1971,[*] to imply that the couple had planned to kill Charmaine. Rose wrote: 'I would keep her [Charmaine] for her own sake, if it wasn't for the rest of the children. You can see her coming out in Anna now. And I hate it.' But she is simply suggesting sending Charmaine to her mother's, rather than murdering her. Fred replies, 'So you say yes to Char, that good. I will see to it when I get out but don't tell her for you know what she is like . . .' He is talking about arranging for Rena to have Charmaine when he comes home which, according to Rose, is what he did. 'He advised me that I would be better off if I was not around,' she said, and so she went to her parents' house when Rena came to

---

[*] The police found the letters stored in a box in the attic at Cromwell Street, along with a newspaper cutting from their trial in 1972, prison visiting orders and other documents they'd saved over the years.

collect the little girl. There were also discrepancies about the date that Mrs Giles had brought her daughter to see Charmaine, and it is possible Fred was out of prison by then. If so, he could have murdered the little girl and Rena by this time.

When Rose left Fred in 1971, she had said to her parents, 'You don't know him, he's capable of anything.' Adding, under her breath, 'Even murder', as she went back out to Fred as he waited in the van. Her parents wrongly assumed she was being overdramatic. In any case, these do not sound like the words of a killer, but of a girl who has been shocked to discover that her boyfriend is. There is always the notion with the wives of serial killers that 'she must have known'. But this is often not the case as, for example, with Primrose Shipman and Sonia Sutcliffe. Mrs Shipman would often drive her husband to his patient's house. She would then wait in the car, unaware, as he gave a lethal injection. On one occasion, she was even asked to 'hold the fort' and wait with the body for the deceased's relatives to arrive, while Shipman went on to the next patient.

The Yorkshire Ripper's wife had no idea that her husband's bloody clothes from each murder went into their washing machine, where their missing kitchen knives went, or that Sutcliffe had sewn himself a revolting undergarment to wear beneath his jeans to make life easier for himself as he bent over his victims, performing his hideous acts on them. Through no fault of their own, Mrs Sutcliffe and Mrs Shipman had no idea what was going on right under their noses, as was the case with the lodgers at Cromwell Street. Fred had also killed Anna McFall before he even knew Rose. The series of murders after-wards bore all the same hallmarks. He had also said Rose was out the night he killed Heather, and as he often sent Rose out to stay the night with other men, this is perfectly feasible. A former worker at the Westward Ho! Holiday Centre has also recently revealed to the author how, during the summer of 1987, Rose had written to the 'Top Camp' to try to get her daughter Heather a summer job there, not realising that the camp had closed down a few years earlier. The letter was sent only a few days or weeks before Heather's murder, and seems more the handiwork of a caring mother than one standing trial for killing her daughter.

Rose, however, didn't help herself by lying in court. Some lies were more plausible but others seemed ridiculous (the cellar was bolted from inside and she could barely remember Lynda Gough, their live-in nanny, who had been the victim of the Wests' first murder together). However, as regards the latter, there was a huge throughput of tenants and their friends at Cromwell Street over the years and, as Rose's daughter was to say of her mother, she had a 'terrible memory'. Rose had even told Mae before the case: 'If I can't remember, that's what I will have to tell them.' As well as lying, Rose made jokes in very poor taste about the deceased. And from being obsequious and manipulative – bowing to the judge and wearing a poppy near Remembrance Day and a gold cross around her neck though she wasn't religious – she would fly into rages. But, though she came across as strange, obnoxious and offensive, liked S&M and was a cruel and abysmal parent, it still didn't mean she was guilty of murder.

The jury, however, decided that Rose wasn't Fred's victim, as she portrayed herself, but that she and Fred had been 'in it together'. Rose was given ten life sentences, one for each of the murders, which has since been commuted to whole life and means she will never be released. In prison, Rose continues to protest her innocence and at one point launched an appeal, but then dropped it as she felt it would be impossible to live a normal life outside or to see her children in peace. 'This is the point where I spell it out for you, I AM INNOCENT OF MURDER!!' she wrote to a pen friend in 2005.* But despite Rose's continued

* Published in the *News of the World*, September 2008

protestations of innocence, there is one piece of evidence that has only recently come to light: an allegation which incriminates Rose in at least one of the murders. In the supplement 'Britain's Worst Serial Killers',* Barry West, who was just 7 at the time his big sister Heather was killed, gives an eyewitness account of her death. Unbeknown to his parents, the little boy was standing behind the door, watching through a crack in it, when his sister came home in the early hours that June.

'It was about 3 a.m. I heard my Mum slap her and I saw my Dad walk round behind her and put his leg out. Then my Mum just booted her. She was kicking and kicking her and calling her a slag. Then when my Dad tried to get her to do things to him [these would be sexual], she refused. I think that's why she ended up dead. When my Dad finished with her, Heather was too weak to get up and my Mum kicked her in the head. I could see blood coming out of her head and her mouth. Then Mum stamped on her head five times and Heather didn't move again. Finally Mum rubbed her hands together saying very matter-of-factly, "Right, let's clear this up. Let's get rid of this ****ing whore." I could hear my Dad wrapping her in some plastic and I could see my Mum scrubbing the floor with a bucket and brush.'

Barry was still only 14 when his mother stood trial for this murder and nine others. His whole life had been turned upside down and he'd had to live with what he'd seen for years. Whether, because of the trauma of this, or out of misplaced loyalty or fear, it is understandable that it is only now he has felt able to talk about it. In his account, Barry also recalled how the next morning his father had asked him to help lay some patio slabs in the garden and to cover them over with twigs. 'My Mum continually lies about her involvement in the hope that one day she'll be free,' Barry went on to say. 'But she knew every detail of what took place . . .'

* Published in the *Mirror*, summer 2010

This ties in with what Stephen West was to say of his mother in court. 'We lived a life and Mum said the total opposite.' And as Mae wrote of her, 'She won't face the truth. She never has.' Quite simply, Rose was and remains in denial. The truth, in any case, will always be hard to get at because Rose, like Fred, has been a compulsive liar from an early age. Rose later denied taking the calls from 'Heather' and even pretended in court not to know that Shirley Robinson was pregnant by Fred. Moreover, if Fred had been out of prison when Charmaine was murdered, that doesn't mean Rose wasn't involved. She had been tying up and abusing the little girl while Fred was away, and it may have been that when he returned home Charmaine was their first torture and murder together: the rehearsal, as it were, before the series of murders.

There has also been speculation that the murders were a result of their sex sessions getting out of hand, using the huge dildos and vibrators that the police took from the house. These would almost certainly have ruptured the young women, who would have died of their injuries. Fred, in fact, near the end of his life, had told his appropriate adult, Janet Leach, that the victims found at Cromwell Street were 'some of Rose's mistakes' that she'd made while he was at work. He told his solicitor that he knew she'd killed some of the victims with a 'vibrator. Pushed in with Rose's foot; that big bastard', he said, referring to a vibrator that was twelve inches long and four inches across. 'She did so much damage to them with that, that she had to fucking kill them,' he continued. 'Obviously she bound their mouths up with that fucking tape round their gobs . . . she'd push the vibrator in as far as she could . . . then get hold of their legs and just push it in with her foot.' And there was no doubt that Rose kicked her children and had shoved large objects, including vibrators, candles and other implements, into some of the surviving victims.

Detective Superintendent John Bennett, who led the investigation, also gives credence to this view when he recently said,

'The whole case was about Rosemary being sexually insatiable. There were huge quantities of pornographic material and sex objects in the house. I firmly believe that Rose murdered the girls and Fred disposed of the bodies.'*

Rose's template, like Fred's, was maladaptive and had been set at a very young age. Both were narcissistic, psychopathic and had antisocial personality traits. Fred was also paranoid. Before Rose met him, she was already a sex offender (against her brothers) and Fred had already killed. The couple also had in common highly toxic family backgrounds, including early abuse by parents, violent, dominating fathers and aggressive mothers. Rose and Fred were also pathological liars.

The fact that two such people should meet in a lifetime was highly unlikely but, if they did, it was always going to be a recipe for disaster.

Having introduced the young Rosie to sexual sadism, she took to it willingly, because she saw it as a way of getting her own back over other young women, and began exceeding even Fred in cruelty. Had she not met Fred, she would have been violent and dangerous to her children, perhaps even to the point of murder, as she had with Charmaine, but it is highly unlikely that Rose would have become a serial killer. Myra Hindley, by contrast, had nothing to mark her out as a potential killer. Living with her grandmother, she had a stable home life, had not been abused as a child, was not a bully, and was not sexually precocious, being a virgin when she met Ian Brady at almost 20. She was also kind to the children she babysat regularly and, up until the point she met Brady, was said to be reliable and sensible. Had she not met Brady, it is almost certain she would not have killed.

Although there are some characteristics shared by serial killers, despite the similar upbringing of Rose's siblings and her children,

* *Mail* Online, 25 January 2008

they did not go on to become murderers. This is because a person's innate temperament and individual experiences differ. For example, unlike Rose, Glenys was bright and had a reasonable relationship with her father; Andy was savagely beaten by his father, but was protected to some extent by his mother as well as his girlfriend and her family. Developmental paths are complicated, but when some ill-fated characteristics come together, linked with relationships and experiences, a serial killer can result – such as happened in the case of Fred and his brother John, and Rose and her father Bill Letts; although two serial killers in each family is *incredibly* rare. That one of them was a woman and that she was an extreme sexual sadist is even more so.

Rose and Fred were also highly organised – even practising their different methods of tying up their victims on Anna-Marie first, and going on dummy runs to pick up young girls. There was also less chance of their being discovered because they buried the young women at their home, and because they were expert at choosing their victims – who were mostly vulnerable young girls, as Rose had been.

However, if we are to prevent such a phenomenon as Rose from happening again, then we must have quality child-protection systems in place. We must also have sympathy for the young Rosie Letts: a little girl with plaits in her hair who was slow, emotionally isolated and abused, preferring to stay at home with her mother and knit rather than be bullied by her peers. And Freddie, too, a small scruffy boy smelling of pigs, going to school to be made fun of with just a raw turnip in his lunch box and being taught by his father how to have sex with sheep at just 8 years of age. Neither Dozy Rosie nor Weird Freddie were protected as children, the fallout of which was to be their hideous crimes together. Although Fred had killed his first wife, Rena, and his mistress, Anna McFall, Rose was never in any danger of being his next victim because he loved her; but Rose appeared entirely devoid of this emotion, as sociopaths are. Lamenting the creature that he and his father-in-law had created, Fred said near the end of his life, 'She's got no feelings at all Rose. She's got no feelings for nothing.'

Rose was and is a mass of contradictions: childlike in her clothes and voice but clever in distancing herself from Fred, and a person who could express herself fluently, even lyrically, in writing. She wrote to her daughter Mae while on remand, 'It's been a lovely day here today. I have a nice view from my window. You want to see the sky sometimes, beautiful colours. Sometimes the clouds are white and fluffy against a clear bright blue sky. We have an airbase nearby . . . air balloons come close over the rooftops. I could see the people quite clearly in the baskets. Or you get jets making patterns against the sky . . .'

Above all Rose is an enigma. As Fred's brother John was to say of her before his death, 'I don't think anybody gets to know Rose. She's just Rose. When you went there you took her as you found her or you didn't take her at all.'

Rose Now

Rose has been taken out of society for the rest of her life and now sits in her cell or her 'bubble', as she calls it, where she spends her days knitting, cleaning, and drinking tea from her china tea set. She also watches television – nature programmes and the soaps – and was quoted in the press as saying, 'I can't watch anything about serial killers! No matter how make-believe.'* Her day also consists of working out in the gym; she has reportedly lost several stone and ditched the oversized spectacles for contact lenses.† In the earlier years, she became friends with Myra Hindley when they were on the prison hospital

* *Mail* Online, January 2008
† *Daily Mirror*, 5 November 2005

wing together, and more recently she has befriended Tracey Connelly, Baby Peter's mother, who she is teaching to cook healthy food 'instead of junk'.* This friendship is not so remarkable, given they are both high-profile prisoners who are reviled by other inmates.

Just like her father, Rose has set up a music club in her cell, where other Category A inmates can listen to and discuss some of their favourite artists.† In Rose's case these include Westlife, Glen Campbell, Helen Shapiro, John Denver and Dusty Springfield. There is also rumoured to be a Rose West cookbook pending for the prison.

In recent years Rose has turned down an offer of marriage from a pen friend when she discovered he had no money, telling him, 'Even a girl in my position needs a man with a little more prospects!' She ended their relationship just as swiftly and completely as she has many others in her life, including the one with Fred. She has also severed all contact with her children, telling Mae in a letter written in 2006, 'I was NEVER a parent and could never be now.' Although this shows an incredible coldness towards her daughter, it is perhaps one of the most truthful things Rose has ever said. She could not have expected to be a parent when she had no idea how to be. Rose does, however, continue to write to her mother and sends her birthday and Christmas cards, although it is not known whether Daisy replies. The only family member who still visits Rose is, ironically, her stepdaughter Anne Marie, whom she horribly abused all her young life. When a prison officer asked Anne Marie why she still comes to see Rose, she replied, 'It's just like visiting someone in hospital . . .'

---

* From Tracey Connelly's letter to a friend, published in the *News of the World*, 2 May 2010
† *Sunday Mirror*, 28 November 2010

EPILOGUE

The Aftermath

IT IS FIFTEEN YEARS since Rose West went to prison but, despite the passing of time, it is impossible to imagine how the families of the victims of the Wests could ever come to terms with the horrendous way in which they lost their daughters, sisters and friends. It is the stuff of worst nightmares. Yet the families of the victims were tremendously dignified and compassionate in reaching out to Stephen West at the victims' inquests in 1995. For Stephen, as well as being the son of the serial killers responsible for the deaths of their loved ones, had also lost his sister, Heather, for whom he and his siblings were at last able to grieve. The West children also lost their mother to a lifetime of imprisonment and their father to suicide, and probably felt confused in their grieving for either parent. As Mae was to say of her father: 'Despite everything, I still love him.' And Anne Marie, who learnt at last what had happened to her mother and little half-sister Charmaine, could grieve for them both and try to come to terms with her loss.

The West children lived a life of the most hideous sexual, physical and psychological abuse at Rose and Fred's hands which, unsurprisingly, affected the ability of some of the children to be able to slot into society and to make 'normal' relationships as they grew up. Stephen was violent towards his wife and the marriage ended almost as soon as it began. He also served a short prison sentence in 2004 for underage sex. As his barrister, Stephen Mooney, rightly said at the time, 'He had one of the most traumatic and distressing childhoods one can imagine, and what happened affected his emotional development. Anyone who has suffered like him has a tendency to remain emotionally less well-developed for his age.' Like his father before him, Stephen has also tried to hang himself.

After difficult teenage years and a failed marriage, Anne Marie grew up to become a refined and dignified young woman, who has done well in her new life. Nonetheless, the terror of the past is still there, and she too has made attempts on her life, jumping into the river Severn in Gloucester.

As one of the surviving victims, Caroline Owens, was to say, 'The attack shattered my life . . . I suffered low self-esteem and tried to kill myself with a tranquilliser overdose.' Caroline also suffered from survivor's guilt for many years.

Leo Goatley, Rose's lawyer, who stopped acting for her in 2004 when she dropped her appeal against the length of her sentence, said he was haunted by the case years later. 'It was something like a horror film, looking at pictures of skulls with plastic tubes coming from the mouth . . . My wife said I could be pretty obnoxious and difficult to live with during the case and now there are times I can't bear to watch TV after the watershed when there's blood and gore in films.'* Legal secretaries who typed up the case were also said to be traumatised by it, as doubtless were the police and many others involved in it.

The West children and their children have been scarred by being closely related to the world's most infamous female serial killer. Mae has since changed her appearance and started a new life with a whole new identity. Tara has her own family now, and she and Louise and Barry have gone back to live in the Gloucestershire area where Anne Marie also lives. Rosemary junior and Lucyanna moved away some years ago, to start new lives in another part of the country.

* *Daily Mirror*, 31 October 2005

There have also been huge repercussions from the case for Rose's siblings and their families. Rose's mother, Daisy, also changed her name in an attempt to escape the past. When the case broke, she dared not go out in the village for a very long time for fear of what the neighbours might think of her, and Andy and Jackie Letts, and Andy's siblings, have all been tainted by association. Andy, a hard-working, honest and reliable man, had problems finding work because he is related to Rose. Sadly, Jackie, who longed for children but suffered a number of miscarriages, now believes this was a blessing in disguise. This is because she feels that any children she and Andy might have had would almost certainly have suffered the stigma of having a notorious serial killer for an aunt.

At the time of Rose's case, Andy also suffered the indignity of being made to strip off by the police. One of Rose's younger children had reported being raped by one of the Letts brothers, and they were looking for a distinguishing feature that she'd reported. Andy didn't have this feature and the police immediately apologised, but Andy said he'd never been so embarrassed and humiliated in all his life. He still also lives with the anger and guilt of not realising the abuse his father was responsible for and doing something about it. 'By God! I'd have let him know about it if I had!' he said.

Aside from Rosie, the legacy of Bill Letts has left most of his children psychologically scarred. Although, like Joyce and Glenys, Andy has done remarkably well, he became fanatical about bathing as a young man and still feels compelled to bathe at least twice a day. The youngest child in the family has had numerous problems. Around the time of his father's death, Gordon had lived with his partner Karen in the Forest of Dean. But the relationship broke down in the most tragic of circumstances. The couple had a baby together who they called Michael, but who died in his cot. He was just 8 months of age. Gordon was accused of murder and held for four days at the police station, by which time Karen had left him and refused ever to see him again. Gordon hadn't murdered the baby and was never charged; according to Gordon Burn, in *Happy Like Murderers*, the baby suffered from eczema and they had put cream on his skin to soothe it. But the cream had stuck the baby's face to the bri-nylon pillow case and prevented him from breathing. Gordon sat on Michael's tiny grave for a week after that. He then bought a puppy but the collar was too big. The puppy slipped his head out of it, rushed into the road and got knocked down by a lorry. 'They done me here,' Gordon was to say of his parents, pointing to his head. 'All I wanted was to be happy at home and see my parents happy at home. None of us got that . . . In the end I gave up. I personally couldn't take it.'

Gordon developed a drug problem early on and still suffers from mental ill-health, spending periods of time in psychiatric hospitals and prison. He was also prosecuted in Plymouth in 2004 for carrying an axe, but said he had to carry it in order to defend himself against the 'death threats' he'd received when people found out who he was.*

Gordon's older brother, Graham, became a smooth-talking charmer, like his father. And like Bill, he too became violent as a young man, frequently beating his wife, Barbara, who had to be moved to a succession of safe houses to get away from him. Graham also became an alcoholic, drug user and thief early on, spending time in borstal and prison. Though at one stage, Rose and Fred offered him advice, of all things, on being 'responsible'.

Rose's eldest sister Pat sadly died of Alzheimer's in her early 50s; Joyce became a nurse and finally a matron of some note. She married a church minister and believes she is the only one to have broken the chain. It is telling that Daisy never suffered with her nerves or from depression after Bill's death. She even

---

* *Western Morning News*, 3 July 2004

met a kindly former Grenadier Guard, Tom Heals, with whom she lived happily for many years until his death in 1994. As Andy Letts said of his father, 'He had a way of twisting things to make it look like it was other people; that it was Mum who was ill, not him.' To outsiders, Bill had been 'always charming'. Like a serial killer – which his quiet young daughter, who took pleasure from knitting, would turn out to be.

Rose had been enjoying reading *The Shell Seekers* while on remand. This is a book about a middle-aged woman looking back over her life as she explores the disastrous effects an inheritance can have on a family. In Rosie's case the legacy that led to tragedy for so many young women and families wasn't about money, or property or other assets, but was of abuse.

Bibliography

BENNETT, JOHN WITH GARDNER, GRAHAM, *The Cromwell Street Murders: The Detective's Story* (Stroud, Glos.: Sutton Publishing, 2006).

BERRY-DEE, CHRISTOPHER AND MORRIS, STEVEN, *Born Killers: Childhood Secrets of the World's Deadliest Killers* (London: John Blake Publishing Ltd, 2006).

BURN, GORDON, *Somebody's Husband, Somebody's Son: The Story of the Yorkshire Ripper* (London: Faber & Faber, 1984).

BURN, GORDON, *Happy Like Murderers: The Story of Fred and Rose West* (London: Faber & Faber, 1998).

DAVIS, CAROL ANNE, *Women Who Kill: Profiles of Female Serial Killers* (London: Allison & Busby Ltd, 2001).

DOWSON, JONATHAN H., AND GROUNDS, ADRIAN T., *Personality Disorders Recognition and Clinical Management* (Cambridge: Cambridge University Press, 1995).

GANNON, THERESA, MARIAMNE, ROSE, AND WARD, TONY, 'Pathways to female sexual offending: approach or avoidance?', *Psychology, Crime & Law* 16:5 (9 February 2010), 359–80.

GEKOSKI, ANNA, *Murder By Numbers: British Serial Sex Killers Since 1950* (London: Andre Deutsch Ltd, 1998).

MASTERS, BRIAN, *'She Must Have Known': The Trial of Rosemary West* (Reading, Berks.: Corgi, 1996).

ROBERTS, CAROLINE, *The Lost Girl: How I Triumphed Over Life at the Mercy of Fred and Rose West* (London: Metro Publishing Ltd, 2005).

SOUNES, HOWARD, *Fred & Rose: The Full Story of Fred and Rose West and the Gloucester House of Horrors* (London: Sphere, 1995).

WANSELL, GEOFFREY, *An Evil Love: The Life of Frederick West* (London: Hodder Headline, 1995).

WEST, ANNE MARIE, WITH HILL, VIRGINIA, *Out of the Shadows: Fred West's Daughter Tells Her Harrowing Story of Survival* (London: Simon & Schuster, 1995).

WEST, STEPHEN AND WEST, MAE, *Inside 25 Cromwell Street: the Terrifying, True Story of Life with Fred and Rose West* (Monmouth, Wales: Peter Grose Ltd, in association with the *News of the World*, 1995).

WILSON, COLIN, *The Corpse Garden: The Crimes of Fred and Rose West* (Reading, Berks.: True Crime Library/Forum Press, 1998).

I would like to pay special tribute to my literary agent Ben Fox Mason and to writer Gordon Burn, who sadly passed away in July 2009.